Rush FAQ

Series Editor: Robert Rodriguez

Rush FAQ

All That's Left to Know About Rock's Greatest Power Trio

Max Mobley

Backbeat
Books

An Imprint of Hal Leonard Corporation

Published in 2014 by Backbeat Books
An Imprint of Hal Leonard Corporation
7777 West Bluemound Road
Milwaukee, WI 53213

Trade Book Division Editorial Offices
33 Plymouth St., Montclair, NJ 07042

The covers of the books *The Masked Rider* (9781550226652), *Ghost Rider* (9781550225488), *Traveling Music* (9781550226669), *Roadshow* (1579401457), *Far and Away* (1770410597), and *Clockwork Angels* (9781770411562) appear courtesy of ECW Press.

The FAQ series was conceived by Robert Rodriguez and developed with Stuart Shea.

Printed in the United States of America

Book design by Snow Creative Services

Library of Congress Cataloging-in-Publication Data is available upon request.

ISBN 978-1-61713-451-7

www.backbeatbooks.com

For the millions of listeners for whom rock and roll is more than just music, and for Tina and Molly, who tolerated the sound of typing and shouting in 7/8 lo these many months

Contents

Foreword

"Rush changed my life."

I hear that a lot from fans, and I can completely understand what they mean, because Rush changed my life, too. Perhaps that seems like a strange thing for me to say; after all, I am the woman who is often credited with discovering them and getting them some of their first US airplay, when I was music director at WMMS-FM in Cleveland; they dedicated two albums to me, and you may have seen me in the documentary *Rush: Beyond the Lighted Stage*. But that is all part of the story, part of how my life was changed by taking a chance on a band from Canada that few Americans had ever heard of.

I never expected that my life would change. When I received that first Rush album on Moon Records, which was sent to me by a Canadian record promoter friend of mine named Bob Roper, I never expected that listening to it would lead to a forty-year friendship with the band, as well as a friendship with several members of their management team (and I'm still in touch with Bob Roper, too). At the time, back in the spring of 1974, I was the music director at WMMS-FM in Cleveland, and there I was, sitting in my office, listening to some new music (it was all on vinyl LPs back then). I was just doing what music directors did, trying to find some interesting new songs for the disc jockeys to play. So, I gave the Rush album a listen. Album rock stations played the long versions of songs, and I dropped the needle on the longest track—"Working Man," and you probably know what happened after that. I knew immediately that this was a perfect song for Cleveland. The audience agreed—when I gave it to Denny Sanders to play, the phones lit up. But I had no idea what would follow. We played several other songs from that album, including "Finding My Way" and "Here Again," and the response was just as positive. I've told the story of how I contacted the band's managers in Toronto to let them know that Rush was becoming popular in Cleveland. I've told the story of how they came to Cleveland to perform live for the first time, and how their then-co-manager Vic Wilson told me, "Donna, we won't let you down." (And even forty years later, I can honestly say they never have.)

What is amazing is the way that the members of Rush kept in touch after that, and how they have continued to be appreciative for the ongoing support I gave them. In those early years, I even called music directors at other stations to turn them on to this new and exciting band. Years later, I worked with several other fans to help them get a star on the Hollywood Walk of Fame, and I lobbied every music critic and journalist I knew, trying to get them inducted into the Rock and Roll Hall of Fame. But even if I hadn't done anything more than jump-starting their careers in the US, they never lost contact with me.

You really have to understand how unusual this is: I spent nearly four decades in radio, and in all of those years, I helped all kinds of performers, getting them airplay, saying good things about their music to music industry magazines, championing the songs I believed in. And about 99 percent of the time I never got so much as a thank you. Now and then, there were some pleasant surprises—Bruce Springsteen was absolutely wonderful to work with, to cite one example. But more often than not, I didn't expect to hear from the performers I had helped; this was part of my job, and my first loyalty was to the audience. I wanted the listeners to hear great new music. So, when Rush kept in touch, it was unexpected. And over the years, I can honestly say they have remained the same down-to-earth, kind, empathetic people I first met in mid-1974. Success has not spoiled them, and they continue to make me proud of them.

So, yes, in a somewhat different way from the average fan, I can truly say that Rush changed my life. In Cleveland, I was not very comfortable with or popular among most of the folks in rock and roll radio—I didn't smoke or drink or use drugs, I taught Sunday School (really), and believe it or not, I am actually very shy, so some folks thought I was standoffish. But once I became associated with Rush, suddenly I found a lot more acceptance and I made a lot of friends I didn't have before. To this day I am in contact with Rush fans from all over the world, and I feel a profound sense of kinship with anyone who loves this band as much as I do. Rush fans are a giant, extended family. We may not see eye to eye on politics or religion, we may not like the same songs, but we all believe the same thing: finding Rush has been a life-changing (and for some of us, life-saving) event.

When Max asked me to write a few paragraphs of introduction for his book, I asked him why he was writing it—not because I didn't think there's an audience for books about Rush (believe me, there is), but because I wanted to hear his story, and I wanted to learn how Rush had changed his life. As it turns out, his story had some elements that were quite similar to mine. I think you are going to enjoy reading his book, and I think it will give you yet another reason to be glad you are part of the Rush community. As for me, I will just end where I began: Rush changed my life, and knowing them, and calling them my friends, is a gift for which I will always be grateful.

Donna L. Halper
Quincy, Massachusetts
April 2014

Donna L. Halper's broadcasting career spans three decades. She is credited for introducing Rush to U.S. rock fans during her time as music director for WMMS in Cleveland. Halper is also the author of six books, including *Invisible Stars: A Social History of Women in American Broadcasting*.

Acknowledgments

Additional research provided by Riley Smith, Jason Deppong, Frank Ross, Chris Bentley, the websites Rushisaband.com, Cygnus-x 1 (cygnus-x1.net) and Power Windows (news.2112.net). Photo help from Yaël Brandeis, williamclarkphotography.org and Fred Gabrsek of freddysfrets.com. Special assistance from Ed Stenger, curator of Rushisaband.com, and Tony Geranios (aka, Jack Secret).

Introduction

first heard Rush at the impressionable age of twelve years old. The son of a preacher who had just moved onto our street, a tough rocker of about sixteen, had brought *2112* to my next-door neighbor's house. An attractive teenaged girl lived there, and the guy thought that by playing Rush's most infamous album he would surely win her heart, or at least a few minutes of make-out time. Naturally, this didn't work. The girl, hated the music, but figured her little neighbor (me), who at this time was living off Kiss *Alive!* and ACDC, would probably enjoy it. So she came and got me. Told me I had to hear this music, which, according to her suitor, was unlike any rock and roll ever played on a turntable before. I was happy to oblige.

The preacher's son (don't remember his name, though I wish I did) made a ritual out of hearing *2112* for the first time. First, he had me study the album cover, including the image of the three weird-looking dudes wearing wizardy-looking robes and looking super serious. Like a cerebral version of soul-possession serious. I took this as a good (though slightly dangerous) sign. After all, outside of Robert Plant, it was a time when rock and rollers were not supposed to be good-looking. And looking weird was as good as looking tough, at least in my book. The preacher kid also had me read the paragraph on the album's back cover about life in a mysterious place called Megadon. The plot had thickened and I'd yet to hear a note.

I listened to side one of *2112* three times in a row that day, with opened album jacket in hand. Per the preacher kid, I was to listen to one instrument each time: drums first, then guitar, then bass. I'm not sure I was able to do that, though I probably acted like I had. Upon each needle drop, the song just seized me and took me wherever it wanted. I thought I heard it all the first time, but on each subsequent listen I heard more and more.

Perhaps it was this combination of a reverential and ritualized first listen coupled with the truly original and bombastic sound of *2112*, but man, I was hooked. I had found my religion. I had found something that spoke to me with such intensity that it was all I could think about for weeks.

Decades later, Rush's music is still something I think about often. I've been fortunate to have interviewed guitarist Alex Lifeson twice, once for the excellent guitar mag *Premier Guitar* and once when I was a columnist for the illustrious but doomed (another Internet casualty) *Crawdaddy!* magazine. And in the hundreds of rock and roll articles and columns I have written for the music press and newspapers, I always seem to slip in some Rush reference that perhaps nobody but a diehard fan would pick up on. This was never intentional; it's just that the band had become part of my viscera, their lyrics a part of my personal lexicon. Like so many Rush fans, I know firsthand how the band's music and lyrics can act as a form of shelter against the snakes and arrows of cruel adolescence (see what I mean?). The best music, or at least the right music heard at the right time, has that ability.

Along with the remarkably original story of Rush's ascent from high school drop-outs stoned on rock and roll to their controversial induction into the controversial Rock and Roll Hall of Fame, *Rush FAQ* also covers the story of the fantastic relationship Rush fans have with the world's greatest Canadian prog-rock Power Trio of all time (sorry, Triumph). These stories are intertwined because that's the only way the story of Rush can accurately be told.

Even more than providing shelter from the storms of adolescence for several generations of teenagers, Rush is a live band. That is how they earned their place in the rock and roll pantheon—one show at a time, and sometimes hundreds of shows in a single year. Because of this, Rush's live work, and the gear used to deliver their music, helps tell this tale of three travelers from Willowdale, and one professor from St. Catharines. With that in mind, cue up your favorite Rush albums and *enjoy*!

—Max Mobley

Rush FAQ

Loud and Polite

How Three Nice Kids Learned to Rock Big and Loud

Who the hell is Rush, anyway? They've been described as the world's most famous Canadian prog-rock power trio of all time. But then, name the *second*-most famous Canadian prog rock power trio of all time. No doubt the name Triumph comes to mind for a handful of music fans—okay then, name a third.

Rush is in the Rock and Roll Hall of Fame, but the band is hardly a household name by the standards of popular music. They may be known in pop culture, but mostly as a joke, thanks to *The Colbert Report* or the hit comedy *I Love You, Man*, or maybe in reference to one of a dozen FM classic rock staples, or even the game Guitar Hero. In fact, their level of fame is actually at odds with their level of success, as told by the following stats. They have sold well over 43 million records worldwide—over 25 million in the US alone. Only the Beatles and the Rolling Stones have more gold and platinum records than Rush, who have an astounding twenty-four gold records and seventeen platinum (including three multi-platinum) records earned over their forty-plus-year career. They have played nearly two thousand concerts in North America alone, most at sellout or near-sellout capacity. Not bad for a band far from the mainstream.

And yet, if, ten years ago, you asked most Americans to name a popular artist who hails from Canada, they'd probably offer names like Alanis Morissette or Celine Dion, or if older than fifty, Gordon Lightfoot or Anne Murray. A few musos may have offered the name Neil Young, who hails from Toronto, although he has lived in Northern California for so long he is considered a California native by many Americans.

Pose the same question to Americans today and you'll likely get the same names, plus Justin Beiber. The point is, it's unlikely anyone will mention Rush's three members (and proud Canadians): bassist, vocalist, keyboardist Geddy Lee, guitarist Alex Lifeson, and drummer Neil Peart, unless, of course, the person you are asking happens to be wearing a Rush concert T-shirt.

Rush is perhaps the modern world's most successful enigma, and certainly the world's most popular cult band. Their Canadian roots, which they proudly cling to much the way U2 remains stubbornly rooted in Ireland, is part of the reason.

For many fans of rock and roll, Rush is as much a mystery as the territories between British Columbia and Ontario (i.e., the bulk of Canada). Their music is fiercely original and defiantly anti-pop (really, anti-categorization, for that matter). It often takes even Rush fans a few listens to fully get all that is looming and lurking inside one of the band's highly arranged tunes. The rhythm section (Lee and Peart) is considered one of rock's best, and it's often one of rock's busiest, yet they strive to make it all work—and it works like nothing else in rock and roll. Guitarist Alex Lifeson has the rare ability among guitarists to play only what the song needs—no more, no less. He is revered among well-known guitar heroes, and yet hardly a household name. The three men of Rush are sponges when it comes to absorbing musical and technological trends, and yet they are fanatical about serving their own muse, always insistent on following the noble equation: art over commerce. The band also invented another equation; let's call it the Rush equation: Bigger = Better. And by any measure, not just the aforementioned stats, Rush is big indeed—in musicianship, in songwriting, in performance, in substance, and as an influence.

With one well-known exception (among Rush fans), Rush songs are not about sex or drugs, but fantasy realms, dystopian futures, steampunk adventure, and more often than not, the hopes and fears of humanity at its noble best and self-destructive worst. The band members are not handsome enough to be on the cover of their own albums (not that they'd want their mugs featured anyway), nor are they ugly enough to be considered outlaw-cool, like a Ramone or a Sex Pistol. Lee, Lifeson, and Peart are the ultimate anti-heroes and anti-rock star muso nerds. For anyone keeping score, in rock and roll, the difference between a true anti-hero and a quasi-anti-hero is that most true anti-heroes never end up on the cover of *Rolling Stone* magazine.

Rush never sought fame or fortune, they just wanted to play their interpretation of rock and roll the best they can on bass, guitar, and drums, and then go home and be exceedingly normal. They don't need fans; they need the music. But since they have fans—a devout and faithful legion millions strong—they insist on taking good care of them by playing three-hour concerts, sometimes fifty or more in a year, and offering loads of content and special features on their albums and DVDs.

Despite Rush's considerable financial success (thanks to one of the most loyal fan bases in all of music), they have never ever taken for granted what they get to do for a living. The band's work ethic has as much to do with their success and fan base as does their talent. That is at the core of their body of work—over forty years of touring, twenty studio albums, twelve live albums, nine live DVDs, and, thankfully, there is no end in sight.

Not bad for three tragically unhip kids from suburban Toronto.

Like Liverpool to the Beatles, Dublin to U2, Southern California to the Beach Boys, and countless other examples, Rush's homeland and their family ties have played a huge role in who they are and how they seized the day.

Rush's Link in the Chain Reaction of Rock and Roll

Musical inspiration within the broad umbrella of rock music has been one long chain reaction, starting with African-American blues and gospel music from the 1950s. That initial link birthed, among other things, what we've come to know as hard rock by influencing artists such as Cream and Led Zeppelin, both major influences of Lee's, Lifeson's, and Peart's. Rock's earliest pioneers, Elvis Presley, Carl Perkins, and Little Richard, who were huge influences on the Beatles (who, in turn, were huge influences on artists too numerous to mention), were likewise directly exposed to blues and gospel growing up.

Though the Beatles and Led Zeppelin couldn't sound more different, both were born from the chain reaction triggered by the exposure to blues and gospel—Zep's influence was more direct, the Beatles only one or two links removed. The point is, in these first few decades of rock music, that influence and sound—the chain reaction—was pretty linear. But for some artists and fans, that linearity was a problem (a musical form of the adage: Familiarity breeds contempt). Mutations were needed for rock and roll to truly evolve, and bands like the Who, Yes, King Crimson, Jefferson Airplane (and even the Beatles, between *Rubber Soul* and *Abbey Road*), were all too happy to oblige.

The members of Rush happened to draw inspiration from both the initial chain reaction (Led Zeppelin and Cream) and its wonderful exceptions, including Yes and the Who. It is this combination of influences that helped Rush derive its early sound.

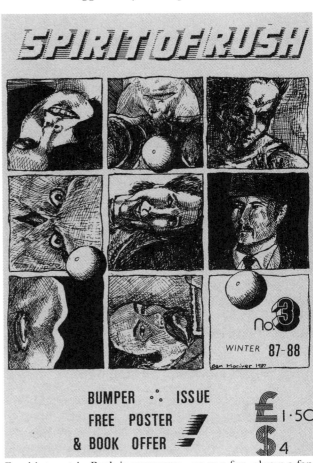

Fans' interest in Rush is evergreen—once a fan, always a fan. Here is a cover from *Spirit of Rush* (Vol. 3), a fanzine dedicated to the group.   *Courtesy of John Patuto and cygnus-x1.net*

The fact that they've kept discovering new influences over the decades has much to do with why Rush's sound keeps evolving.

Clearly, a Zeppelin-esque form of the blues can be heard in Rush's 1974 self-titled debut album, and little else. However, it's worth keeping in mind that most of the songwriting for that record happened when Lee and Lifeson were teenagers under the spell of their favorite bands, rather than progressives forging their own path. This is not to say that Rush's first record is a throwaway; it certainly is not. "Working Man," a track from that album, is the song that cracked open the door to an American fan base for Rush. It being played on WMMS FM radio in Cleveland in 1974, thanks to Rush's patron saint Donna Halper, who decided the track was ideal for her working-class, Zep-loving audience (and also long enough for a bathroom break), caused the station's phones to light up and the lives of Rush's members to be changed forever. The song has been in and out of setlist rotation ever since.

After that first album, however, Rush rightfully (and thankfully) abandoned any semblance of blues-rock for the opportunity to progress rock and roll musicianship, and the rock and roll landscape. In other words, the band created a new link for others to connect to and react to in rock's infinite chain reaction. As such, every single record Rush made after their debut album bears little resemblance to rock and roll's well-defined blues and gospel roots. And it is those albums, especially *Fly by Night* through *Signals*, that can be cited as inspiration for many artists considered significant in popular music, and many more that will never lay claim to fame. The list is as impressive as it is diverse, and includes: Pearl Jam, No Doubt, Foo Fighters, Primus, Wolfmother, Red Hot Chili Peppers, Muse, Porcupine Tree, Metallica, Queensryche, Rage Against the Machine, Tool, and the Smashing Pumpkins. Add to this list the number of drummers influenced by Rush's legendary stickman Neil Peart, and the list grows exponentially.

Rush's influence on rock music cannot be overstated, and yet, had it not been for the shocking inhumanity of World War II, Alex Lifeson and Geddy Lee may never have met. Had they not, rock and roll would likely be very different than it is today. Such is the contribution of Rush as innovators, co-conspirators, and inspirations to countless musicians across the broad spectrum of working-class music.

From Horrors to Happiness

Gary Lee Weinrib was born to Morris and Manya (Mary) Weinrib on July 29, 1953, in the Willowdale suburb of Toronto, Ontario, Canada. The Weinribs were from Nazi-occupied Poland. At the ages of twelve and thirteen, respectively, Morris Weinrib and Manya Rubenstein, along with their family members and neighbors, were marched from a Jewish ghetto in their hometown of Starchvitzcha, Poland, to the town's labor camp. It was there that Weinrib and Rubenstein first met. Most young people meet at school or some social place, but Lee's parents, like millions of other Holocaust survivors, were not so lucky. Soon after, they were sent to the notorious Auschwitz concentration camp. Their crime: being Jewish. Somehow, amid the unimaginable horrors of a Nazi-ruled concentration camp, romance bloomed between them. Morris Weinrib would bribe guards to deliver little gifts of precious food and shoes to Mary. Soon after, he was transferred to the Dachau concentration camp, where the Nazis were exterminating Jews at the rate of 200 per day. Around the same time, Mary Rubenstein was transferred to Bergen-Belsen, where upwards of 50,000 Jews had been killed, including 35,000 from starvation and Typhus. A sign of how bad the conditions were at Bergen-Belsen, another 10,000 Jews died in the first month after the camp was liberated by the British Army. They were simply too weak and ill to survive.

Surviving the Holocaust was blessing enough; that Morris and Manya would ever see each other again seemed impossible. Mary, in fact, had assumed that Morris had not survived. In the midst of such atrocities, she also assumed that humanity itself was in its desperate last throes. But, somehow, Morris Weinrib *did* survive—for a time, anyway. Like a story out of a movie, as soon as he was able, he made his way to Bergen-Belsen to track down his true love. He married Manya Rubenstein there in 1945, inside the liberated-but-still-reeling camp at Bergen-Belsen. They started their life together in a former Nazi officer's quarters as they awaited their place in the world. Like so many other immigrants, they had originally set their sights on America. But, at the last minute, they decided on Canada. They heard it was nice. They settled there in 1947.

Upon settling in the Toronto area, Mr. and Mrs. Weinrib opened and ran a discount variety store in the Toronto suburb of Newmarket. Sadly, in 1966, a few years shy of Rush's earliest incarnations, Morris Weinrib finally succumbed to the wounds he had suffered in the camps, and the widowed Manya Weinrib, who started going by Mary when they moved to Toronto, had no choice but to keep the store going and keep the family strong. Following the Hebrew tradition, young Gary spent eleven months and one day mourning for his father. This included visiting the synagogue twice a day, and shunning forms of entertainment, including all music. According to Mary, Lee dutifully fulfilled his mourning obligation, and when it was over he emerged quite the young man. The following Christmas, Mary was so impressed with how her son had handled the obligation of mourning, how he had matured, and how hard he had worked alongside her during the holidays at the family store that she wanted to buy him a present. She asked her son what he would like. The next-door neighbor was selling an acoustic guitar with palm trees on it. He told his mom he wanted it, and God bless her, she obliged. This was just a few years before young Gary would meet his lifelong friend and partner in crime, Alex Lifeson.

It was also around this time when Gary Lee Weinrib earned the nickname Geddy. The derivation is simple: Mary Weinrib's thick Polish accent was such that whenever Gary's friends heard her say his name, it sounded like Geddy. Friends started calling him Geddy as a tease, and it stuck. Years later, Gary

Lee Weinrib had his name legally changed to Geddy Lee. Rumors that he had changed it to Geddy F***ing Lee are simply not true. That is just how he is known to a legion of rock bass players.

Lifeson's Immigrant Song

Alex "Lifeson" Živojinović was born in Canada on August 27, 1953, to Nenad and Melanija Živojinović. Both were Serbian immigrants who met in Canada after their families emigrated from war-torn Eastern Europe. The country of Yugoslavia was completely unprepared for the Macedonian invasion by Nazi, Hungarian, and Bulgarian forces that overran the Yugoslav army during World War II. After the war had ended, things did not improve as the country became trapped under the iron fist of a pro-Soviet Communist regime. For those who could, leaving their homeland was a good idea. Like the Weinribs, Lifeson's parents also chose Canada. Fernie, British Columbia, to be exact—about as far away as one could be from Toronto and still be in Canada.

Upon arriving in Canada, tough times persisted. Nenad, a coal miner, had lost his first wife shortly thereafter. He met Melanija (Mellie) at the restaurant where she worked; they married a year later. After Nenad suffered a back injury, he and Melanija moved their family to Toronto with the hopes of finding more work and, perhaps, even a shot at prosperity. After bouncing around a few different Toronto neighborhoods, the family moved onto the same street as Rush's original drummer, the late John Rutsey. A skinny Jewish kid lived around the corner. His name was, of course, Gary Lee Weinrib. Funny how fate works, eh?

Young Alex was five before he started speaking English, and it was not until he began school that English became an important language to speak well. He was twelve years old when he got his first guitar—a cheap acoustic by Kent that cost his father ten bucks. It was a Christmas present.

The guitar was a gift in the most significant meaning of the word. It allowed young Živojinović to discover his function lust. It helped him figure out who he was and what path he should take, and there are few gifts more important than that. The path of music was so important to Živojinović that, prior to receiving that first guitar, he was trying his best to learn the viola. Once that guitar entered the house, however, the viola lessons quickly fell by the wayside. At the impressionable age of twelve, it was hard for young Živojinović to find any music featuring guitar players who rocked a cheap acoustic, though one of the first riffs he learned to play was the jingle from a cigarette commercial, and his first 45 was the corny "Sink the Bismarck," by Johnny Horton. Živojinović was driven by rock and roll, which was decidedly electric. He was therefore faced with a choice—dive into acoustic music (hey, folk music was huge in 1965, at least in North America) or rock out on a guitar not meant for it by electrifying it. Živojinović chose the latter—he managed to wedge the needle of a record player into the body of his Kent, and he rewired the family's television to accept the signal. It worked—sort of. Živojinović's innovations grew more ambitious over time, eventually causing the destruction of the guitar (good thing he didn't want to be a doctor). His parents soon replaced the busted acoustic with an electric model made by the Japanese company Conora. Alex and his parents had made a deal: a good report card for an electric guitar. Both sides kept to the bargain, despite finances being stretched and Nenad and Mellie having to borrow the money to pay for it. It was another cheap, entry-level instrument, but it was electric. And that was huge.

Having an electric guitar in the house meant the need for a guitar amp, something the Živojinović's didn't own. Luckily, Lifeson was able to borrow his neighbor's amp. Wanting to emulate the musicians with whom he was growing more and more familiar, he used black electric tape to create a Vox logo on the amp's grille. At this time, Vox was an amp brand made famous by the Beatles, and (to a lesser extent) Led Zeppelin. It's hard to find a more well-known piece of rock and roll gear.

Later, young Alex would borrow an amp from his neighbor and schoolmate Gary Weinrib. Although the two became fast friends in middle school, having bonded over middle school humor and an innate goofiness, it wasn't until Alex started playing with neighbor and friend John Rutsey that Weinrib would become a significant part of their musical clique.

When rock and roll became Alex's main pursuit, he saved rock music journalists an untold number of typos and mispronunciations by changing his name from Živojinović to Lifeson. He based the change on the literal translation of his surname: son of life.

Neil Peart Discovers His Superpower

While Lifeson and Lee were living the life of immigrant children in a city where, like all big Western cities, anti-Semitism lurked, Peart was busy being a hippie farm boy with a big brain and a temper. That may sound harsh, but in his own words, including his highly autobiographic travel book, *Traveling Music*, Peart recalled that, as a young teenager, he had discovered a love for words and language; he also admitted that he had a formidable temper that needed to be managed. True to form, he did so.

As a teenager, Peart dressed more like someone hanging out in Golden Gate Park in the sixties than a farm boy in a small Canadian town. His hair even went past his ears. And, of course, there was that impressive and intimidating brain—an endowment to be sure, but, like a superpower discovered at a young age, it was a gift that he had to learn to control, and that, at times, made it hard to assimilate. Luckily, Peart did not give a damn about assimilation. Being on the outside-looking-in is a familiar vantage point for artists, especially writers and musicians, and Peart is clearly both. So he quickly learned how to master himself—at least within reason.

Neil Elwood Peart was born on September 12, 1952, to Glenn and Betty Peart of Hagersville, Ontario. When he was two years of age, he moved with his

Fly by Night introduced rock fans to the drumming and lyrics of Neil Peart. Peart's Rush debut revealed new possibilities for the band and rock and roll in general.   *Courtesy of Max Mobley*

family to St. Catharines, where his father took up running a farm-equipment dealership. Childhood and family life were fine, if uneventful, for the brainy, introverted Peart. This began to change, however, when he saw the 1959 biopic *The Gene Krupa Story* on television. Krupa was a legendary jazz drummer with a flamboyant style. He was one of the first drummers capable of stealing the show in a Big Band environment. Captivated by the film's portrayal of a legendary drummer and the fabulous noises, rhythms and showmanship that were available from behind a drum kit, Peart found a pair of chopsticks and began banging on every surface of the family home.

His uncle Richard was also an early musical inspiration. Only one year older than Peart, Richard drummed in a band called the Outcasts. They played what is now considered classic rhythm and blues: Sam and Dave, Wilson Picket, James Brown, and the like. Watching and listening to them play live, Peart felt the power of both the music and the beat. It was also around this time that Peart discovered the Who and the manic magic—both visual and rhythmic—of Keith Moon tearing up a drum kit with bombastic aplomb. The spark of musical inspiration lit by Sal Mineo portraying Gene Krupa had now grown into a flame fueled by one of rock's most iconic and influential drummers. Inspired by Moon, both as a player and as a showman, and likewise inspired by the artistic qualities of a beautiful drum kit (Moon's famous *Pictures of Lily* drum kit, which inspired Peart's *R30* drum kit), Peart created fantasy drum kits by laying out magazines on his bed, which he would then play as ersatz drums and cymbals. This went on around the clock for months until, at age thirteen, he was finally rewarded with the freedom to stop taking piano lessons and start learning drums, or drum, as the case would be: he was given only a pair of sticks and a practice pad. It was enough. A year later, he had proved himself worthy by refining and focusing his tendency to beat things within the confines of his practice pad instead of the furniture, walls, carefully arranged magazines, various pots and pans, and his sister's playpen. The reward for such discipline and diligence was a drum set—a Stewart kit in red sparkle with one tom, one floor tom, one snare, one kick, and three cymbals (four, if you count each hi-hat cymbal separately). A picture of a young Neil Peart behind this kit has circulated on the Internet for years. It reveals a young man filled with earnest joy and genuine pride. The emotions captured in the photo were perfect for the moment, and an augur of the life the young man would one day lead. Indeed, the photo should be captioned: "Young Man Finds Special Purpose."

It was clear to anyone within earshot that Peart had a gift behind the drums. Don George, his teacher from the Peninsula Conservatory of Music, noticed this and began challenging young Peart with drum parts advanced for his age and experience.

Peart had quickly outgrown the Stewart set, and had become enamored with a gray ripple Rogers kit at the studio where he was taking lessons. He worked on getting his dad to sign for the kit, which was a pricey $750. Before the elder Peart agreed to the deal, he met with the drum teacher to inquire about his son's potential. Don George confirmed the budding talent he saw in his pupil, and the kit found a home in the Peart household. Neil was still on the hook for the monthly payment of $32, which he earned by mowing lawns and playing the occasional gig.

In the late sixties, most kids seeking music had to be content with AM radio, playing pop hits over and over. Before fully immersing himself in rock and roll, Peart listened intently to whatever he could get his hands on, from his dad's jazz records to Top 40 tunes. In a 1994 feature in his hometown paper, the *St. Catharines Standard*, Peart mentions going to bed with an AM radio pressed up against one ear so he could surreptitiously bask in the magic of new music heard by fresh ears. As would always be the case, it wasn't just rock and roll that moved Peart—it was music in general. But, upon hearing bands such as the Who (his first "favorite" band), Cream, and the Jimi Hendrix Experience, he had found a kind of music that spoke directly to him and his generation—and via drumming, and, later, lyric-writing, he spoke back.

No teenager wants to be an outsider. At some point during adolescence, however, all teenagers feel that they are. Peart was no exception. More often than not, it truly did not seem to bother him. Keep in mind that Peart was a gangly kid with a staggering degree of intelligence. The price for that intelligence was entering high school (Lakeport High School in St. Catharines) at the awkward age of twelve. No matter, music and English classes were all he cared about; the rest were little more than a distraction. There were exceptions of course—kids can be so goddam cruel. A famous example of this occurred at Lakeside Park (yes, the same Lakeside Park referenced in the song with the same name found on Rush's 1975 album, *Caress of Steel*), on the shore of Lake Ontario. An adolescent Peart nearly drowned after swimming many yards out to a diving dock. Bullies that had taken over the dock refused to let him hold onto the side of the structure to catch his breath and rest. He had no choice but to turn around and swim many yards back. Thankfully, friends saw him in distress and helped him to shore.

At the age of fifteen, Peart played his very first gig—a Christmas pageant at St. John's Anglican Church Hall, in Port Dalhousie. That same year, he earned respect (at least temporarily) from his peers by playing in a rock trio called the Eternal Triangle at his high school variety show. The band's set included an original number ("LSD Forever") that featured a drum solo. It was one of the first times Peart experienced acceptance in the high school halls. And there is nothing like validation at a young age to help set one's life trajectory.

Peart's parents were very supportive throughout, as shown by Neil's father signing for his first proper kit—that gray ripple Rogers kit. The kit, and the drum solo played on it at his high school variety show, landed him in the band Mumblin' Sumpthin'. They played blue-eyed soul songs—with a bourgeoning prog-rocker on drums. When Peart wasn't playing one of their many gigs, he was either practicing or taking drum lessons. School still fit in the mix, but it was far from his *raison d'être.*

Peart then joined another blue-eyed soul group, Wayne and the Younger Generation, who quickly changed their name to the Majority (probably so their name would fit on a marquee). When the Majority disbanded, Peart wisely started hammering on members of J. R. Flood, one the more popular local bands in the area. They gave him a shot. He nailed the audition and became their new drummer straight away. J. R. Flood's music was a better fit for Peart, and vice versa. By this time, Peart had added a second kick drum, and he had removed the original wrap on the Rogers drums shells and replaced them with chrome-colored wallpaper to make the drums look more like Keith Moon's kit from The Who's *Tommy* era. It was also around this time that Peart, now seventeen, was allowed to quit school and follow his passion. Peart's first official attempt at lyric writing came when he was a member of J. R. Flood. The band even recorded in future Rush producer Terry Brown's Toronto Sound Studios. J. R. Flood was happy with their local success. They were busy with gigs. They were popular. They were big fish in a wee pond. And Peart wanted something more.

Melancholy in the UK

Hendrix was ignored in the States until "discovered" in England. The Who, Cream, and the Yardbirds were English born and bred. Better still, by 1971, prog rock had actually become an accepted genre, thanks to English bands like King Crimson, Genesis, and Yes. And each of those very English bands had exceptional drummers that fit Peart's tastes to a tee. Feeling that he had more in him than being the best drummer in the greater St. Catharines area (though still true today), in July of 1971, Peart (once again with his parents' support), followed his muse all the way to England where he fell flat on his face (figuratively speaking), lived poor, and occasionally went hungry—important steps in the life of most artists. Peart's father helped him build a crate for his drums, and along with his record collection and two hundred dollars, Peart arrived in England where he met up with friend and fellow Canadian Brad French. French was kind enough to offer him a couch to sleep on until Peart found a gig. The only problem was, Peart never really found a gig. He pounded on the doors of record labels only to be told, no thanks (and the occasional "Bugger off!"). He went on a few auditions sourced from local music magazines—nothing. He managed to land a few session gigs, but nothing that came close to paying the bills. He played a lounge gig for a business dinner with a room full of obnoxious drunk suits. He hated it with a passion, and the experience helped him realize that, no matter how poor he was, and how desperate for a gig, he would compromise neither his integrity nor his music ever again. This marks an early example of a member of Rush strictly following the noble equation that served them so well for over forty years.

Broke and disillusioned, Peart bumped into an old friend from back home, a man by the name of Sheldon Altos. Altos ran a souvenir shop in Carnaby Street in Soho, and he gave Peart a job. Although far from drumming, it allowed Peart to scrape by.

Carnaby Street was one of the most fashionable streets in all of London—still is today. Working there exposed Peart to connections that helped him land a spot in a band called English Rose. In October of 1971, Peart quit his position in Carnaby Street to hit the road with his new band.

Unfortunately, the gig was much less than Peart hoped it would be. His bandmates seemed to be little more than reprobates who stole their gear and had no qualms with getting into trouble. The band wasn't that good, and as the gigs dried up, so did Peart's already meager cash flow. It got to the point where his bandmates were giving him small amounts of questionably attained cash just so Peart could eat. Soon after, he returned home.

This is something that happens to most artists sooner or later, and it fuels the muse that feeds the drive to make the music—so it all worked out in the end. But at the time, moving to England to chase a rock and roll dream and returning with that dream unfulfilled had to be painful for anyone, especially for such a deep thinker as Peart. All told, Peart spent eighteen months beating his dreams

"An evening with Rush"—four words that every Rush fan loves to read. *Courtesy of Joe Pesch*

against the cynicism he encountered in the same country that bred artists he revered. He left with his head high however, for he was not compromising his art, only his ambition—he would play the music that inspired him, and return to his father's dealership in Canada.

It wasn't long after Peart had returned to his father's business that he had found himself in a working band again called Hush. They were a busy "bar band" working the southern Ontario club scene. The one thing he failed to do in England just seemed unavoidable back in St. Catharines. Soon after joining the band, he got a call from another band ending in "ush." The members of Hush tried to talk him out of joining the much more successful band, this one calling themselves Rush. Hush minimized Rush as just some Zeppelin wannabes. Perhaps they understood what they would be losing.

After much consideration, Peart agreed to the Rush audition. He and Geddy Lee hit it off immediately; Lifeson and he, not so much. Peart was clearly still a gangly young man, and as Lifeson admits in the documentary *Rush: Beyond the Lighted Stage*, he didn't think the brainiac drummer was cool enough. It didn't help that Peart had shown up in a beaten-up Ford Pinto crammed full of drums, cymbals, and stands. Thankfully, Lee talked his buddy Lifeson down, and the rest is Rush history. The audition, which Peart describes as disaster, included a jam that eventually evolved into the first track on 1975's *Fly by Night*—"Anthem." Ian Grandy claims to have recorded the audition the best he could, although that recording has yet to see the light of day.

Peart officially joined Rush on July 29, 1974. Two weeks later, on August 14, he played his first gig with Rush in front of 11,000 people at Pittsburgh's Civic Arena. It was the largest crowd the trio had experienced by a factor of ten (at least). The show kicked off their first US tour, in which they were the opener for Uriah Heep and Manfred Mann. Peart celebrated the new gig by purchasing a new Slingerland kit with double bass drums. He played that kit from Rush's first US show through the 1976–77 tour in support of their live album *All the World's a Stage*, though by then it had been augmented with more toms, cymbals and percussion pieces, and a used Slingerland Artist Snare drum. That snare remains one of Peart's most coveted drums, and it can be heard on every Rush album from 1975's *Fly by Night* through 1993's *Counterparts*.

2

The Ballad of John Rutsey

Rush's Unsung Steady Starter

O riginal Rush drummer John Rutsey was far more than Canada's answer to Pete Best. (Best was the Beatles' first drummer. He was let go shortly before the band became the biggest thing since electricity.) Rutsey had a pretty-boy glam-rock look that contrasted nicely with the hard-rock hippie style of a young Geddy Lee and Alex Lifeson. Rutsey also had a solid rock and roll voice that nicely backed up Lee's emotive wails. As a "front man from behind the kit" during the band's early days, Rutsey's rock and roll good looks and glam-rock hair and wardrobe were put to good use onstage. Same goes for his rock-solid groove-oriented drumming. This can be seen in the Laura Secord Secondary School concert footage available in the special features of the DVDs *Rush: Beyond the Lighted Stage* ("Best I Can," "Working Man") and *Time Machine 2011: Live in Cleveland* ("Need Some Love"). The emerging glam-rock look is also evident in very early pictures of the band.

Rutsey and Friends Start a Band

John Rutsey was Lifeson's classmate and neighbor. They played hockey on the streets together before they played music together. But music was to be their ultimate bond. Together they formed the band the Projection when Lifeson was only fourteen years old. The Projection never made it out of the basement and the occasional teenage party. Lifeson thought the band was terrible, so limited performances were arguably a good thing.

The Projection played covers, including "Louie, Louie," by the Kingsmen, "For Your Love," by the Yardbirds, and "Hungry," by Paul Revere and the Raiders. Reports vary on the band's lineup. Some Rush historians claim Rutsey and Lifeson were the Projection's only members, with friends filling in. However, in an interview with *Guitar International* magazine, Ian Grandy, a childhood friend of Rutsey and Lifeson who ended up working for Rush for fifteen years (he is listed in album liner notes from *Rush* to *Signals*), lists the 1967 lineup as Al Grandy (Ian Grandy's brother) on bass, Bill Fitzgerald, "Doc" Cooper, Rutsey, and Lifeson.

In 1968, Rutsey and Lifeson were hanging out in the basement of the Rutsey home, talking about music (what else?), when they decided to call the band Rush—the name proffered up by Rutsey's brother, Bill. Outside of the occasional amp loan (Lifeson had yet to own one), Lee was not yet in the picture. He and Lifeson had jammed a few times together at this stage, and they were good school friends who shared a mutual love for the same rock and roll bands, but that was all. When Lifeson and Rutsey tried to make a go of their new band, Rush, it was their friend Jeff Jones (Ocean, Red Rider) who filled out the lineup on bass and vocals. Their first gig together was also their last. It was a teenage drop-in center, dubbed the Coff-In, located in the basement of a neighborhood church. St. Theodore of Canterbury Anglican Church, to be exact. The date was September 19, 1968. Though Jones technically provided bass and vocals at this inaugural gig, Lee is rightfully credited with being a founding member as Jones was only in Rush for a matter of weeks. He quit right before the band's second gig at the same place a week later. Quit may be putting it kindly. There is a longstanding rumor that Jones was too drunk to play that second gig. Not a rumor is that Geddy Lee was called by Lifeson to fill in. After a short, impromptu practice, Lee, Lifeson, and Rutsey had parked on a few blues covers they could play over and over for the gig. Thus, Jones's influence and participation in Rush is virtually nonexistent. This is not meant as a slight: he just wasn't the right guy for Rush, and Rush wasn't the right band for him. Case in point— in 1971, as part of the band Ocean, Jones enjoyed pop-music success with the band's gospel hit "Put Your Hand in the Hand," which peaked at #2 on the *Billboard* Hot 100. That same year, Rush was in the nascent stages of their never-ending evolution, and they had yet to record a thing.

John Rutsey brought glam style and good looks to Rush's early days, as shown in this flyer for one of the band's early club gigs.   *Courtesy of Max Mobley*

Lee, Lifeson, and Rutsey, Ready to Take Over the World

Understandably, that first Rush gig with the agreed-upon original lineup of Lee, Lifeson, and Rutsey was far from glamorous. They played for a few dozen teenagers drinking coffee and eating donuts. Lacking a proper microphone stand, they had to tape the vocal mic to a lamp stand. The gig earned the trio twenty-five bucks. In their eyes, that meant they were professionals. They took the cash and went to Pancer's Deli, where they ordered the Canadian delicacy of chips (french fries) and gravy. The conversation was one that any person who has ever been in a rock band can relate to—reliving the gig and plotting world domination through rock and roll.

The next few years found the band playing every damn place that would have them, with setlist of covers the band liked and a growing list of originals. They got good this way, just like the Beatles got good playing Hamburg's Reeperbahn every night for a couple of years. This was also the time when a young man named Ray Danniels entered the picture. He remains the band's manger today, and is the founder and CEO of their company and label SRO-

Rush's music was never 45 rpm-single friendly. That did not stop the labels from trying, as shown with this promo-copy single of "Finding My Way." *Courtesy of Joe Pesch*

The band's first-ever pressing, shown here, has become a rare and highly coveted item. *Courtesy of Joe Pesch*

As this ticket stub illustrates, in 1975 you could see Rush in a small venue almost for free.   *Courtesy of Joe Pesch*

Anthem Entertainment Group (SRO is an acronym for *standing room only*). When he met Rush, he was a free-spirited runaway who believed in the band's music, even when the audience sometimes didn't. (Lee has mentioned that Rush ruined more than one prom by playing their bombastic, undanceable, raw rock and roll for stunned and disappointed high school seniors.) Danniels started getting a cut right away in exchange for promoting the band, one heavily fliered light pole at a time.

Since the drinking age was still twenty-one, there were few places for teenagers to go see a band. Rush and Danniels took advantage of that the best they could, though Rush's music was never a coffee-and-donuts kind of soundtrack. Then, in 1971, the drinking age in Ontario was lowered to eighteen, and bars and clubs suddenly needed fresh music that matched the age and temperament of their new patrons. Once again, Rush and Danniels were more than happy to oblige, and it was a superb fit. Rush played their asses off, and Rutsey, due to diabetes and a lifestyle at odds with the disease, sometimes struggled to keep up. Still, it was his love, his band, and his friends. How could anyone quit that?

Who the Hell Is Hadrian?

In 1969, Rush rather inexplicably changed their name to Hadrian for a short while, and, even more inexplicably, booted Geddy Lee from the band. Joe Perna was his replacement. Lee started his own blues-rock band called Olgivie, which, perhaps for obvious reasons, quickly changed their name to Judd. Both bands were managed by Danniels, who found himself doing better with Lee's band, though at this stage, no one was really making much money. At Lifeson's request, Hadrian added Lindy Young on keyboards (his sister Nancy is Lee's wife of a zillion years). The band fell apart rather quickly, the final nail being Young quitting Hadrian to join up with Judd, which was faring better. With Hadrian officially disbanded, Lee was asked to return, with the band being called Rush once again. All involved did their best to forget that the personnel changes had ever happened. Well almost all—since Danniels was central to Lee's temporary ousting, Lee jokingly admits that he still reminds him of it now and then.

Two years later, in 1971, still trying to establish a baseline personnel, Lee, Lifeson, and Rutsey tried out a two-guitar lineup, with a guy named Mitch Bossi on second guitar. This lasted for about four months, until Bossi moved on, returning the band to the trio status it needed to be.

Rock and Roll Is Hardest on a Drummer

Rutsey played his last gig with the band in July 25, 1974, at Centennial Hall in London, Ontario. He had a significant influence on the band's music, and their emerging glam-rock look. Clearly, it is the latter that the band seemed to miss the most. Rutsey was a very solid drummer—not on the level of Neil Peart, but what drummer back in the late sixties and early seventies was? Being replaced by one of the greatest drummers in the history of rock and roll has overshadowed Rutsey's skills as a musician. His Gretsch kit may have been smaller than Peart's, but it fit his no-nonsense, straight-ahead style quite well. While Rutsey's drumming on Rush's first single (Side A, a remake of Buddy Holly's "Not Fade Away," Side B, the original "You Can't Fight It") and the band's debut album is excellent, upon hindsight, it's clear that his style would not sustain the band's evolutionary arc. Lifeson and Lee knew the direction in which they wanted to go, and, despite what Rutsey brought to the band, they knew they could not get

Rush's debut album, featuring John Rutsey on drums, remains a mainstay at record stores.   *Courtesy of Max Mobley*

there with him on drums. The fact that Rutsey suffered from Type I diabetes, and was living a life at odds with the disease, helped confirm what was a difficult choice.

"Need Some Love" was the first original song recorded by the band (outside of rare board tapes). According to Lifeson's 2011 interview with MusicRadar, the song was written by Rutsey and Lee, though Lifeson is often credited as Lee's writing partner for the number. The song was not included in Rush's debut album. In fact, the eponymously titled *Rush* does not list Rutsey as a songwriter, though he was assigned the role of chief lyricist prior to the recording sessions. A sign of his temperament, Rutsey was so unhappy with his writing that he tore up his lyrics sheets just prior to the recording session, before even Lee and Lifeson could see them, forcing them to come up with their own.

John Howard Rutsey died of a heart attack on May 11, 2008, just three days before his fifty-fifth birthday. He had stopped playing drums shortly after departing from Rush. His solid drumming can still be heard regularly on US radio, thanks to "Working Man" being a permanent FM staple. While history has shown that Lee and Lifeson made a wise choice in replacing him, it is clear that he played a key role in the band's birth and early years. As Ian Grandy has said, "There would be no Rush without John Rutsey."

3

A Trio of Breakouts

Rush's Three Most Pivotal Albums

Most successful bands can attribute their success to a breakout album. For some bands, the breakout album is also their debut album. In such instances, the debut album breaks new ground and redefines the landscape of popular music and rock and roll. *Please Please Me* by the Beatles, *Van Halen* by Van Halen, and *Are You Experienced* by the Jimi Hendrix Experience are classic examples of breakout debut albums. Each one earned an enormous fan base for the artist and changed rock and roll music forever—and for the better.

Recording and releasing a breakout record is usually a singular event. Once a band breaks out, they've arrived. Once you arrive, you cannot arrive again without disrupting the space-time continuum. But Rush is a band that apparently does not know the rules of physics or rock and roll. They are the only band in the history of rock with not one breakout album, but three: 1976's *2112*, 1981's *Moving Pictures*, and 2007's *Snakes and Arrows*.

This is not hyperbole, just another unique claim to fame by one of rock and roll's most unique bands. It also raises the question: How can a band so reviled by critics, and so outside the mainstream have one breakout album, let alone three? To answer that question, we need to examine the changes and impact that accompany each of the aforementioned records.

Breakout Number One: *2112*

Leading up to Rush's fourth album, *2112*, the band was in a tight spot. After starting strong with their debut album (thanks, in large part, to WMMS FM Cleveland and Rush's minor FM staple "Working Man"), and with the new guy (Peart) on drums, the band had hit a decent plateau (for twenty-something Cana-

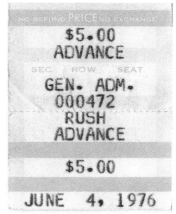

Hard to believe that it only cost five bucks to see Rush play in support of one of their most important albums. This ticket stub is from the Amarillo, Texas, stop of the *2112* tour. The opener that night was Iron Butterfly.

Courtesy of Scott Burgan

dian musicians) with their follow-up album *Fly by Night* (1975). They were far from rich, but their gigs were getting bigger and better, and they had another minor hit with *Fly by Night*'s title track. That same year the band released *Caress of Steel*, and things started sliding backwards. The album, which preceded *2112*, was the band's first attempt at long-form concept pieces. Unfortunately, the concept escaped much of Rush's growing fan base. It also brought in poor returns for Mercury / PolyGram Records, the band's label. To make matters worse, the tour in support of *Caress of Steel* was an arduous one, and punctuated by long, uncomfortable van rides between venues and lousy sleeping arrangements. Young rock bands could usually suffer such drudgery as long as they were rewarded with a good show in front of admiring fans, and proper payment. According to Peart, in a 2004 interview with *Classic Rock* magazine, by the end of the *Caress of Steel* tour, the band could neither pay themselves nor their crew, and the crowds were getting smaller instead of bigger. One of the pain points of the tour was that, over its six-month course, the band shared the bill, either as an opener or headliner, with over a dozen different bands, ranging from Mott the Hoople to Kiss.

Caress of Steel was Rush's first foray into large-concept pieces. The album ended up putting the band into a do-or-die situation for their next record. *Courtesy of Max Mobley*

2112—A Great Year for Prog Rock

With the tour over, the band all but destitute, and a persnickety record label demanding the concept for their next album be one of profits and hit singles, à la Bad Company, Rush headed into Toronto Sound Studios to lay down their fourth record. The rock world was about to be changed forever. And there would be no going back.

Rush and producer Terry Brown ended up making an album that had as much in common with Bad Company as *Lord of the Rings* does with *50 Shades of Grey*. In fact, *2112* was the polar opposite of what Bad Company was doing at the time artistically speaking, and what the record label was expecting. By deciding to make the record that was in them instead of one deemed necessary by their label, Rush delivered an album that was true to their muse and their musicianship. And it broke them out of a downward spiral.

The album was a huge success by 1976 hard-rock standards. Here are a few stats:

- RIAA Certified Gold, November 16, 1977 (a big deal during vinyl's glory days).
- RIAA Certified Platinum, February 25, 1981 (the same month and year Rush released *Moving Pictures*).
- RIAA Certified 2x Platinum, December 1, 1993.
- RIAA Certified 3x Platinum November 17, 1995 (only two years after earning 2x Platinum status).
- First Rush album to make the *Billboard* Top 100 (peaked at #61, previous best chart position for a Rush album was #105 for *Rush*. All subsequent studio albums by Rush have charted higher).
- Peaked on Canadian music charts (RPM) at #1 (previous best was #37 for *Fly by Night*).
- Listed as #10 in IGN's list of Top 25 Prog-Rock Albums of All Time.
- Listed in *1001 Albums You Must Hear Before You Die.*
- Reached #2 in *Rolling Stone* Readers Poll for Best Prog-Rock Albums of All Time.
- Listed as #24 in *Kerrang!* magazine's 100 Greatest Heavy Metal Albums of All Time.

While these are compelling stats for any rock or pop group, they are monumental for a 1976 release by a struggling Canadian prog-rock trio. However, sales alone do not signify breakout status. One also has to consider where the band was prior to the release, and where they ended up after.

No doubt about it, prior to *2112*, Rush had one foot in the land of "almost was," and they knew it. Their attitude during the making of *2112* was, if they were going to go down in flames, let it be flames of their choosing. Peart has since stated that he would rather have gone back to working at his father's

Rush's first breakout album, *2112*, is considered by many to be the band's definitive album. *A Rolling Stone* Reader's Poll listed it as the #2 prog-rock album of all time (after Dream Theater's *Metropolis Pt. 2: Scenes from a Memory*).   *Courtesy of Max Mobley*

farm-equipment dealership after making music he respected than have a successful career making albums of hopeful singles that were artistically disingenuous. Of the things Rush figured out early on, principal among them was that they did not have what it takes to fake it. They could—and would—only make Rush music, not the music envisioned by record executives, however well-meaning they might be.

2112 Aftermath

The new album expanded Rush's fan base exponentially, evidenced by both record sales and concert attendance. They played far more headline shows on the tour in support of *2112*, with emerging prog- and hard-rock bands, such as Styx, Max Webster, and Thin Lizzy opening. The band also played a handful of shows as an opener for Kansas, Blue Öyster Cult, and Aerosmith, all of whom were enjoying success with major hit singles: "Carry on My Wayward Son" (Kansas), "Don't Fear the Reaper" (BOC), and "Back in the Saddle" (Aerosmith).

The dark, fantasy-sci-fi concepts of *2112* resonated deeply with Rush fans and coming-of-age rock lovers. This cover of the fanzine *Spirit of Rush* (Vol. 4) exemplifies that.

Courtesy of John Patuto and cygnus-x1.net

So while *2112* was changing (or fulfilling) the fate of Lee, Lifeson, and Peart, and redefining the rock and roll horizon, it was doing so without the benefit of a hit single (the title track was the most popular number, and it's over twenty minutes long). It was also doing it without favorable reviews from the press (no surprise there), without much FM airplay, and without marketing or promotional help from Mercury / PolyGram, who, at the time, was convinced the album would be a financial loss. (Neil Peart had seen the label's financial forecasts around the time of *2112*'s release, and Rush was not even mentioned.) So not only was *2112* a breakout album done on the band's own terms, it happened without label help or FM airplay. It happened via word-of-mouth from a fan base that started to not just "get" Rush, but that was also swearing allegiance to them. That same allegiance helps define the Rush experience today.

Breakout Number Two: *Moving Pictures*

Including Rush's first live album, *All the World's a Stage*, recorded during a three-night stint at Toronto, Canada's Massey Hall during the *2112* tour in early June of 1976, only four albums and four years separate *2112* and *Moving Pictures*, Rush's second breakout album. Musically speaking, the gap is much wider.

Two of the three studio albums following *2112*, 1977's *A Farewell to Kings* and 1978's *Hemispheres*, were as proggie and concept-oriented as their breakout predecessor. This was the kind of music Rush's burgeoning fan base (mostly males born in the late fifties and early sixties) had come to expect—long epic works containing complex arrangements, odd time signatures guiding heavy, melodic riffs, and literary, high-concept lyrics. The band had cemented themselves among male hard-rock fans as the band to see and hear live during this time (and still to this day). Anyone who has seen Rush live in person or via DVD can tell you that this reputation is earned. It also may have been helped along by rumors of Rush's contemporaries being too wasted or burned-out to perform well live. It was, after all, a time when Jimmy Page, Keith Richards, Keith Moon, and Ozzy Osborne (among others) were almost as well known for their drug use as their music.

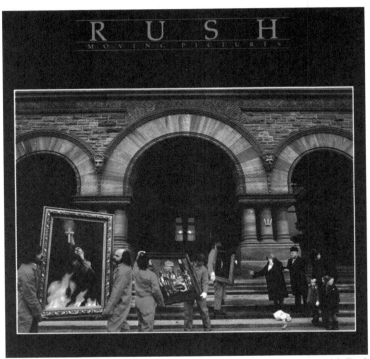

The songs from 1981's *Moving Pictures* have become synonymous with Rush and prog rock in general. *Courtesy of Max Mobley*

Permanent Waves, the 1980 studio album preceding *Moving Pictures*, signaled a departure from the long-form, highly conceptual songs that made up the last four studio records. Little did fans know that *Permanent Waves*' opening track, "The Spirit of Radio," was a sign of things to come. The song made it to #51 on the *Billboard* Hot 100, and an astounding #13 on the UK singles chart (quite high for a Rush song in the UK), setting the stage for another breakout—this time into crossover audiences, and much wider acceptance.

Moving Pictures brought Rush very close to mainstream popularity. They were now a constant entity on FM radio, and in some cases on the cars themselves, that blasted those modern rock and classic rock stations.   *Courtesy of Rob Silverberg*

Permanent Waves was a transition album for the band. Fans expecting twenty-minute epics were assuaged by the intense musicianship heard on the album's heavier numbers: "Spirit," "Freewill," "Jacob's Ladder," and "Natural Science." It helped that "Jacob's Ladder" and "Natural Science" were long songs (7:28 and 9:16, respectively) with distinctly separate parts that resembled the style and substance of the previous four prog-heavy studio albums. *Permanent Waves* remains a cherished record by fans, and it shifted Rush's trajectory toward breakout number two.

Moving Pictures Really Moves

The band was strong and healthy after their first breakout album, *2112*. They were steadily earning hard-rock fans, and keeping them. They had a few songs sparsely but consistently played on FM radio (mostly "Working Man" from *Rush*, "Closer to the Heart" from *A Farewell to Kings*, and "The Spirit of Radio" and "Freewill" from *Permanent Waves*). They had a bit of money in their wallets, and a few gold records on the wall. And then, on February 12, 1981, everything changed. That was the day *Moving Pictures* was released.

Once again, things would never be the same for the band. A legion of new fans from a new generation leaped on board the private club cars of the Rush train to the sound of sweeping synths and an angry mob—partly from the ersatz mob noises that open "Witch Hunt," the sixth song on *Moving Pictures*, and partly from longtime faithful fans expressing concern that their secret world of Rush had been discovered and invaded.

The momentum could not be stopped. Rush was now taking on an entire new fan base that didn't resemble the one already established. Stranger still, it wasn't entirely male-centric and hard-rock oriented. The more accessible material, shorter, radio-friendly songs, iconic synth sounds, and slick production that was *Moving Pictures* was embraced by a new generation and a new kind of music lover. One who had a strong interest in New Wave music, and the new soundscapes derived from emerging music technologies. Another breakout had occurred, and once again, sales records and new ground had been broken for the ever-evolving band. For rock and roll, new textures, sounds, instrumentation, arrangements (and even playing styles) had entered the lexicon. Here are a few stats:

- RIAA Certified Gold, April 13, 1981 (just two months after the album's release).
- RIAA Certified 1x Platinum, April 27, 1981 (less than three months after its release—a first for the band).
- RIAA Certified 2x Platinum, October 12, 1984.
- RIAA Certified 4x Platinum, January 27, 1995.
- Listed as #3 on *Billboard* Top 200 albums chart (highest position at the time of the release).
- A run of sixty-nine weeks on *Billboard* charts (including reissues).
- Listed as #3 on UK album charts.
- Listed as #1 on Canadian charts (RPM).
- Listed in *1001 Albums You Must Hear Before You Die*.
- Listed as #10 in *Rolling Stone* Readers Poll for Best Prog-Rock Albums of All Time.
- Listed as #43 in *Kerrang!* magazine's 100 Greatest Heavy Metal Albums of All Time.
- Two *Billboard* Hot 100 hits: "Tom Sawyer" (#44) and "Limelight" (#55).

Moving Pictures Aftermath

Moving Pictures brought Rush to the edges of mainstream. And that was plenty close as far as Rush's original fan base was concerned. The devoted following they had earned between their first and their sixth studio album (*Hemispheres*) saw the band as anti-establishment, anti-corporate, and indifferent to mainstream acceptance. Whether the band actually felt that way is debatable. But one thing was certain—the band made the music they wanted to make, and they didn't give a damn about writing hit singles. And yet now, thanks to *Moving Pictures*, they had two.

This second breakout album for the band gained them a larger, more diverse following, the ability to play larger venues in more cities, and status as prog-rock icons. Lee reflects in *Beyond the Lighted Stage* that Rush was the band to see the year they toured in support of *Moving Pictures*. Indeed, the tour saw the band playing the same large venue for two, three, and sometimes four nights in a row.

Alex Lifeson (right) and *Moving Pictures* producer Terry Brown, making more than just memories.

Courtesy of Yaël Brandeis

While Rush did not become a household name immediately after *Moving Pictures*, the song "Tom Sawyer," with its signature sweeping synth sounds (played on an Oberheim OB-X), became instantly recognizable and can still be heard all over the place, including movies, television, sporting events, shopping malls, and, of course, on the radio. One sure sign of the song's iconic status is that if you ask almost anyone under 55 to make the synth sound from "Tom Sawyer," they'll know exactly what you mean, and probably do a fair job aping it. Another is that many synthesizers and keyboards made today include a version of the Tom Sawyer patch.

Breakout Number Three: *Snakes and Arrows*

In the twenty-six years between the release of *Moving Pictures* and 2007's *Snakes and Arrows*, the band had stepped well away from the edges of mainstream. They still served the Rush muse and their now multi-generation fan base with bombast, mirth, and aplomb, but the band's evolution had tapered off some. Rush followers know that the band spent some of these years in the shadows of terrible personal loss. It could have gone either way—retirement or rebirth. Thankfully, it was the latter. Still, it would be a slow climb out of the ashes—not so much a phoenix rising as an egg cracking open with the delicate life inside it easing into the unfolding of wings. The recovery and renewal was evidenced by the 2002 release of *Vapor Trails*, an album of great material exploring new sonic textures for the band. Unfortunately, the album also suffered from production and mastering issues (see the chapter on this album for details). While *Vapor Trails* may have been somewhat disappointing due to these technical issues, it signified a triumphant return for a band whose fans had feared that the Canadian prog-rock party was over. This was in evidence during the sixty-seven stops of the *Vapor Trails* concert tour.

That evidence became the stuff of Rush legend when the band headed to South America, on little more than a whim, to play a few shows.

Brazilian

The US leg of the 2002 *Vapor Trails* tour was somewhat typical—the band was their usual best, and the fans were their usual passionate selves. But, partially out of respect, and partially due to this tour being the first outing since the tragic events, there was a subtle but palpable air of solemnity lurking in the crowd's roar. For one thing, fans didn't want to perturb the man behind the kit who had been through hell, and who was far from comfortable with fandom on his best day. For another, no one onstage, behind it, or in front of it, was ever going take the experience of a Rush concert for granted again.

And then the band played Brazil.

Due in large part to the amount of CD sales within Brazil's healthy black market, the band and its management had no idea of how popular their music was in that country. So imagine Lifeson's, Lee's, and Peart's surprise and gratitude when they played for crowds three times the size of a typical show in the US. What's more, the crowd arrived hours early, were even more passionate and fervid than US audiences (in part, because bands such as Rush rarely visit South America), and they sang along to entire shows—even the instrumentals! If there is any doubt that Rush had come back but was not the same (they were better), see the *Rush in Rio* concert DVD.

Feedback and Resonate

Thanks to the success of *Rush in Rio* and the *Vapor Trails* tour at large, Rush was back in a big way. But they weren't looking forward just yet.

Eager to get on the road and celebrate their 30th anniversary, the band followed up *Vapor Trails* with 2004's *Feedback*, an EP of well-known rock and roll songs members of the band covered as teenagers. Some of these songs were played at Rush's very first gig at the Coff-In teen hangout in a church basement back in 1968.

Feedback was fun, and an unexpected twist from the Rush formula of studio album-tour-break-studio album-tour-break that fans had grown accustomed to in those three decades. Fans dug it, and eagerly awaited the *R30* anniversary tour, which turned out to be one of the more memorable ones. (See the chapter on it for the glorious details.)

With all that out of their system, and the oldest fans honored by the *R30* tour setlist, the band was ready to look forward in a huge way.

Rush Slays with *Snakes and Arrows*

With demons exorcised, debts paid, and musical and personal bonds deeper than ever, Lifeson, Lee, and Peart were invigorated and eager to get back to work. That work produced the band's third breakout album, *Snakes and Arrows*.

Interviews with band members published during and immediately after the making of this album, including those found in *Classic Rock* magazine, *Jam! Music*, *Billboard*, and the *Toronto Sun*, reveal the band to be in a new headspace, or at least more willing to talk to the press about their creativity. Watching *The Game of Snakes and Arrows*, the 2007 "making-of" documentary found on the MVI version of the album, shows the three band members relaxed and confident, as if finally, after all those years and all those songs, they no longer had anything to prove—to themselves or anyone else. This did not mean that they took the

Rush's third breakout album was also one of their heaviest, 2007's *Snakes and Arrows*. It was the first album with producer Nick Rasculinecz, who grew up rocking out to the band's music.   *Courtesy of Max Mobley*

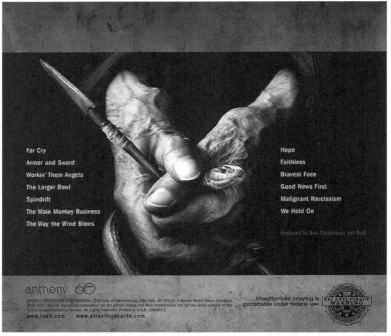

Far Cry
Armor and Sword
Workin' Them Angels
The Larger Bowl
Spindrift
The Main Monkey Business
The Way the Wind Blows

Hope
Faithless
Bravest Face
Good News First
Malignant Narcissism
We Hold On

The title *Snakes and Arrows* was inspired by the ancient Hindu game Leela. The album's lyrics focused on the positive and negative aspects of a religious-based society.   *Courtesy of Max Mobley*

job of writing, playing, and recording an album's worth of words and music any less seriously—clearly, that will never change. But their new groove seemed to allow the band to take some chances and branch out in different directions. Chief among these changes was the inclusion of hiring a die-hard Rush fan to co-produce the new album.

Boojze = The Sound of *Snakes and Arrows*

Nick Rasculinecz is a respected member of the modern rock establishment, having produced albums for the Foo Fighters, Velvet Revolver, and the Exies. He is also a serious Rush fan, which made him a smart yet bold choice as the co-producer for *Snakes and Arrows*. He loved the band's music, he understood their legacy, and he had the balls to be honest with them—one of the most important jobs for any record producer.

Boojze (the nickname Peart assigned Rasculinecz based on his air-drumming vocalizations), helped the band realize their renewed vision without trying to make them something they were not. The bombastic, heavy riffs, the big transitions, the intense musicianship—all hallmarks of the best Rush albums—remain front and center on *Snakes and Arrows*, thanks in part to Rasculinecz's involvement. Here are a few stats:

- It was listed as #1 on the *Billboard* rock album charts—a first for the band. *Clockwork Angels*, the record after *Snakes and Arrows* also debuted at #1.
- It reached #3 on the *Billboard* Top 200 (the highest position ever for the band).
- It was #3 the *SoundScan* Top 200 album chart in the first week of release.
- It reached #2 on *Billboard*'s top Internet albums.
- "Far Cry," the single from the album, made it into the top 25 on the *Billboard* Hot Mainstream Rock Tracks chart.

Glaringly absent from this partial list of stats are RIAA gold or platinum awards. It's true—Rush's last RIAA award for US sales of a studio album was 1996's *Test for Echo* (all Rush albums continue to score at least gold status in their native Canada). No doubt the steep rise of single-song digital downloads, and the recording industry's slow, uncomfortable, and well-publicized transition to a digital medium plays a role here. However, there may be more to it. For example, Rush's live albums and DVDs continue to sell very well (the *R30* live recording was awarded 5x platinum status, and the *Snakes and Arrows Live* DVD was awarded 2x platinum). Perhaps it is the band's history as a live act (remember, their first breakout, *2112*, was earned through their touring) is a contributing factor to this downturn in studio album sales.

Snakes and Arrows Aftermath

While the sound and attitude of *Snakes and Arrows* may have been rooted in the band's earliest and heaviest material, it broke new records for the band as illustrated above. It also brought a heightened level of mainstream acceptance well beyond that of *Moving Pictures*. Thanks in part to Rush's TV appearance on Stephen Colbert's *The Colbert Report* in the summer of 2008; the band being a key plot point in the popular 2009 feature-film comedy, *I Love You, Man*; and the overwhelming success of the 2010 rock doc, *Rush: Beyond the Lighted Stage*, mainstream success had finally become a permanent feature of the Rush landscape. Proof of this can be found in the band's induction into the Rock and Roll Hall of Fame in 2013, a full six years after the release of their third breakout album (and after their twentieth studio album), a breakout that appears to have stuck.

Post-*Snakes and Arrows*, Rush had become a part of the mainstream lexicon. TV commercials, having their music played at sporting events and in cutaways during sports broadcasts, being the highlight of a Foo Fighters' concert, and, ultimately, their acceptance into the Rock and Roll Hall of Fame, highlight the fact that, like it or not, a whopping thirty-seven years after their first breakout record, Rush is finally on the inside, looking out. Just like all their other successes, the band earned it the hard way. And while not a single fan begrudges them their much-deserved success and accolades, some, especially those who were there from the beginning, and some who possess a false sense of proprietorship with regards to the band's music and ethos, do begrudge the tearing down of the walls hiding rock and roll's greatest secret—Rush is badass.

4

What's with All the Keyboards, Man?

Rush's Love Affair with Technology and Sound

Synthesizers and keyboards made their first appearance as part of the Rush sound with the iconic intro to the overture of *2112*'s title track. That sci-fi soundscape was created by Geddy Lee and Rush's album art designer, Hugh Syme, using Syme's Arp Odyssey synthesizer. The Odyssey was part of the early synthesizer revolution taking place at the time. Its main competition was the Moog Minimoog, the first professional "affordable" synthesizer (at fifteen hundred dollars a pop). The Odyssey was known for giving users sliders and buttons over all its various parameters, and for being duophonic (the ability to play a whopping two notes / sounds simultaneously, depending on the sound; the Minimoog was monophonic—one note / sound at a time—period).

Despite having twice-weekly piano lessons as kid for a couple years, Lee was new to keyboards. When Rush was looking to fatten up and embellish their sounds, Lee, who fondly recalled his sister's talent at the piano, immediately gravitated toward keyboards. Though really, what was a good alternate choice? Saxophone? Backup singers? The timing of Rush's earliest keyboard experiments coincided with the advent of the synthesizer in modern music. So it was easy for Lee to be seduced by emerging synth technology and the new textures and soundscapes it offered. However, it was Hugh Syme who played the keyboard parts heard on *2112*, including the Mellotron's woodwind, horn, and strings sounds heard on "Tears." According to a 2012 *Classic Rock* magazine *Special Edition* that included an interview with the legendary album art designer, Syme had been invited into the studio during the making of *2112* to come up with and record the aforementioned Mellotron parts. He arrived with his Mellotron and Arp in tow, and, in between sessions, he and Lee killed time fooling around with the Arp Odyssey. The results are part of prog rock's recorded history as heard in the ethereal opening moments of *2112*.

Since the minimal but crucial role on *2112*, the use of synthesizers in Rush's sound grew to include keyboards as an instrument for melody and solos, and not just for embellishments and textures. It would be difficult to think of Rush's most iconic hit, "Tom Sawyer," without thinking of Lee's signature keyboard melody from that track, and the iconic sweeping note that kicks off the tune, played by Lee on his Oberheim OB-X.

A Farewell to the Guitar / Bass / Drum Sound

While *2112* was a groundbreaking album for both the band and for rock and roll music, Rush's next studio album, 1977's *A Farewell to Kings*, bore little resemblance to the bombastic *2112* sound. This can be attributed, in part, to the amount of keyboards found in the mix, along with the heavy use of acoustic guitars and symphonic percussion.

Kings introduced keyboard as a melody and not just a texture. The synthesizers of choice were a Moog Minimoog and Moog Taurus Pedals, and they can be heard on all six tracks of the album. They are prominently featured on the infamous "Xanadu," the melancholy "Madrigal" (including a pretty keyboard solo by Lee), and the Elizabethan intro to the title track.

Hemispheres, which followed *A Farewell to Kings* in 1978, had strong sonic similarities to its predecessor, despite Rush's persistent evolution. It helps that the sidelong track, "Hemispheres," is a component of the two-part "Cygnus X-1"opus that began on the final track of *A Farewell to Kings*. "Cygnus X-1 Book I:

A Farewell to Kings, from 1977, introduced synthesizers as a key element to Rush's sound—a trend that would grow.   *Courtesy of Max Mobley*

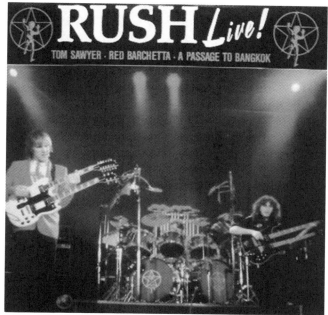

While the sound of *A Farewell to Kings* would be impossible to achieve without synthesizers, it would also be impossible to play live without Lifeson's Gibson double-neck guitar (six- and twelve-string), and Lee's Rickenbacker double-neck (bass / guitar), shown here from a live promotional album.   *Courtesy of Joe Pesch*

The Voyage" is the last track on *Kings*, with "Book II: Hemispheres" being comprised of the eighteen-minute, six-part opening track on *Hemispheres*. Along with Lee's Minimoog and Taurus pedals, an Oberheim 8-Voice synth was added to help accommodate the increasing presence of keyboards in Rush's sound. Once again, keyboards featured prominently on every track—a trend that would continue, much to the growing chagrin of Alex Lifeson.

Prior to bringing the Oberheim 8-Voice onstage, Lee kept it backstage on tours, and Terry Watkinson, keyboardist from the Canadian band Max Webster (a perennial opener during Rush's earliest headliner days, whose members were also good friends with Rush), spent time with Lee helping him grasp the fundamentals of analog synthesizer programming. It is important to remember that in these golden days of analog synthesis, to get a particular certain sound, one had to dial it in by hand. Unlike today, when a simple patch change requires a single button push, in the seventies and eighties, the tweaking of up to a dozen different knobs, switches, buttons, and sliders, was required to change from one sound to the next. Imagine doing that while playing a busy bass line and singing complicated lyrics about Greek gods in space in front of a few thousand fans.

The Permanent Wave

Permanent Waves, Rush's 1980 release, is considered by many to be one of the band's best guitar albums. (Let the arguments begin!) The album opens with Lifeson's signature guitar lick—the manic, opening hammer-on-pull-off feast from "The Spirit of Radio."

In many ways, especially in those first seventeen seconds of the song (perhaps the most intense seventeen seconds in all of progressive rock), "The Spirit of Radio" is all about guitar, bass, and drums. And yet keyboards are present throughout, including those jaw-dropping opening moments. But in the opening track, they are mostly long string pad sounds lurking deep in the mix, making them easy to miss—unless you took them away. Their presence grows throughout the song, including a melodic interlude prior to the reggae section, and as a rhythmic countermelody alongside the main riff played in the song's chorus.

As has now become standard practice, keyboards play a role on every song on *Permanent Waves*, including a beautiful piano part played by Hugh Syme on "Different Strings."

Once again, Geddy Lee's keyboard rig grew in sync with advancements in synthesizer technology, which, in turn, gave the band more sounds and textures to choose from. Lee added to his Minimoog, Taurus pedals, and Oberheim 8-Voice polyphonic synthesizer, an Oberheim sequencer, and an Oberheim OB-1. In the studio and in concert, Lee's Taurus pedals were interfaced to control the Oberheim 8-Voice. On the *Permanent Waves* tour, Lee used two sets of interfaced Taurus pedals live, one beneath his keyboard rig, and one beneath his main mic when playing bass guitar.

Rush's Synth Technology So Far

During live performances, Lee played the majority of the band's synth sounds with his feet, using those two sets of Taurus pedals so he could play bass guitar with his hands. Using keyboards in this way was rarely seen in the seventies and up to 1980, when Rush toured in support of *Permanent Waves*. That setlist contained an awful lot of songs that contained synth parts, which in turn required a highly sophisticated live setup for the band. Back then, interfacing synthesizers so they would work together was no easy feat. Everything was proprietary by brand, and primarily analog, so no two pieces from different manufacturers would talk to each other. Except for a couple of expensive studio pieces, digital was still the domain of calculators and wristwatches. For anyone under forty-five, this is nearly impossible to comprehend, and the challenges and instability of analog technology is mindboggling compared to today's perfect-replica digital audio world. And yet Rush was fearless in pushing forward with it, not just because it was their mindset, but because their music (and their muse) demanded it.

To be able to pull off the music from *A Farewell to Kings* through *Permanent Waves* (and beyond) live, Lee had to interface two different keyboard systems from two different manufacturers a full three years before the debut of the keyboard interfacing technology known as MIDI (Musical Instrument Digital Interface), which would greatly simplify such connectivity. MIDI has since become the standard means to connect and control various keyboards and synthesizers from the same or different manufacturers. Music, as we have come to know it, would not exist without MIDI. The technology is taken for granted today, and is used in everything from websites to controlling stage lighting rigs. Rush was a band that helped reveal the dire need for this technology, and used its kludgey precursors several years before MIDI-capable products were available to the public. How's that for envelope pushing?

At this point in Rush's music, Geddy Lee and his chief keyboard tech to this day, Tony Geranios (aka, the infamous Jack Secret), had created a very solid and sophisticated keyboard rig for the band. According to a 1980 interview in *Guitar Player*, Lee had also divvied up the roles of each of his synth-based instruments. His trusty Minimoog, which could now be heard on three Rush albums, was used for keyboard melody and lead lines; the Oberheim 8-Voice was used for horn and string parts; and the Oberheim OB-1, which was connected to Lee's Oberheim sequencer, was used for sequenced parts (think of that rhythmic countermelody in "The Spirit of Radio") and "weird sounds."

It bears mentioning that in Rush's tour books for *Permanent Waves* and *Hemispheres*, Lee lists a Roland Space Echo as part of his synthesizer rig. The Roland Space Echo is a classic and a highly regarded piece of gear, but it is a tape-echo effect, not a synthesizer.

The Most Famous Synth Sound in All of Prog Rock

BUUROWWWwwwwwwww . . .

Many who claim not to know or like Rush are nonetheless familiar with the growling intro note that kicks off Rush's most popular hit, "Tom Sawyer," from 1981's *Moving Pictures*. It is one of the most iconic single notes in rock and roll. As mentioned previously, the sound was played by Lee on his Oberheim OB-X. Lee discovered the sound before a single note of "Tom Sawyer" had been written. Lee has mentioned in interviews that the sound helped inspire the song's creation. That note also announced to fans that keyboards would now have equal footing with guitar and bass and drums in the Rush sound. Previously, their role was more supportive, with a few sparse, carefully placed melodies. But "Tom Sawyer" is nearly as much a synth song as it is a guitar song, or bass song, or drum song. And while the album *Moving Pictures* still emphasizes guitar bass and drums, Rush's fifth album to use keyboards has the keys up front in the mix, to the point of being cornerstones. "Tom Sawyer," is, of course, an excellent example of this, with both the infamous growling note and the hooky lead line preceding the guitar solo, which also helps close the song. Other examples of keyboards being front and center include "Vital Signs," "The Camera Eye" (the first full Rush song written on keyboards), and the epic, Grammy-nominated rock instrumental "YYZ" (which lost to the Police's mundane-by-comparison "Behind My Camel" from *Zenyatta Mondatta*).

Though once again, and pretty much forevermore, synthesizers are present on every track of a Rush album, *Moving Pictures* also makes good use of organic sounds. Rush had been using environmental and organic sounds since *A Farewell to Kings* (the birdsong in Wales, recorded at Rockfield Studios and used in the intro to the title track, is a good example). But, like their synth melodies and counterpoints, organic sounds were key elements in *Moving Pictures*. Specifically, the "angry mob" noises the band and crew simulated at Toronto's Le Studio, where the album was recorded, and the city sounds that open "The Camera Eye," which were lifted from an episode of *Superman*, where Clark Kent is walking the downtown streets of Metropolis on his way to the offices of the *Daily Planet*.

Perhaps one of the biggest signals revealing the role keyboards would play in Rush's music over the next decade can be found in the *Moving Pictures* tour book. Geddy Lee's gear page puts keyboards at the top of the list, followed by basses and amplification. Coincidently, a *Keyboard* magazine reader's poll listed Geddy Lee as "Best New Talent" of 1981. That would have been the same year *Moving Pictures* was released, and the year Rush released their second live album, *Exit . . . Stage Left*. The latter album was recorded during the *Moving Pictures* tour.

Lee's keyboards for the *Moving Pictures* album and tour were: Oberheim OB-1, OB-X, and 8-Voice Polyphonic; two sets of Moog Taurus pedals (one set under the keyboard rig, another beneath his main vocal microphone) interfaced to control the 8-Voice. He also had his trusty Minimoog, and, for the first time, a pair of Roland sequencers, which, when triggered, could play multiple notes and parts from the above-mentioned synths.

New World Sounds

One of the things that feeds Rush's perpetual motion machine is that Lee, Lifeson, and Peart remain tuned-in to rock's persistent evolution. *Signals*, the band's release of 1982, serves as an excellent example of this, both stylistically and musically. Once again, Rush followed their most keyboard-heavy work to date with an album featuring even more keyboards. *Signals* is also the first Rush album in which listeners find Lifeson's brilliant playing slipping deeper into the mix. The camel's back was not yet broken, but it was starting to bend uncomfortably.

The keyboard heft of *Signals* is reflected by Lee's ever-growing keyboard rig which, for the *Signals* session and its subsequent tour, consisted of a Roland JP-8 synthesizer; a Roland 808 drum machine (used to trigger the JP-8 arpeggiator while sending a synchronized click to Peart's headphones so he could play drums in lockstep with the arpeggiated synth parts); an Oberheim Xa synth (an updated version of the Oberheim OB-X that Lee added during the *Moving Pictures* era); an Oberheim DSX sequencer; the Moog Minimoog; the requisite two sets of Moog Taurus Pedals, now interfaced with the OB-Xa; and a custom-made switching box, courtesy of Tony Geranios.

With the exception of the opening track, "New World Man," which was written and recorded in the studio over the remarkably short span of two days, every track on *Signals* has large amounts of keyboards. And three of the eight songs on the record were mostly written on keyboards ("Subdivisions," "Chemistry," and "The Weapon").

If *Moving Pictures* signaled a key role for synthesizers in Rush's ever-evolving sound, *Signals* revealed a greater mastery of synthesizer playing and programming—especially pro-

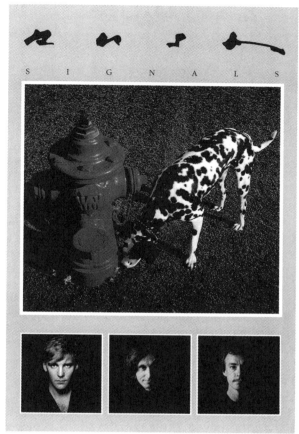

Signals, from 1982, marked the end of the Terry Brown era. Synthesizers played a sizeable role in both the album and the departure of the man who helped guide Rush's sound during their most pivotal releases.   *Courtesy of Max Mobley*

gramming, as Lee considered himself more of a synthesist than a keyboardist. The late seventies through the early nineties represented a sort of "space race" of synthesizer and digital keyboard technology. It was quite similar to the speed and innovation with which personal computers and the Internet itself evolved during the late nineties and into the 2000s. In fact, the evolution of keyboards and synthesis as it pertains to technology and to modern music can be traced by listening to Rush's studio albums, from *2112* through *Power Windows*. In between, there was *Grace Under Pressure*.

Guitars Under Pressure

By 1984's *Grace Under Pressure*, Lifeson had expressed his dissatisfaction with the amount of space keyboards were taking up in Rush's sound. As a result, *Grace Under Pressure*, while still keyboard-laden and very much an album of the time (the lush and texture-filled New Wave eighties mingled with the ska and reggae rhythms of that other power trio, the Police), marked a correction (albeit a temporary one) in Rush's sonic trajectory. This correction gave Lifeson more room to get his guitar mojo up in the mix.

Rush has never been afraid to make mistakes in their exploration of music and musicianship, and is often the first to learn from them. *Signals*, another fan favorite, had revealed a problem in laying down all those fat analog keyboard sounds within the confines of a guitar-heavy band with a hyperactive rhythm section. The problem was one of mud. The guitars and analog synths were sharing too many of the same frequencies and timbres, and it caused what was an otherwise great album to sound, at times, muddy, with the guitar not being up where it should be. Lifeson seems to agree. In a 1987 interview in *Kerrang!* magazine, he states that *Signals* is "hard to listen to." Fortunately for fans, material from that album are mainstays in Rush's live setlists.

The solution to this problem, as heard in *Grace Under Pressure*'s eight tracks, was to shift the keyboards into both higher and lower frequency ranges that were outside of, or at least not integral to, the guitar's domain. Another part of the solution came courtesy of the evolving keyboard synthesizer technology—an excellent metaphor and complement to Rush's ever-evolving sound.

Lee had smartly employed a PPG 2.2 Wave synthesizer for the much of the keyboard sounds of *Grace Under Pressure*. Unlike the fat, gritty Oberheim and Moog analog synths previously used—at times because they were the only technology of the time—the PPG was a wavetable synth, relying on digitally produced single cycle sound waves generated either from a digital recording (a sample), or from a digital oscillator. Lee's PPG 2.2 synth had both. The result was a clearer, more-defined synth sound than its analog counterparts. As a byproduct of that clarity, the sound is more crisp than fat, with more highs than the beefy analog synth sounds. It also offered a higher degree of flexibility than its analog counterparts. The PPG Wave synth was a cutting-edge piece of technology in 1984, and once again, Lee was an early adopter who made great use of it. This technology was so important to cleaning up the mud found on *Signals* that many keyboardists agree it could not have been done without the use of a digital, wavetable synthesizer. Another huge bonus of this technology was that now, finally, after five studio albums of analog synths and their myriad buttons, sliders, dials, and switches, the PPG had the ability to call up dramatically different sounds with a single button push. Ahh, saved by technology again, which, as many Rush fans and music lovers know, is a Faustian salvation at best.

Another key component that helped return Alex Lifeson's guitar work to its rightful place in the Rush soundscape came from Lee giving parts written on keyboards to Lifeson to play on guitar. It was a recipe that worked. And, true to form, it would not last for long.

During the writing and recording sessions of *Grace Under Pressure*, Lee, the eternal sonic explorer, began to push his keyboard skills even further. He had already mastered the difficult programming skills required of professional synth work. The next logical step was to play like a keyboard player and not like a bass player. This meant rhythmically independent control for both left and right hands. Out of this push, Lee began to write bass lines on his keyboard to be played exclusively with his left hand (on a different keyboard no less—one of those fat analog ones!), while his right hand played melodies and lead lines. Because of this, the *Grace Under Pressure* tour was the first in which Lee took off his bass guitar entirely for a song or two.

Keyboards, keyboards, keyboards! They were now everywhere it seemed—all over Rush's sound, and all over their stage. Their use in Rush's music was so significant, in fact, that Lifeson had a keyboard rig onstage to help satisfy the sound of *Grace Under Pressure*. Needless to say, the brouhaha between keyboards (which aren't even real instruments, according to Lifeson in the Rush doc *Beyond the Lighted Stage*) and guitars (with effects that are just keyboards without keys, to paraphrase Lee from the same documentary) was far from settled.

Lee and Lifeson's battle for balance between keyboards and guitar was largely internal, though it had been growing since *Moving Pictures*. However, by 1984, a few outward signs were showing. In a September 1984 cover story on Geddy Lee in *Keyboard* magazine, Lee, regarding the use of effects, states that "if you've got a good idea, you don't have to junk it up with toys and effects. I'm not a guitar player and that's why I think that way. Guitar players all think the other way: Got to have effects and toys, and this, that, and the other thing." While at a glance that quote sounds like a dig, it is entirely possible that it was also nothing more than an inside joke between two best friends, a joke that flirted with the dangerous topic of keyboards battling guitars over the soul of Rush.

As was the tradition, Rush's keyboard rigs (plural!) had evolved in step with the music and the technology. Lee's two Moog Taurus pedals were in their traditional places below the main vocal mic and Lee's keyboard rig, only now they were connected to Lee's Oberheim OB-Xa, which had officially replaced the cumbersome Oberheim 8-Voice that Tony Geranios referred to as a "white elephant." The Moog Minimoog was also still onstage (a rig stalwart since 1977), and the Roland (Jupiter) JP-8 first used on *Signals* had also returned, as did the Roland 808 drum machine used to control the JP-8's arpeggiator while feeding a click to Peart's headphones. The Oberheim DSX sequencer was also still in use.

Lifeson's keyboard rig consisted of two Oberheim OB-Xas each controlled by a dedicated Oberheim DSX sequencer and Lifeson's very own set of Taurus pedals. Rumor has it guitar and bass rigs were also onstage somewhere in the backline . . .

Do Digitally Sampled Guitars Still Count as Guitars?

With 1985's *Power Windows*, the keyboard tide had turned again, and this time it was not in Lifeson's favor. Both Geddy Lee's muse and cutting-edge technology were at the root of it. With *Grace Under Pressure*, Lee had pushed his keyboard skills to the next level by using his left hand for bass lines. A year later, he clearly had missed playing bass guitar, so he made sure to leave room for it on *Power Windows'* eight songs. It was one of the few instruments on the record that was not sampled prior to recording. That may sound strange by today's standards, but 1985 was a big year for keyboardists and synthesists, thanks to significant improvements in digital sampling technology, which offered seemingly limitless sound-creation possibilities. Sampling equates to digitally capturing (recording or "sampling") a snippet of sound that can then be looped to play endlessly and then spread across a keyboard with each key playing the sample at different pitches. While sampling had been around for a few years prior to 1985, the year *Power Windows* was released (Lee's PPG Wave synth had a sampling component), the technology needed to mature before it could be considered nimble enough and portable enough for songwriting, production, and touring. For example, the Fairlight CMI was one of the first samplers to be used in popular music as early as 1980 (Peter Gabriel, Thomas Dolby, Stevie Wonder). It sold for almost thirty thousand dollars, was very limited (but brilliant for its day), extremely complicated, and not suitable for being moved around, or even glared at. But, in 1984, Dave Rossum's E-MU Systems was on their second-generation Emulator, the vastly improved Emulator II sampling keyboard, which boasted fidelity specs that were about half of the quality of today's compact disc. The deluxe version also boasted a whopping twenty megabytes of memory. That is less than 1 percent of the memory of a typical iPod. And yet it was huge for its day. The Emulator II (E II, for short), sounded great, was reasonably easy to use, and, at a mere eight grand, it was a bargain to boot.

Digital samplers, including Emulator IIs, were all over *Power Windows*, helping the album achieve its keyboard-layered, crystalline sound. The band had also brought in bona-fide keyboardist Andy Richards to program and perform the intricate keyboard parts heard on the album. Richards was a heavyweight, having worked with Frankie Goes to Hollywood, Tears for Fears, and the Pet Shop Boys—all hugely popular synth bands from the eighties. This explains the giant leap in keyboard sounds and parts heard on *Power Windows* compared to prior Rush albums—fans were hearing a level of keyboard playing beyond Geddy Lee's skills. In turn, this seemed to free Lee up to lay down some of his best bass lines, which ended up fitting perfectly with the keyboard foundation. In addition, Peter Collins produced *Power Windows*, and he was much more of

Though Rush had been using synths and keyboards with increasing regularity on the three studio albums prior to 1985, *Power Windows* ushered in a new-synth sound for the band, thanks to the bright and crystalline sound of digital-sampling technologies. *Courtesy of Max Mobley*

a pop producer than the band had heretofore worked with, which also lent to the heavy keyboard flavor of *Power Windows*.

In *Grace Under Pressure*, Rush had learned to keep the keyboards out of the guitar's way by moving keyboard parts into frequencies that did not compete with electric guitar. The use of digital synthesizers over fat resonating analog synths also opened space up for Lifeson to do his thing. With *Power Windows*, Rush did the opposite—there were simply too many keyboard parts to move out of Lifeson's way. So, to keep a good, pop-centric mix, it was the guitar that had to adjust. That meant a brighter, cleaner, thinner sound was required by Lifeson for his instrument to be heard. Prior to this, his entire rig was dedicated to chunky, lush, heavy rock guitar sounds. To accommodate the myriad keyboard sounds filling up Rush's new sound, Lifeson had to go direct (guitar straight to an amp) and forgo his many effects, which could make the guitars too lush-sounding. It was an old-school method which, thanks in part to Lifeson using guitars with more attack and brightness, allowed the keys and guitar tracks to coexist. Some Lifeson fans protested his new, mostly clean tone, but it worked perfectly in serving the songs and sound of *Power Windows*. The guitar work on

Tony "Jack Secret" Geranios surrounded by Emulator IIs backstage. During the show, his job was to continuously load floppy disks of samples into multiple units for the next song while other units were being triggered by Geddy Lee onstage.

Courtesy of Tony Geranios

Power Windows is stellar, per usual. And the heavy use of keyboards played mostly by Richards, who had the same level of musicianship as Lifeson himself, pushed him to create highly innovative progressions and melodic, texture-filled solos. Because of this, several *Power Windows* album reviews boasted a return to Rush's roots, which, of course, could not have been further from the truth. But the album did illustrate a return to Lee focusing on bass, Peart's complex rhythms dominating in the mix, and Lifeson pushing the envelope with regards to modern and innovative guitar rhythms and leads.

As if it wasn't enough to be deprived of your rig and have to contend with a master musician on keyboards who wasn't even in the band, the guitar also risked getting squeezed out by an entirely new element—live string and choral sections. Along with the samplers, and various analog synthesizers, Rush had also brought in a live string section and a live choir, which was used extensively on the track "Marathon." Live strings can also be heard on the third chorus of "Middletown Dreams." The string orchestra was Rush's idea—they wanted to work with Art of Noise's Anne Dudley, who directed and arranged the string parts for the band. According to a 1985 interview with Geddy Lee in *Canadian Musician*, the choir was their producer's idea: "Peter Collins wanted to add the choir, we'd already used everything including the kitchen sink. Most people won't notice, it's all in the last thirty seconds [of "Marathon"]. I was there and saw pregnant women and old men sing our song. I'll never forget it." The twenty-five-member choir was recorded in a church that Collins had selected for its acoustic properties. The thirty-piece orchestra was recorded in the legendary Abbey Road Studios, much to the delight of the band.

Sampling technology was put to excellent use on *Power Windows*, with samples of guitars, percussion, and even Neil Peart vocalizing a drum roll, being captured, manipulated, and then incorporated into the mix. In order to play *Power Windows* live, it required multiple samplers, sequencers, and, of course, both Lifeson and Lee playing keyboards. One sure sign that the camel's back was starting to break was that when performing live, Lifeson found himself triggering samples of his guitar work instead of actually playing guitar. Still, it would be another record before keyboards slunk back to what many feel is their rightful place: behind Alex Lifeson's guitar work.

A byproduct of the digital keyboard revolution coupled with the advent of MIDI, which allowed a high degree of interfacing and connectivity options, was that keyboard rigs got smaller and yet did more. Lee's rig had been augmented noticeably as a result, but it had also grown. He now relied on several Emulator IIs (he fails to mention exactly how many), and Rush's live show required several Emulator IIs offstage, so that Jack Secret could alternate loading sounds from floppy disks into each, always leaving one loaded and ready to play. Lee also had a Yamaha DX-7 keyboard—a favorite piece of gear during the eighties, along with a Yamaha QX-1 MIDI sequencer, the PPG Wave 2.3 used on the previous tour and album, and the Roland JP-8. AMS hard disk samplers were also used in the studio, and a myriad of MIDI boxes for syncing and interfacing it all together, including two Yamaha KX 76 controllers. Lee's Moog Taurus pedals, which were decidedly not MIDI, were swapped out for Korg MPK-130 pedals, which looked and behaved an awful lot like Taurus pedals, with the added bonus of being MIDI capable.

Lifeson's side of the stage also had a set of Korg MPK-130s, and an Emulator II controlled by a Yamaha QX-1 sequencer.

Yipes.

Hold Your Balance

Hold Your Fire, or "The Red Album" as some fans call the 1987 album (see the album cover picture), could be considered a companion piece to *Power Windows*. Some fans consider the album a bit too poppy in production and tone (many felt the same way about *Power Windows*), however, the album's mix shows that Rush had finally achieved the proper balance between the competing elements of copious keyboards and prog-rock guitar, or, looked at from a different angle, modern music technology and organic instrumentations. Though pound for pound there were more keyboards (or at least louder keyboards) on *Power Windows* than *Hold Your Fire*, both albums relied on them for their mojo. As an example of how Rush uses music and technology first and foremost to serve their collective muse, *Hold Your Fire* is an introverted, moody record compared to the spry, effervescent tone of *Power Windows*. This naturally pushed the role of keyboards on *Hold Your Fire* toward more underlying textures and counterpoints, which, in turn, allowed Lifeson's virtuoso guitar skills to lead rather than follow. This may have helped temper his attitude toward keyboards in Rush's sound. Lifeson's guitar tone still allowed room for the synths and samplers in the mix, and once again, the Rush fans who were predominately guitar lovers and players, and fans of Lifeson's riff-work from early albums, openly missed the crunch and chunk that helped earn him the reputation of being one of rock's best guitarists. Critics of Lifeson's sound during the eighties should also remember what was musically going down at the time, and what acts the members of Rush were then listening to: Ultravox, Peter Gabriel, Trevor Horn, the Fixx, and the Police, to name a few. They were all highly respected artists (with good reason) from the colorful and happy eighties, and their guitar sounds were crisp, glassy, and cutting. In short, the tone was one that served the ethos of the era and the synth-heavy sound of New Wave.

Once again, Andy Richards was brought in to pinch-hit on keyboards, and bringing back Peter Collins as producer caused the project to lean toward a more synth-pop sound. But this was Rush, dammit, and Alex Lifeson's guitar skills are a force to be reckoned with, which is why so much of the flavor and drive on *Hold Your Fire* comes from the guitar department and not the keyboard section. Once again, the guitars had to contend with a live string section, though upon listening you can hear that Lifeson's superb playing won all sonic battles. Collins also recorded (with the band's blessing, but not with their input) a brass ensemble for "Mission," his favorite track on the album. However, the brass section never made it into the final mix. Maybe one day . . .

The keyboard tools used in the studio for *Hold Your Fire*, and live for the subsequent tour, were mostly samplers. Seven Akai S900s had replaced the Emulator IIs, though an Emulator 3 was employed in the studio. The S900 was stable, and being a rack-mounted sampler, relatively compact, which made it more road worthy and more amenable to loading in the one hundred different floppy-disk–based sample libraries now required to pull off a Rush show. It also made it easier for Rush to travel with a duplicate backup rig in case the live

All this and badass bass and vocals, too. Tony Geranios stands amid Geddy Lee's keyboard rig, which Geranios designed and created with Lee's help. The massive rig was a requirement to be able to play Rush's heavy-synth material from the eighties. Lee's rig today uses two keyboards that, combined, have more power and sound than all the knobs, switches, sliders, and keys shown here.

Courtesy of Tony Geranios

keyboard rig misbehaved. Lee had also added a Prophet VS synthesizer made by Dave Smith and Sequential Circuits (Smith is the man behind the invention of MIDI; he won a Grammy for it in 2013), two Roland D-50 keyboard-synthesizers (one for backup), two rack-mounted Roland D-550 synths, two Yamaha DX-7s (one as a backup), a Yamaha KX-76 MIDI controller, two Yamaha QX-1 sequencers, a Yamaha MFC1 foot controller, two Korg MPL-130s foot pedals, the PPG Wave keyboard, and, making a comeback, Moog Taurus pedals. Most of this gear was offstage, and it required a complicated MIDI network that made early NASA command modules seem like toys.

Hold Your Fire was also the first album on which Lee had begun to write music using a Macintosh computer running Performer, a MIDI sequencing software by Mark of the Unicorn, and a predecessor to their popular digital audio workstation platform Digital Performer.

Lifeson's keyboard rig included a Yamaha KX-76 MIDI controller, a Yamaha DX-7, at least one Akai S900m, a Yamaha QX-1 sequencer, and a set of the Korg foot pedals.

Neil Peart, who had been using electronic Simmons drums since *Grace Under Pressure*, was enlisted to fire off synth and keyboard samples in order to satisfy the sound requirements of the *Power Windows* and *Hold Your Fire* material. Peart employed a MIDI DrumKat, which was a pad-based MIDI controller designed for drummers and percussionists. It fired off samples loaded into a dedicated Akai S900.

The Weight of Digital Sound

The requirements of playing songs from *Power Windows* and *Hold Your Fire* live proved to be more than the three men could handle without sacrificing the high degree of joy that comes with performing. Not only did each member have to play their own instruments at the level they were known for, they also had to play keyboards, trigger samples, and engage with and be enslaved to, sequencers playing pre-programmed sections. Rush performing live during this era was a bit like an all-synth band (Kraftwerk?) playing live while also spinning plates and baking a difficult cake. It was simply too much, and resulted in making the tours for these records more grueling and less fun that they otherwise would have been. The camel's back had finally been broken by technology and girdled by MIDI cables. The grand experiment was officially over. Rush had learned how much music they could make as a threesome without being overloaded. They had also expanded the definition of progressive music, and the role keyboards could play in what was still essentially a guitar, bass, drums lineup. They helped an entire industry discover how the brand-spanking new music technology of digital keyboards, digital sampling, wavetables, and MIDI could work in live situations. Like all great experiments there were more than a few explosions and singed eyebrows along the way (including Jack Secret eviscerating Lee's keyboard rig at the start of the *Power Windows* sessions when he forgot to factor in the voltage differences between North America and the UK). The failures were as important as the successes and, if Rush's music from the eighties is any indication (including the imperfect but wonderful *Signals*), Lee, Lifeson, and Peart, along with the supporting cast of keyboard tech Tony Geranios, Jim Burgess (another keyboard tech and programmer deeply involved with Rush to this day), Andy Richards, and Peter Collins should feel very proud indeed. It was the sonic equivalent of making it to the moon. But the question remained: Could they make it back?

The Melodic Mission of Geddy Lee

As mentioned previously, some Rush fans did not (and still don't) get Rush's keyboard-heavy music. They wanted the big, brash, ballsy power-prog music that put Rush on the map. That was the kind of Rush music that early fans had first been introduced to. That was the music that made them the diehard fans Rush is known for having. But even those early albums, from one to the next, showed that Rush's music was in a constant state of flux. They were continually evolving, not just as musicians, but as individuals. And the muse they passionately chased was a shape-shifter with a voracious appetite for new music, new technology,

While the band's use of keyboards have dimmed significantly since the eighties, Rush's music would not be the same without them. Geddy Lee's keyboard rig from 2010–11's *Time Machine* tour is much more powerful and much more compact, thanks to modern technology.   *Courtesy of John Carretta*

and new sounds. So, while there are those Rush fans who prefer to skip over some albums from this period (usually *Power Windows* and *Hold Your Fire*), they should be neither surprised nor disappointed that Rush's musical path ventured from the dark forests of fat, heavy analog synthesis to the crystalline waterfalls of digital processing and sampling. Upon hindsight, it was an obvious path for the band to take.

There is no doubt that Geddy Lee was the driving force behind Rush's great technological chase during the eighties. And who can blame him? Looking back over the music Rush made during this time, it was clear that Lee, while falling short as a virtuoso keyboardist, was a master of melody. And bass is arguably the last instrument of choice for someone gifted with the ability to create melody. Bass is, after all a rhythm instrument—well except in the hands of Paul McCartney, Chris Squire, and, of course, Geddy Lee and a few others. But despite Lee's ability to lay down some incredible melodies using a bass guitar and its relatively limited tones, textures, and frequency range, it was only natural that he would have a love affair with keyboard technologies and their genuinely limitless melodic capabilities. What Lee accomplished in bringing keyboards to Rush has since proven to be a wonderful gift to the band, its fan base, rock and roll music, and even the innovators who design and create musical instruments. Thankfully, he never fully traded his bass for keyboards, and he was secure enough to admit that he would never be a keyboardist in the ways he is a bassist. But thanks to all he learned during this era of Rush, he could now orchestrate, program, and write melodies with the best of them. Lee cared, and he was driven. He even took piano lessons around the *Hold Your Fire* sessions in order to improve his chops. But, in the end, he would have to settle with being rock and roll's greatest bass player. Oh, well . . .

Though Rush had eight more studio albums to make (at least as of this writing), the keyboard concern had been settled, and they had learned much and exceeded their own perennially lofty expectations. Keyboards would always play a role in Rush's music to some degree. And, now, the band knew exactly how to make it work.

Thus ends this part of the story. Well, at least the interesting part.

5

Rush Milestones on TV and in Film

Prog-Rock Icons' Decades-Long Screen Test

For most of the band's career, the members of Rush have maintained a reputation for being reluctant participants in television, and, to a lesser extent, film. Conversely, conventional wisdom has it that these visual mass mediums have tended to ignore the band in favor of acts with better haircuts and more accessible ditties. But upon further study, it turns out that both of these claims are simply untrue. Since 1974's Laura Secord Secondary High School performance (Rush's Canadian TV premiere) featuring the late John Rutsey, to their show stealing induction and jam on the 2013 Rock and Roll Hall of Fame ceremony broadcast, Lee, Lifeson, and Peart, as a band and individually, have appeared (or have been referenced) dozens and dozens of times on TV and in film. While some of these are as a prog-rock punch line, more often than not it is either to celebrate or to promote the band's work. In addition, some of these appearances seem designed to feed their love of show biz (yes, including the usually elusive Neil Peart) as not all of these appearances are music related.

Polite Rebellion

What has since turned out to be an historic coup for Rush fans, especially Alex Lifeson fans, Rush's legendary guitarist appeared in the 1972 Alan King documentary, *Come on Children*, filmed between 1969 and 1970. The film is a sobering and sometimes glaring look at disaffected youth in the hippie era coming of age and rebelling against parents who had grown up during World War II.

One especially powerful scene in the film comes when a young Lifeson is at the dinner table arguing with his nonplussed father, a hard-working immigrant and WWII survivor, over quitting school in order to pursue music. A portion of this scene can be found in the documentary, *Rush: Beyond the Lighted Stage*. Notable in the scene is all the young people at the table smoking cigarettes (Lifeson's sister has a particularly hacking cough) while Lifeson and his father go at it about his quitting school to follow music. Obviously, Lifeson got it his way and it paid off in spades. But, as he would note, many years later, his parents were right.

The film features several performances by Lifeson, who is clearly consumed with the guitar, though he has yet to master it and control it in the ways for which he is known. At one point, he plays an early Rush song, "Run Willie, Run," on acoustic guitar, and makes an earnest attempt at capturing Hendrix's psychedelic bombast while playing the guitar god's version of "The Star-Spangled Banner," replete with string gnawing. In both scenes, Lifeson's potential is evident, as is the effect his playing has on his peers.

Secondary Schoolhouse Rock

In 1974, four years after young Lifeson was filmed arguing with his parents over rock and roll liberty by documentarian Alan King, a Rush performance was videotaped by a Toronto TV station. The venue was Laura Secord Secondary school in, ironically enough, Peart's home town of St. Catharines. It is not, however, Peart behind the blue sparkle Gretsch kit, but John Rutsey. This early hard-rockin' performance features glittery wardrobe, Lee at his high-pitched best, sporting platform shoes and an impressive amount of chest hair. The audience was made up of perplexed young women and dozens of teenaged boys politely rocking out while seated. This video is considered a treat among Rush fans as it features Rutsey playing the front man role from behind the kit. It is the only footage that proves Rutsey had the looks and the chops to be a proper rock star (though he was no Neil Peart—but then, who is?). This recovered gem was found in the SRO-Anthem "Vault" (aka basement). The video had been mislabeled "Pink," which SRO assumed was a reference to Rush's 1979 Pink Pop performance. Two songs from this archive, "Best I Can" and "Working Man," are included as special features in *Rush: Beyond the Lighted Stage*. A third song, "Need Some Love," is included in the special features of Rush's concert DVD, *Time Machine*. It is unknown if more footage exists or will someday be released by the band.

This footage is about as close as a fan can get to experience what Rush was like in their club days. The three songs captured here reveal Rush's heavy bar-band vibe from their early days, including Lee boogieing on his bass to a straight drumbeat, and Lifeson pounding out riffs to a somewhat stunned audience.

Don Kirshner's Rock Concert

Long before MTV, the Internet, and the digital age, most Americans were stuck with four or five channels on their bulky televisions—the three big networks and one or two local channels (if the market was big enough to support them). That was it, and they all signed off around one a.m. On weeknights, talk shows closed out the night. On weekends, it was, on one lucky channel, *Don Kirshner's Rock*

Concert. Kirshner was a veteran television producer who left ABC's *In Concert* TV show, which featured lip-synched pseudo-live performances of pop-rock acts, to start his own syndicated show. *Don Kirshner's Rock Concert* debuted in 1973. It was the real deal for rock and roll fans whose opportunities for catching their favorite band in a live performance were few and far between. The show featured rock's best, including bands (like Rush), that were far outside the TV pop-music world. The Rolling Stones appeared on the show's debut, and over a hundred bands were featured on the ninety-minute show over its eight-year run. The lineup ranged from Joan Baez to Alice Cooper, Led Zeppelin to the Byrds, the Sex Pistols to Santana, and, of course, Rush, who appeared on October 9, 1974, when they shared the bill with Pure Prairie League. They played the requisite three songs, "Best I Can," and full versions of "In the Mood" and "Finding My Way." Unfortunately, poor-quality videos of these performances are all that remain. "In the Mood" and "Finding My Way" can be found in the special features of Rush's *R30* DVD.

Despite the poor quality, the performances are remarkable, showing how Rush played balls to the wall from first note to last, riding on the very edge of losing control of all that music. The performance is also noteworthy for it being one of Peart's earliest performances in the band (Peart had joined Rush only two months prior).

It is important to note that Rush's performance on *Don Kirshner's Rock Concert* occurred the same year as their Laura Secord Secondary School performance. A comparison of the two renditions of "Best I Can" provides, arguably, the best example of how Peart changed the band's sound, style, and substance. Where Rutsey's groove was solid and steady, Peart's groove was defined by adding flourish after flourish, filling up additional space in the song to the point of changing its energy and its flow—for the better. This also appears to have had an impact on Lee and Lifeson's performance. The Secord performance shows Rush being Rush: big, bombastic, loud, but also just the slightest bit awkward, as if they were still getting their legs under them. The *Don Kirshner's Rock Concert* performance reveals Rush being Rush in all caps, so to speak—BIG, BOMBASTIC, BUSY, and LOUD! There is an intensity and a sense of confidence that just isn't evident in the Rutsey performance. While it's true the venues and audiences were dramatically different, it's doubtful, from a musician's perspective, that that had any bearing. For most working rock musicians, once the music starts, it's all about rocking and rolling. The difference in venues does, however, reveal how Rush was gaining momentum in the US while still confounding the Canadian music scene. That would soon change . . .

Rush Speaks

After the *Don Kirshner's Rock Concert* appearance in 1974, the members of Rush appeared on TV in the US and Canada with increasing regularity. Unfortunately, they weren't doing what they do best: that is, playing their instruments. Instead, they were being interviewed. Chronologically, the next video of Rush speaking was an Alex Lifeson gear rundown backstage at the Paramount Theatre in Portland, Oregon. The video shows UFO as the opener on the marquee, so it's safe to assume this was filmed in September of 1977. The interview and taping was conducted by legendary rock photographer Buck Munger.

In 1979, during the Tour of the *Hemispheres*, Geddy Lee was interviewed by a Canadian TV reporter during setup of Rush's gig at Wynne Stadium in Hamilton, Ontario. This interview is available in the special features of the *R30* DVD. Lee comes across as very laid back, yet cerebral and intelligent—more like a stage manager or director than a badass bass player. (In truth, many musicians would rightfully argue that laid back and cerebral is exactly how badass bass players tend to be.) During this same stop on the *Permanent Waves* tour, Rush's manager, Ray Danniels, sporting an impressive Canadian mullet, was interviewed for the Canadian music channel MuchMusic. However, the actual broadcast of this interview includes music video snippets from 1982's *Signals* album, denoting that the Danniels interview sat on the shelf until Canada (or the band) was ready for such coverage.

Le Studio Le-Interviews, Le-Stoned Le-Lifeson

One of the first in-depth video-taped interviews of the band was made in 1980, shortly after the release of *Permanent Waves*. It was conducted at Le Studio outside of Morin-Heights, Quebec, the studio where *Permanent Waves*, among other key Rush records, was recorded. The interview captures the band members as they were before one of the biggest moments in Rush history—the recording, release, and reception of *Moving Pictures*. As rumor has it, the interview also happens to capture Rush, well, incredibly stoned. Lee, Lifeson, and Peart, despite his cerebral-nature, do appear altered. Lack of sleep? Early AM call time? The fragrance of Afghanistan? No one but the band knows for sure. Lifeson seems the most out of it; maybe it was the chemicals from his new perm. His contribution to the piece consists of a few mumbles and long fruitless attempts to meld into the scenery. Luckily, a stoned Neil Peart is deeper, more thought-provoking, and more intellective and honest than most musicians, sober or not. Lee hands things over to Peart at the top of the interview, and he runs with it. It is an early glimpse into how naturally bright the man is. Wielding a thorough understanding of the current state of music, and the dysfunction of the music industry, Peart inadvertently eviscerates the interviewer at times. His candor, coupled with the band's everyman attitude, seems to befuddle the reporter who starts strong, ends weak, but does a fair job trying to get the band (well, Lee) to talk about their use of technology.

The timing of the interview is noteworthy in itself. Not only does it find the members at ease with the success they have earned on their own terms and shows them as they were before the impending, hugely life-changing moment that was *Moving Pictures*, it also captures a time when rock and roll itself was in

Lee, Lifeson, and Peart making music at Le Studio, something they preferred more than talking about it.   *Courtesy of Yaël Brandeis*

the midst of a rebirth. In 1980, New Wave crashed hard onto the airwaves, altering rock's soundscape forevermore. Listening to Peart and Lee during the interview, it is clear that they are neither threatened nor alarmed by the new musical movement, as the interviewer seemed to expect them to be. Quite the contrary: they seem to fully understand and embrace it. It is this part of the interview when Lee really comes to life, and the camera finally goes for a two-shot, granting Lifeson a seemingly much-desired reprieve from the spotlight. Here, Peart and Lee correct the interviewer's misguided notions that New Wave bands are simplistic, and the music they make, uninteresting. Peart and Lee kindly but emphatically point out that New Wave is progressive, original, and often contains complicated arrangements, citing the Boomtown Rats and the Talking Heads as examples.

As if pre-planned, Peart and Lee make an excellent joke in unison out of a question posed to them by the interviewer that they must have heard dozens of times previously. The interviewer points out that, with the addition of Peart to the band, Rush's music had "turned over . . ." to which Peart and Lee interject, "Turned over and died!" This is an early glimpse into the band's comedic side, a side that would bloom in subsequent decades.

Rush's Early Videos

Moving down this impressive list (by prog-rock standards, anyway), it's good to keep in mind that the key difference between a music video and other footage capturing Rush performances is that music videos are created solely for promotional purposes. Rarely do they show the band actually playing live, and, if they do, the live audio is often replaced with the studio recording. A live performance video, however, captures part of an actual Rush show (or performance). For example, the Laura Secord videos capture a performance and are not considered a music video. Same goes for the *Don Kirshner's Rock Concert* footage. With that in mind . . .

"Anthem" "Church" Video (1975)

Truly promotional (music videos were a marketing tool for labels, big and small, long before MTV), this video shows the band playing their asses off on a set seemingly built for a Black Sabbath tribute act. The song captured and promoted was "Anthem," the opening track on 1975's *Fly by Night*, and one of the band's most intense non-stop barrage numbers. The song and the video are testament to what Peart would bring to the band over the next thirty-plus years. In fact, Lee and Lifeson had the opening riffs to "Anthem" back when Rutsey was in the band, but he couldn't get a feel for it, so it had lain fallow. It took a drummer like Peart to be able to finish the song.

Clearly this video was recorded on a soundstage, clearly the band is truly playing and singing, and clearly the live music, if recorded at all, was replaced by the album version of the song.

This early video has some great close-ups of Peart in action behind his chrome Slingerland kit, garbed in wardrobe suitable for a wizard's apprentice, or perhaps a Renaissance Faire bard (Huzzah!), with his head down as he bashes away on the song that marked his arrival into the annals of prog rock.

"Fly by Night" "Church" Video (1975)

Hey, while the cameras are rolling, why not shoot another song? Same set, same wardrobe, same energy, different song.

"Fly by Night" from the album of the same name, is somewhat more straight ahead and less manic than "Anthem," making it an excellent contrast. This was arguably closer to hit-single potential (indeed, "Fly by Night" did receive a bit of FM airplay), and so this was probably Side A of the two-song video session, with "Anthem" being the B-side. Once again, the band is clearly playing live, and once again, the album version of the song is dubbed in.

These two videos, often referred to as "the church session videos," are not to be confused with Rush's first gigs in a church basement of St. Theodore's of Canterbury. They are understandably popular within the Rush fan base, especially with first-generation fans who latched onto the band during the seventies, an era these videos capture well. Gearheads in and out of the Rush multiverse appreciate the videos for the classic gear they reveal. Lifeson is playing his Gibson ES-355 through Marshall JMP stacks, and Lee is playing a white Rickenbacker 4001 through two Ampeg SVT stacks. Lee and Lifeson are sporting two amp stacks each. Most likely, one was live and the other a backup, or each was dialed in for a different sound, and therefore each was used separately.

Both of these videos are on disc two of the *R30* DVD.

"A Farewell to Kings" and a Hello to Prophetic Robes (1977)

The interval between the release of 1975's *Fly by Night* and 1977's *A Farewell to Kings* seems too large for the band to have escaped making a promotional video, especially given the huge success (by Rush standards) of the independence-earning, groundbreaking, barrier-shattering *2112*, the studio album preceding *A Farewell to Kings*. Perhaps this is because *Caress of Steel* followed *Fly by Night*, and it fell flat as far as the label was concerned, and therefore may not have been considered promo-video worthy. And *Caress of Steel* was followed by *2112*, the album that had Rush giving the finger to their label in the form of a twenty-minute prog-rock opus as the opening track. Twenty minutes is damn near an eternity when it comes to making a promo video, though arguably "Something for Nothing" or "The Twilight Zone" would have worked well as promo-video material, as would "The Temples of Syrinx." After *2112* came Rush's first live album, 1977's *All the World's a Stage*, which was released on the heels of *2112*'s surprising (and surprisingly huge) success. Too bad there are no official video or film recordings from that timespan.

However, the multiple locales and costume changes found in the 1977 music video for "A Farewell to Kings" possibly makes up for it. Or not . . .

The video opens with Lifeson playing the song's beautiful classical guitar opening from a well-hidden spot in a pine forest. Had he not been wearing a bright red

Three of the six tracks from *A Farewell to Kings* received the promotional video treatment. It was a good chance to witness Rush during their grandiose wardrobe period.

Courtesy of Joe Pesch

robe (or possibly a kimono), he may have been hard to spot. Long crossfades are featured in these opening moments, including some shots of Bodian Castle in East Sussex, England. These shots fit rather well with the tone of the intro, as well as the lyrics to "A Farewell to Kings." Once the song gets heavy, it reverts to the tried-and-true "live" soundstage setting, with Peart and a bare-chested Lee sporting their infamous white satin, "absurdly prophetic robes," to quote Geddy Lee. In an attempt to portray a more authentic concert experience, the video's wide shots contain the silhouettes of a few hairy heads. The curly hair of the fellow in the middle resembles Rush's longtime tech and current lighting director, Howard Ungerleider.

The video is quite dark, making it hard to see the band's gear. The stand-outs are Lee's black 4001 Rickenbacker and Lifeson's white Gibson ES-355, the guitar he has been most associated with. Through the shadows one can also make out Peart's black, twelve-piece double-bass Slingerland kit (his last Slingerland), heavily augmented with orchestral percussion pieces such as tubular bells and glockenspiel. There are also a few nice shots of Lee's Minimoog synthesizer.

"Xanadu" (1977)

Following the standard practice of promo-video production, as shown in the church session videos, "Xanadu" was also taped during the same session as "A Farewell to Kings" (Seneca College Theatre in Toronto). The same dark lighting comes into play, though the addition of fog from the dry-ice machines helps brighten things up somewhat. Again, the band is playing live and, again, the studio version of the song was dubbed in.

One of the most remarkable things about these videos is that both songs are quite long by music-video standards (though far short of *2112*'s twenty-minute sonic journey). Both songs take time to develop and contain fairly long passages devoid of vocals. While such arrangements are celebrated by Rush fans, they are usually maligned by marketing video producers. Both "A Farewell to Kings" and "Xanadu" can be found on disc two of the *R30* DVD. The video is fun to watch as it shows both Lifeson and Lee playing their double-neck guitars.

"Closer to the Heart" (1977)

One of Rush's biggest hits, "Closer to the Heart," also from *A Farewell to Kings*, was taped during the same sessions as "Xanadu" and the album's title track. Destined for singledom, this video is given a socio-political intro not found in the "Xanadu" and "A Farewell to Kings" videos. It opens with a video mask revealing Geddy Lee's deep-set eyes while political figures, ranging from Mao Tse Tung to Gerald Ford, fly in and out of frame.

This video is by far the best lit of the three; you can actually see all that should be seen, which makes one wonder why "Xanadu" and "A Farewell to

Kings" did not get the same treatment. This version of "Closer to the Heart" can be found on the *Chronicles* video compilation DVD where it is listed as "Closer to the Heart (Live)." They may be playing live on the video, but the music heard is that of the studio version from the album.

Three songs from *Hemispheres* were given similar treatments to the three music videos from *A Farewell to Kings*. Again, the band appears to be playing live (this time with much better lighting), and the audio is all album versions. *Hemispheres* is a four-song album. "Cygnus X-1 Book II: Hemispheres" is over seventeen minutes long, narrowing down the video options to the remaining three tracks: "The Trees," "Circumstances," and "La Villa Strangiato." "Circumstances" and "La Villa Strangiato" can be seen on disc two of the *R30* DVD.

Rush on MTV

A theme throughout this book is how Rush's influence, impact, perception, fan base, and even the attitude of their detractors changed after the release of *Moving Pictures*. Up until that point, Rush's presence in front of any video camera was a rare event, and many of the aforementioned appearances had been forgotten and not missed until released on recent DVDs as part of the Special Features material. (And make no mistake: Rush fans are grateful that they have been found, especially the Laura Secord and *Don Kirshner* performances.) In the years after *Moving Pictures*, it was a different story. That album was released in February 12, 1981. Just under six months later, on August 1, MTV was born. Those who were old-school rockers during the eighties remember that date and the excitement that followed because it was a station dedicated solely to rock and roll. MTV was literally music television, twenty-four hours a day, seven days a week. It played almost nothing but music videos (like the ones mentioned earlier although, with minor exceptions, none of those

LAV-FM97

RUSH

TICKETS ON SALE TOMORROW!

WINGS STADIUM   NOVEMBER 11 8PM

TICKETS: $10.75 (plus 25¢ parking chg) Reserved Seats and Festival Floor On Sale at Wings Stadium Box Office; Boogie Records, Kalamazoo: Choker Records, Battle Creek; Believe in Music, Grand Rapids; Disc and Tape, Muskegon; Woodmark Records, Holland and Crazy Bob's, Jackson. For Info Call (616) 345-5101.

Prior to MTV, there was a better chance of seeing Rush live than there was on television, despite their growing body of video.   *Courtesy of Joe Pesch*

THROUGH ANY WINDOW

Any window but television, that is. Though Rush's handful of videos remained in rotation on MTV and its sister station, VH1, Rush was far from a TV-friendly band.   *Courtesy of Joe Pesch*

were ever played on the network). But in October of 1981, Rush released "Tom Sawyer" as a single and the music video for it made its way onto MTV's regular rotation in between all that new wave and ska. Prior to this, "Limelight," the first single released from *Moving Pictures*, could occasionally be found late at night on the fledgling network. Once "Tom Sawyer" was out and being pushed as a single, it was, surprisingly enough, not that hard to catch Rush on the network, much to the chagrin of all those college girls wanting Duran Duran and the Go-Gos. Even the music video for "The Trees" received the occasional airing during the wee hours.

By the mid-eighties, the members of Rush were making semi-regular appearances on MTV, usually to promote a new video, which marked the release of a new album or single. None of those appearances were for songs on *Moving Pictures* or the following release, *Signals*, though the video for its single, "Subdivisions," received scant MTV love. This is surprising given that *Signals* sounds as if it was inspired by the early days of Music Television.

By the time *Grace Under Pressure* and *Power Windows* were out, Rush could be seen, not only in their growing number of videos on MTV, but in interviews and specials on the network. While their appearances pale in comparison to MTV favorites, like the Police (who were intentionally antithetical to what Rush was all about), they did all right for semi-nerdy anti-rock-star prog musician icons. Incidentally, the members of the Police, who have occasionally maligned Rush in the media, inspired the band and helped shape their evolution. Rush has since eclipsed the Police's influence and impact. The fact that Lee, Lifeson, and Peart admire and even socialize with a band who dissed them (former Police drummer Stewart Copeland and Neil Peart are chums who have jammed together on more than one occasion) speaks volumes to their character.

Indeed, as the eighties progressed into the nineties, Rush videos were in B-level rotation on MTV. Some of the more popular videos were "Time Stands Still" (featuring fellow Canadian Aimee Mann) from *Hold Your Fire*, "The Big Money" from *Power Windows*, "Distant Early Warning" from *Grace Under Pressure*, and (finally) "Subdivisions" from *Signals*. "Tom Sawyer," "Limelight," "Red Barchetta," and even the rarity "Vital Signs," all from *Moving Pictures*, would still crop up now and then, though more so on MTV's sister station, VH1 Classic. Many of Rush's videos from this era were not on par with the band's music or music production. At times the concepts found inside the videos seem designed to hide the fact that Rush was not a group of "pretty boys." And, at times, the lip-synced performances seem forced, as if the band was trying to play along with the eighties stylistically, but were often uncomfortable doing so.

By the release of the album *Presto* in 1989, Rush (and the video producers they hired) had finally found their mojo. Unfortunately, by this time, MTV's interest in music videos was beginning to wane, and there was such a glut of videos available—some of them very high caliber—that Rush's appearance on the network returned to a rare event. More's the pity, since the band ended up producing some excellent videos during the late eighties and much of the nineties, especially "The Pass" from *Presto*. Other notable Rush music videos from this era include "Superconductor" and "Show Don't Tell" (both also from *Presto*), "Roll the Bones" (with its controversial rapping skull) from the album of the same name, "Stick It Out" from *Counterparts*, and "Driven" from *Test for Echo*.

Like many of Rush's efforts that bore fruit, they figured things out as they went, which, as a performing act, results in capturing for posterity the occasional mistake. One could argue that such is the price of sincerity in art, coupled with three men unwilling to rest on their laurels. Their earliest videos were honest and basic—the band playing live with the live audio replaced by the studio version (i.e., the best-produced version of the song). Then, as videos became a full-on medium, much like a 45RPM single, they found themselves on cheap sets acting like something they weren't while playing to a pre-recorded track—so much so it's sometimes hard to watch. Then, they let themselves be themselves (the one Rush recipe that constantly pays off), and they once again produced excellent art via videos, and looked much more comfortable in the process.

These days, catching Rush on one of their live DVDs produced over the past ten years, or seeing them on the shows where they've had cameos, it's clear that they seem to have embraced their inner ham. And, for a few moments, it seemed as if they wanted to be actors (or perhaps more accurately, comedians, à la Monty Python or Kids in the Hall) more than they wanted to be musicians.

The Serious-er Side of Peart

Outside of music videos and the occasional taped interview, the members of Rush appeared infrequently on television and in film throughout the nineties and into the early 2000s, while references to them steadily increased. These range from hearing a Rush song (usually "Tom Sawyer") played at a professional sporting event, to the occasional Rush T-shirt or poster sighting on a sitcom or in a stoner film. Two standouts during this time was Rush being feted as the Artist of the Decade (the eighties) on the 1990 Juno Awards, and being inducted into the Juno Hall of Fame four years later, in 1994. In 1997, the members of the band received the Order of Canada, the country's equivalent to being knighted.

Surprisingly, during this time, it was Neil Peart who had the most unique TV appearances. In 1994, he appeared on Comedy Central's *Politically Incorrect*,

Neil Peart's interviews confirmed what fans suspected based on his lyric-writing: he's not just smart for a drummer; he's smart for a human being!

Courtesy of Joe Pesch

hosted by Bill Maher. The show was essentially a roundtable political talk show with humor, similar to Maher's popular HBO show *Real Time with Bill Maher* (but without the cussing). Peart came across as well informed and scholarly, and, well, not that funny. One year earlier, in 1993, he conducted a remarkable interview with Canadian Prime Minister Jean Chretien for Canada's MuchMusic television network.

Canadians Gone Wild

As documented elsewhere in this book, the first decade of the 2000s proved to be a big one for the band. This was especially true concerning their film and television appearances. A steadily growing presence on Canadian TV (such as a one-hour biography special in 2002 on MuchMusic), Rush, starting with Alex Lifeson, began to show what they were truly capable of doing in front of the camera. In 2003, the Canadian network Showcase (Showtime of the

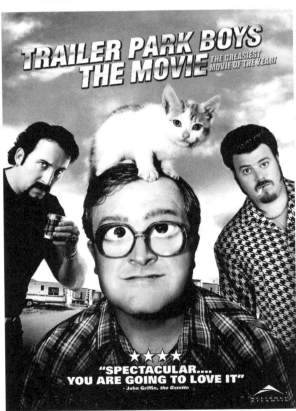

Great White North) had a hit series on their hands with the irreverent, occasionally trashy, always funny, faux docu-comedy, *Trailer Park Boys*. The show featured life in a rundown Nova Scotia trailer park that was home to a handful of colorful losers. In a 2003 episode aptly titled "Closer to the Heart," Alex Lifeson played himself being kidnapped by one of the show's main characters (Ricky). Rush in concert is featured briefly near the end of the episode. That same year, Jack Black, in the starring role of the Hollywood film *School of Rock*, made a big fat Rush plug by handing a young music student a CD of *2112*, citing, "Neil Peart, one of the great drummers of all time, study up."

Years went by, a few more sitcom references, references in cult animation shows, few odd appearances related

Alex Lifeson's scenes in both the *Trailer Park Boys* series and movies steal the show, at least for Rush fans.
Courtesy of Max Mobley

to sports, wine, weather, books, and of course music, and then on July 16, 2008, something very, very big happened in the world of Rush. The band appeared and performed on the popular American late night comedy show *The Colbert Report*. It was mainstream redemption at its finest. It was epic. And it was hilarious.

Stephen Colbert's faux news show, *The Colbert Report*, is an American institution loved by all, even by those it satirizes and mocks. Rush's performance of "Tom Sawyer" on the show was the first time they had played on American TV since *Don Kirshner's Rock Concert* in 1974. The entire thirty-minute show was filled with Rush jokes that the band and fans adored, such as Colbert's theme song being replaced by the song "Limelight," and Colbert's script being replaced by the lyrics to "By-Tor and the Snow Dog" ("Tobes of Hades lit by flickering torch—JIMMY!"). All three band members were interviewed simultaneously (a rare event). They laughed as hard as anyone at the Rush and prog-rock jokes. The interview included questions such as, "Have you ever played a song that was so long, that by the end of the song, you were influenced by yourselves from the beginning of the song?" The show ended with Rush playing an extended version of "Tom Sawyer," and the following day's show opened with Rush playing the last note of the song from the previous night—another joke referencing their tendency for long songs.

Rush's appearance on *The Colbert Report* was important for several reasons: millions of viewers around the globe got to see the band, giving them a chance to shatter the myth once and for all that they take themselves too seriously; *The Colbert Report* is a popular, hip show with an equally hip audience; and Rush's first US television performance in more than thirty years made it feel like viewers were watching history being made. But it was also important because Rush fans (and prog-rock fans in general), who have been taking it on the chin for loving this often-misunderstood band and their music, and for loving a maligned genre considered dorky and nerdy, were finally able to let their guard down and laugh about themselves, their favorite music, and their musical heroes. They were able to relax their defenses and not take this part of their lives so seriously. And holy Syrinx, it was genuinely liberating. Given the appearances and references of Rush thereafter, it was clearly liberating for the band as well.

More Trailer Trash

Alex Lifeson was such a big hit in the aforementioned episode of *Trailer Park Boys* that many fans of the show, along with Rush fans (quite an overlap there), expected him to make a cameo in the show's 2006 film, *Trailer Park Boys: The Movie*. Lifeson, who plays a cop in the film, does not disappoint. His partner was Gord Downey from the Canadian band the Tragically Hip. In the 2009 sequel, *Trailer Park Boys 2: Countdown to Liquor Day*, Lifeson once again plays a cop, this time an undercover cop in drag. Lifeson's natural comedic talent shines through in his scenes.

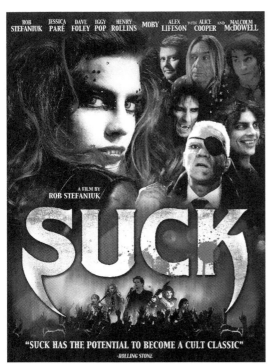

ROB STEFANIUK JESSICA PARÉ DAVE FOLEY IGGY POP HENRY ROLLINS MOBY ALEX LIFESON WITH ALICE COOPER AND MALCOLM McDOWELL

A FILM BY ROB STEFANIUK

"SUCK HAS THE POTENTIAL TO BECOME A CULT CLASSIC"
-ROLLING STONE

Alex Lifeson's acting in the cult film *Suck* was top-notch. Director Rob Stefaniuk even encouraged him to pursue acting as a profession.
Courtesy of Max Mobley

Rush Suck—in a Good Way

Lifeson also made an appearance in the 2009 rock and roll vampire comedy, *Suck*. The film hasn't quite reached cult status, though it arguably should have given the great rock and roll cast, including Iggy Pop, Henry Rollins, Alice Cooper, Moby, and, of course, Lifeson, who underplays his scenes as a border patrol office to fine comedic effect. He turned in such a good performance, in fact, that the film's director, Rob Stefaniuk, actually encouraged Lifeson to take up acting full time. Thankfully, he didn't listen.

I Love You, Man Loves Rush

John Hamburg's 2009 hit "bromantic comedy," featuring two dudes, Peter (Paul Rudd) and Sydney (Jason Segal), who bond over their love of Rush, was as big a moment in Rush history as the band's appearance on *Colbert*. It debuted in the number-two spot at the box office and remained on the top-ten list of moneymakers for five weeks. It went on to gross over $27 million. Rush factors big in the film's plot, being the catalyst for Peter and Sydney's relationship. A key moment in the film takes place at a Rush concert, which was the Los Angeles stop of the *Snakes and Arrows* tour, on May 11, 2008. Peter and Sydney have the time of their lives at the concert (like Rush fans do), while Peter's fiancée, Zooey (Rashida Jones, daughter of Quincy Jones), feels left out. (Jones cited this as her favorite scene in the film.)

Hamburg, the film's director and screenwriter, is a big Rush fan who has played the group's music in cover bands. He went out of his way to make Rush happy and comfortable during the production of the one scene in which they appear, though he needn't have bothered—the band was very happy to participate. When Hamburg explained to Geddy Lee what the main characters would be doing in the scene—rocking out and bonding while the girlfriend feels bored and ignored by her boyfriend—Lee responded, "So it's just like any one of our concerts."

Paul Rudd revisits his Rush superfan role from the bro-mantic comedy *I Love You, Man* for the closing video of the *Time Machine* tour.   *Courtesy of John Carretta*

The storyline and characters from *I Love You, Man* were brought back during Rush's 2010 *Time Machine* tour. Rudd and Segal, in character as Peter and Sydney, appeared in a short film at the end of the concert, entitled *I Still Love You, Man*. The two are backstage in the green room at the end of the concert when the band walks in and discovers their "biggest fans in the universe" eating their food. This may not qualify as amazing comedy by any stretch, but it was still good to see the characters of this much-loved film in a scene with their (and our) favorite band.

Rush: Beyond the Lighted Stage

The 2010 rockumentary *Rush: Beyond the Lighted Stage* is to fans of fantasy-inspired prog rock what Peter Jackson's *Lord of the Rings* trilogy is to, well, fans of fantasy-inspired prog rock. Okay, well, that was a bit of a joke, but it contains some truth. The *Lord of the Rings* movies legitimized fantasy fiction, and its legion of fans, many of whom were often ostracized as dorks and Dungeons & Dragons-playing fanatics. A high percentage of this group also tends to like Rush. And Rush fans—especially diehard Rush fans—can relate to a similar form of ostracism that became their badge of honor, a secret handshake, a key to a secret club. The 2008 *Colbert* appearance was like having the address to that club printed and published for anyone to find. It seemed to start speculation among what Rush fans consider as outsiders—the millions of music lovers who "don't get" Rush, or downright hate them—that this Rush thing may be worth looking

The band you know. | The story you don't.

Beyond the Lighted Stage showed rock fans of all genres that Rush is revered by both their fellow musicians and their fans, and that their story is one of the most original and endearing in all of rock and roll.   *Courtesy of Max Mobley*

into. They seem to be having a good time, and, well, Stephen Colbert seems to love them (he also loves *Lord of the Rings* and has publicly schooled Peter Jackson, on LOTR trivia more than once). Maybe there's more to this prog-rock band than screeches, solos, and well-mulleted fans.

So, after *Colbert*, a well-kept secret became something like a rock and roll life-hack: *Wanna have a rockin' time? Be sure and check out Rush, live!* Rush fans noticed the difference at shows, but these curious adventurers made a point to fit in, right down to the air-drumming and the ubiquitous Rush concert T-shirts. So it was cool. There were a lot of newbies around, but they just wanted to be like "real" Rush fans, so it was sort of a compliment. (Notice how the band is getting forgotten in this bit? More on that later.) Rush fans agreed that the presence of these new Rush bandwagoneers was worth it: suddenly, it seemed, stumbling across Rush sightings in popular culture had become a lot more common. It was a fair tradeoff, and no one really noticed that the trend was growing. In fact, this temporary phenomenon seemed to have plateaued, confirming that it was indeed temporary. Around this time word got out that a Rush documentary was in the works by Scot McFadyen and Sam Dunn, the same guys who made *Metal: A Headbanger's Journey*, a solid documentary that metal-heads and rockers really dug. That rock-doc did not make a single wave outside of the rock and metal scene, which is what Rush fans expected for the documentary about their band—perfect. Then, a funny thing happened on the way to DVD. *Rush: Beyond the Lighted Stage* began earning critical praise.

The film debuted at the 2010 Tribeca Film Festival in New York City and won the coveted Heineken Audience Award. It was also voted an Audience favorite at the Toronto Film Festival. There were a number of public screenings of the film, including an especially memorable one in the San Francisco Bay Area. Seeing Rush fans lined up around the block outside the theatre felt oddly familiar. The faces, the T-shirts, the occasional wafting smells—definitely a Rush show was happening that night. Having the close seats fill up last seemed a bit bizarre, but there were only happy, eager faces wherever you looked.

And then the lights went down.

And the crowd cheered just like it was a Rush concert.

After a revered glimpse into the band's pre-show ritual, an ancient intro Rush fans know well from the first live album, *All the World's a Stage*, spoken by the late Skip Gildersleeve, was heard. And then, in grainy black-and-white, and more importantly, in loud, clean 5.1, a 1970s version of three travelers from Willowdale (well, technically one was from St. Catharines) took over the cinema with the opening riff to "Bastille Day." Every minute of the film that followed these incredible opening seconds was perfect. No wishes for anything different or anything more, no armchair critiquing—just basking in a spot-on story about a band worshipped by grown men of differing generations. We came to see Rush on film and a story many fans already new. Fans left the same way they leave the best Rush shows—changed forever. And there would be no going back for anyone involved—Rush, Rush fans, and lovers of rock music.

The opening sequence was from a 1976 show in Passaic, New Jersey ("Anthem" from that same show was included in the special features of the *Time Machine* DVD). It was culled from a black and white bootleg that had surfaced in the early 2000s, but was hard to watch because it had time code and "ME-48" burned into the video of a young Lee, Lifeson, and Peart climbing the first rungs of their ladder to success. McFadyen and Dunn did an amazing job of removing that burn-in (or finding a version that did not have it) and restoring the audio to near-perfection. It captured a moment in Rush's history, both sonically and visually, making it a perfect opener for what fans had come to see.

Rush Did All That?

It would be good to remember that, until this documentary, it was pretty rare to see and hear the members of Rush talking about Rush, at least for a band as big as they had become. At the time of this writing, it is generally agreed that the Beatles, the Rolling Stones and Led Zeppelin are the only bigger bands in rock history—thus far. Zep is notoriously media-shy. Plant and Page are omnipresent personalities in rock and roll simply because their music is in constant heavy rotation, and they've been huge influences on the course of hard rock. And hours and hours of well-known footage exists of the Stones and Fab Four talking about themselves. But there had been very little available prior to this documentary of the members of Rush talking about anything, let alone talking about their band. Keep in mind that the previously mentioned interview footage was largely unavailable prior to the release of *Rush: Beyond the Lighted Stage*. Just seeing Rush talk about Rush was a big deal for fans.

Many Rush fans believed they knew the story. They had read Peart's books, and the three popular Rush websites—rushisband.com, Power Windows (news.2112.net), and Cygnus-x1.net are well respected, well-loved, and often-visited by the Rush community. Each of these sites do a great job of archiving the Rush story. So imagine Rush fans' collective surprise when new information about the band was revealed, not least among it, how Lee, Lifeson, and Peart really and truly care for one another and interact with each other. The band's dynamic leaps from the screen and is largely responsible for the popularity of the film among non-Rush fans.

You're a Rush Fan? Hey, I'm a Rush Fan, Too!

Another major highlight in *Rush: Beyond the Lighted Stage* is the well-known rock musicians who talk openly and from the heart about what Rush means to them and their music. There is an especially intimate moment when Billy Corgan (the Smashing Pumpkins) talks about sitting his mother down to have her listen to Rush's "Entre Nous" with the hope that Peart's lyrics and the band's sound would help a mother better understand her son, and find the beauty in the music he loves. This is something many Rush fans feel firsthand. The misunderstood youth theme is rampant throughout the story, from Lifeson and Lee being outsiders and immigrants in middle school, to Peart trying to handle being the oddball in his family and among his fellow teenagers, all of whom were (or at least appeared to be) much cooler than teenage Peart could ever hope to be. Even Rush manager Ray Danniels is part of this backstory as, during Rush's early days, he tries and fails to get the band some gigs (let alone some press) and simply cannot understand why promoters and labels do not get or like the band. There are also a few moments when Rush fans tell their story of how being a Rush fan didn't exactly help their popularity or their standing with the opposite sex.

Merely Players

One element that makes the Rush doc work so well is that it features some highly respected musicians (and Jack Black) talking about how important Rush was to them musically and as a shelter from the snakes and arrows of adolescence. Here is this geeky band that simply could not and would not be cool, who would rather just be themselves and make their own music their own way, being vaunted by artists all the cool kids adored. It was the sweetest redemption.

Artists and players appearing in *Beyond the Lighted Stage* include:

- Sebastian Bach (vocalist Skid Row)
- Jack Black (actor, comedian, guitarist / vocalist—Tenacious D)
- Jimmy Chamberlin (drummer—the Smashing Pumpkins)

- Les Claypool (bassist / vocalist—Primus, Frog Brigade, and many other Les Claypoolish bands)
- Tim Commerford (bassist—Rage Against the Machine)
- Billy Corgan (founder, vocalist / guitarist—the Smashing Pumpkins)
- Kirk Hammett (lead guitarist—Metallica)
- Taylor Hawkins (drummer—Foo Fighters)
- Kim Mitchell (vocalist / guitarist—Max Webster)
- Vinnie Paul (drummer—Pantera, Hellyeah)
- Mike Portnoy (drummer—Dream Theatre, Liquid Tension Experiment)
- Trent Reznor (Oscar winning composer—Nine Inch Nails)
- Gene Simmons (bassist / vocalist—Kiss)
- Matt Stone (co-creator—South Park)
- Zakk Wylde (guitarist—Ozzy Osbourne, Black Label Society)

Beyond *Beyond the Lighted Stage*

After the release of the documentary, there was a shift in the Rush space-time continuum. The band was different, and so were the fans. It wasn't just that they had nothing left to prove. It was that Rush now had a new form of respect they had decided long ago that they could live without. Suddenly, not shagging a bunch of groupies after a gig and not overdosing between shows was considered cool. Reading books in hotel rooms after a bigass rock show now seemed perfectly acceptable. This was true because of how Rush was portrayed by the filmmakers and their peers in the film. It was also true because the film came out when geek-culture had gone mainstream, thanks to Bill Gates, Mark Zuckerberg, and the legion of nerds (many of whom happen to be Rush fans) who write and produce today's films and TV shows, and operate the zillions of key cogs that make up our modern interconnected world. And, as it turns out, Rush boasts one of the most interesting and original success stories in all of rock and roll: theirs is a tale devoid of sex and drugs. Instead, we see three nice guys who, if they lived on your street, would probably feed your cat and pick up the mail for you while you're on vacation, and you wouldn't worry once about it while you were gone. (How many rock musicians could you say that about?)

Rock music's prototypical darlings are cherished and held up as examples of honesty and integrity in art, of being imperfect and having no choice but to let that imperfection show. This is the ethos of punk, and the polar opposite of prog bands like Pink Floyd. Honesty and pain is attributed to bands like Radiohead and the Clash, not Yes, or Led Zeppelin, or Rush. And yet, as *Rush: Beyond the Lighted Stage* shows, no band was more honest, more imperfect, more ostracized, more principled (and, after July 4, 1997, more in pain) than they. While critics rarely admit they were wrong, and Rush will never be (and never want to be) critical darlings, this documentary proves that the critics were wrong as could be about the Rush ethos. And fans around the world were vindicated for loving something that, it turns out, was highly substantive and hugely influential on the sound and shape of rock and roll—and more authentic than bands like the Police or Wilco.

Yipes.

In other words, though they never really looked the part, never took the drugs or required the subsequent rehab, Rush is—according to rock and roll's definition of the word—*cool*. The secret club was now open to anyone willing to pony up the new, higher ticket prices. And, boy, did they! The cult was now considered legit, like some sort of Canadian Buddhism. And for many Rush fans, especially first-generation Rush fans, it was a hard pill to swallow. After all, Rush concerts, and their music, and the private nature of the mass Rush ritual, was the reward for being on the outside of rock and roll (and sometimes societal) acceptance. Now diehard fans have to line up for beer behind some guy who can't name what album "The Spirit of Radio" is on. Now there are things called Geddicorns (females who find Geddy Lee sexy). But there are also fathers taking their sons and daughters to see something that mattered hugely to them, hoping for a pair of sticks the way a dad at Wrigley Field has hopes to snag a foul ball. The club has grown, of that there is no doubt—just look at Rush's impressive tour stats in the post-*Beyond the Lighted Stage* era. But there is also a club within the club. And some fascinating overlap like a Venn diagram, laid out across an amphitheater smelling of beer and weed smoke.

6

The Clubs of Rush

Big Music Requires a Big Tent

W hen a band tours as much as Rush does, and fills amphitheaters and arenas as much as Rush does, it makes sense that their audience would be quite diverse. This is truer today than in their early tours, when the band was in the nascent stages of their evolution.

Original Fans

The original fans, or "first-generationers," are those who attended a Rush concert before *Moving Pictures*. These fans likely discovered Rush via *2112*, and then went out and purchased the three prior albums and everything that came after—on vinyl, because that was the premier option during this time. These fans are well-experienced in vinyl's rituals, which differ dramatically from the world of MP3s. It was an era when buying an album was more than just buying a collection of tunes. The liner notes, the artwork on the cover and inside the fold, the lyrics, those little messages from the artists lurking about—all symbolic of the bigger picture of what albums represented at that time. In addition, playing a record during this era was a commitment—big, bulky, hands-on, and beautiful in its way. The whole thing added a sort of reverence to the music and the band that helped cement a relationship between listener and artist.

Rush largely earned their fan base through constant gigging. This is especially true for "first-gen" fans. This poster marks the band's first gig with Peart, a night very few Rush fans can say they witnessed firsthand.   *Courtesy of Max Mobley*

First-generation fans proudly wear symbols of their affiliation however they see fit, such as this Rush belt buckle.
Courtesy of Scott Burgan

This image of a rock-and-roll fan with his Rush T-shirt and massive record collection captures the look and style of "first-gen" Rush fans who came of age during the seventies and early eighties.   *Courtesy of Scott Burgan*

Rush ticket stubs, like the ones in this photo, are badges of honor for fans.   *Courtesy of Joe Pesch*

These "first-generationers" are the senior fellows of Rush's Diogenes Club. They have the best bragging rights, the oldest concert T-shirts, the biggest bellies, and the baddest backs. These fellows (of which I am a proud member), can only take about twenty-five minutes of slow mall-walking before their backs give out, but they can stand in one place and rock out at a Rush show for more than three hours, and their bladder expansion techniques have broken new ground in medical science.

Second-Generation Fans

Second-generation Rush fans discovered the band around the time of *Moving Pictures*, which was still early in the Rush *oeuvre*. These members love to hear stories from generation-one members, and many also hold impressive jobs in computer sciences. Like original fans, and *all* Rush fans—cliques, really—they hold a sort of reverence for what Rush does. This club usually has the best weed, and they are excellent at sussing out the shortest lines for the loo. (Sydney and Peter, from *I Love You, Man*, are members of this club.)

Many second-generation fans have seen more Rush concerts than first-generation fans. They came of age at a time when rock concerts were in greater abundance and more accessible, and they somehow manage to see multiple Rush shows during the same tour. They are lucky fellows, for sure.

Rush Fans, the Next Generation

Rush Fans, the Next Generation, arrived at the party years after the release of *Moving Pictures*, though chances are "Tom Sawyer" was their invitation. These bold fans have no qualms about using the traditionally vacant women's restrooms found at Rush concerts. They also have some of the most impressive air-drumming and air-guitar and bass skills. As Rush started playing larger venues, it is these fans who help to sell out those shows. Outside of *2112* and *Permanent Waves*, Rush music prior to *Moving Pictures* holds little interest for them.

The New Muso Generation

For serious rock musicians in their teens and twenties, Rush matters enormously. What playing Frisbee was in the seventies, playing rock guitar is today. This is due in part to the sheer number of cheaply made, decent-looking guitars available online, in big box stores, in music stores, and in online big box music stores. They may not play well, stay in tune, or even sound that good, but that's okay: there are plenty of boxes to plug into to help compensate for that—well, at least in part. Generally speaking, few rock musicians have the luck or cash to start rocking out on a nice instrument. And today's inexpensive guitars are all-the-way-around much better than their cheap

The fanzine *Spirit of Rush* (Issue 34) celebrated RushCon, the convention for Rush fans of all walks of life, held annually in Canada.

Courtesy of John Patuto and cygnus-x1.net

Today's Rush concert features young and old, male and, on occasion, female. But regardless of age or gender, all respond enthusiastically to a Rush show.

Courtesy of Max Mobley

predecessors. Anyone serious about becoming a decent rock musician will get past the limitations of their first instrument and, sooner or later, end up with something respectable, regardless of its country of origin. Many of these musicians, whose numbers are legion, are apt to become Rush fans for obvious reasons. Slightly less obvious is the fact that, for young musicians looking to be inspired, it is hard to find artists of their generation who have the ability to inspire the way Lee, Lifeson, and Peart have for over four generations. So these young, talented musicians with eager muses and much to say turned to classic rock groups, such as Black Sabbath, Led Zeppelin, and, of course, Rush. YouTube is filled with their videos, teaching Rush licks and beats. While at Rush shows they feel that playing air-drums and air-guitar is a weird, slightly embarrassing tradition, they arrive with high hopes and leave more than satisfied. Their reverence for Rush stems from studying masters of the craft. Rush's message is of secondary importance. They are there to study the hands and feet of Lee, Lifeson, and Peart.

Industry Accommodators

Today, Rush is a big deal, and a big business with a product line and a bottom line. Some fans, especially first-generation fans, may be in denial about this; after all, who wants to look at the business aspect of their heroes?—the commerce and capitalism side required to make a good living as a musician, and put on numerous incredible and expensive shows and release high-quality products in the form of DVDs, CDs, and books (oh, yeah, there is music in there somewhere . . .). Just because Rush, or, more accurately, Rush's corporate entity, SRO-Anthem, is beholden to profits, just like any other corporation (many would argue, perhaps rightfully so, as it is their obligation), it does not mean that Rush has sold out—at least not musically. Yeah, a band that can make as much money as Rush does on a tour can (and do) demand a high ticket price. And ticket sales, at least in the US, are controlled by a monopoly that does questionable things like sell a portion of good seats at face value to a subsidiary who can then sell them to the highest bidder. Ticketmaster, the well-known ticket company in the US, owns several resale ticket agencies where a Rush fan can by a new Rush ticket that was never available at face value for five times that face value.

> Controversial practice? You bet.
> Big business? Hell, yes.
> Rush's fault? Nope.

They aren't the only ones, either; just ask Bruce Springsteen, in between numbers, about working-class struggles and "41 Shots."

Though it may be justifiable to hold on to the dream of such high ideals that a band like Rush would not allow for such a thing—rock music is, after all the art form of the working class, and it would certainly be interesting to see them say no to ticket selling controversies and go it their own way, like they have all

Many who work in the music industry know that Rush concerts feature some spectacular moments, as shown in this image from the *Clockwork Angels* tour.   *Courtesy of Joe Pesch*

these years with their music. But how would they sell their tickets, then? And how does one even make sure that Rush fans have first access, and that the seats are not just filled with the well connected and those making profits off the Rush moneymaking machine? Rush does it through swag-packed pre-sales events that get Rush fans to the front, for a price.

And that brings us to our next Rush club: The Industry Accommodators.

Industry accommodation is the name the music industry (and probably other industries as well) use for an inside deal. For example, if you make guitar amps for a living, you can probably buy electric guitars direct from the builder, or at a special price from the stores that carry your amps because you will do the same in return. Translate that to a Rush concert and you have a host of related industries expecting (and often getting) free tickets to shows, special access to select seats, and special pricing on tickets. These industries include PR and the press (a big chunk these days because Rush is so damn HUGE, and press is a key component to getting the word out). The rest of the industry accommodators include instrument and gear manufacturers, makers of swag, venue-related industries, legal, security, and sundry corporate-related friends, colleagues, and employees. Given all that, is it any wonder so many Rush fans end up on the lawn? One thing about this practice that is not controversial (keep in mind that this is standard practice for most artists): because so much of the music industry is made up of musicians, many with their own dashed dreams of rock star success, most of the Industry Accommodators Club love Rush, or, at least, love a Rush show (it would be hard not to).

Geddicorns

Yep, Geddicorn is a thing. According to urbandictionary.com., a Geddicorn is: "A good-looking female that attends a RUSH concert without having to be coaxed to do so by a dude. She is turned on by Geddy Lee and not afraid to show it."

Boom. There you have it. They exist, they love Rush, their numbers are small and growing, they have excellent taste, and my wife is not a member.

Working Musicians

Few get as much out of a rock concert as a musician. To them, a rock concert is a clinic. It is about guitars, amps, pedalboards, even strings and sticks and cables. It is also about the sound, the tone, the chords, the notes, the words, the mix, the FOH (front of house) hardware, the placement of monitors, the stands, and most of all, the music and musicianship. All rock concerts are clinics for musicians, and a Rush concert is the ultimate master class. So much is learned and enjoyed by this group that their post-show high is as gracious as it gets.

Drummers

Drummers, musicians will tell you, are not musicians. They just hang around musicians, getting things all broken and dirty. Okay, that's more joke than truth, but some drummers feel the same way. And at a Rush concert, drummers are definitely their own club. While they never seem to have money to help pay for a rehearsal space, or for their own beer at practice and at gigs, and they often need to borrow cash to pay for sticks or new heads, they always somehow end up in the best seats at a Rush concert—just a few rows back, dead center. From their vantage point they stare at Mr. Peart all night and play right along, sometimes as if trying to outplay him. They are especially meticulous about hitting the odd time fills, and placement of each air hit is of critical importance. Before and after the show, and at intermission, they are usually found holding two beers. This is remarkable, as beer isn't even sold after intermission.

The Christo-Libertarian Club

Whether it is just a sign of the times, or unique to the band, Rush's fan base includes a surprising number of evangelical Christians (or at least those who take their religion very seriously) who tend to also be Ayn Rand–influenced Libertarians. The Rand reference is key here. Though Peart admits to simple curiosity and the naïveté of youth when he wrote lyrics inspired by Rand ("2112," "Anthem," "Something for Nothing," and one could make a solid argument for "Bastille Day" also fitting that mold), he has since described himself as a bleeding-heart Libertarian. That is, individualism with compassion, and not at the expense of the liberty or happiness of others. No jokes here (this tends to be a group that does not take jokes well), but it is interesting that some of Rush's most devout fans belong to this club, given the fact that the band has been accused of being satanic more than once (even though Geddy Lee is Jewish), and Peart's lyrics from *Snakes and Arrows* call into question the values and potential dangers of religion (check out the words to "Armor and Sword." Peart never goes fully negative in lyrics that discuss religion. His style is far more subtle and philosophical, and his intellectual curiosity about humanity guides his pen. That he has written about such a polarizing topic and yet the band has maintained devoutly Christian fans is a testament to both groups.

Rush's Alleged and Ill-Conceived Satanic Affiliations

It's true: Rush's first truly epic album, *2112*, has a star that resembled a pentagram on it, although the circle around the star actually makes it closer to a pentacle. But, as Peart himself pointed out in a letter about this topic, it's neither; it is simply an open star atop a circle. Pentagrams and pentacles have straight lines, drawn from point to point. That does not describe Rush's red

Rush's symbolism and imagery as shown on the cover of issue 13 of the *Spirit of Rush* fanzine has been misinterpreted as evil and demonic by some religious groups. Rush fans, however, know better.   *Courtesy of John Patuto and cygnus-x1.net*

Rush fans are fiercely loyal, and quite invested in the band, as shown by this collection of swag by Rob Silverberg.   *Courtesy of Rob Silverberg*

star. The pentagram and pentacle are supposed to be satanic, at least according to those who generally feel rock and roll is the work of good old Beelzebub himself (or maybe he was just the manager). Forget the fact that the pentagram's use as a symbol can be traced from ancient Babylon, through ancient Greece, the New Testament (the five wounds of Jesus), and right up to the US Air Force and US Congressional Medal of Honor. And forget the fact that the satanic version of the symbol (so overused it has become cliché) is inverted, with the single point aiming toward hell—or Australia, if you're looking at one while in Canada. The point is, Rush's red star logo (again, not a pentagram), which first appeared on Rush's prog masterpiece *2112*, is pretty flimsy evidence that the band has ties to the hoary red scamp.

Nonetheless, thanks to *2112*, Rush earned the wrath of a small number of people who truly believed that rock and roll was a vessel for Satan, and that Lee, Lifeson, and Peart (especially Peart—he wrote the lyrics, he has the darkest kimono, and he wore that devilish moustache) were not in it for the music; they were in it for the tasty souls of innocent young men.

An early salvo on this issue came from an editorial written by Jim Hanklin and published in a University of Texas newspaper called the *Daily Texan*. The circa 1979 piece was published by a group that held seminars dedicated to revealing how the mission of rock and rollers was to turn young people away from Christ, and toward all things satanic. The red star on *2112* with a naked man resisting (or potentially worshiping) it, dystopian sci-fi lyrics, and objectivistic themes were apparent fodder for those who believed rock music was evil. One could argue that the stoner anthem "Passage to Bangkok," and the ode to Rod Serling, "The Twilight Zone," on *2112*'s side two, did not help matters any. However, what really gave this early accusation some legs was Peart's well crafted but somewhat snarky rebuttal to the editorial. In it, he points out the symbol found on *2112* is not a pentagram, and that most of the rock musicians singled out for being Satan's little helpers were actually too narcissistic and lazy to do the horned one any good (he makes a strong point there). The rebuttal, which can be found on the Internet, reveals a young Peart wielding a pen much mightier than any allegedly Christian sword, describing "grim-faced hypocrites . . . stirring around in the dark places of life hoping to find something—anything—dirtier than their own reflection. And if they can't find anything—no problem—they'll just make something up!"

Ouch.

The lines "Brotherhood of Man," and "Hold the Red Star proudly high in hand," both from the song "2112," are also misguided examples of the completely false notion that Rush cares about Satan. The truth was, is, and always will be (thank goodness), that Rush cares only about their music and their fans. While that should quell any rumors related to the occult, it is a controversy that lingers in the fringes of evangelical Christianity, the mere existence of which seems to bolster Peart's questions about the validity of religion more than it

Rush fans, young and old, gladly stand for the duration of an evening with Rush, as shown here at the Concord Pavilion, in California, during the *Time Machine* tour.

Courtesy of Tina Davey

lends credence to some fire-and-brimstone allegiance between Canadian prog rockers and Abaddon.

These controversies occurred backwards—the rare practice of recording something with the tape flipped over, so that when you flipped it back, it would play backward and be impossible to understand—unless you're Satan, or the unprotected subconscious—was at its peak. The live version of "Anthem" from *All the World's a Stage*, is said to contain the phrases: "Oh, Satan, you are the one who is shining. . . . Walls of Satan, I know it is you are the one I love" (*sic*). Besides the sheer lunacy it required to think that Rush leans toward some organized evil, it's also impossible to believe that Peart would write such ham-fisted doggerel to honor a dark lord.

The bottom line is, it's a big world with its share of loons who simply need something to rail against—so why not Rush?

While the whole satanic thing never really took off for Rush the way it did for Ozzy or Jimmy Page, it did seem to briefly resurface with the alleged satanic art and occultist imagery found on the album *Clockwork Angels*, and, to a lesser extent, *Snakes and Arrows*. (Snakes = devil in some circles.) And, if you happen to worship the devil, you already know that Rush is an acronym for Rule Under Satan's Hand. (Not really.)

Brazilians

The different fan "clubs" mentioned above all have their own version of Rush pride and Rush concert-going enthusiasm. For some, it's quite intense (Rush geeks unite!), and it doesn't always settle back down when the concert is over. It's been this way for years, and over all, it is proper source of pride.

And then there are the Brazilians.

These Rush fans, introduced to all the other Rush fans via the live DVD *Rush in Rio*, are their own thing. And all other Rush fans remain in awe of them. For more details, see the chapter *Rush in Rio*.

7

All the World's a Stage—But Especially North America

A Double Live Introduction to Rush in Concert

R ush earned their success one show at a time, one fan at a time. Despite their success in the studio, and on FM AOR rock radio, they have always been a live band, first and foremost. Because of this, Rush's live albums make an excellent catalyst for telling their story over the decades.

Though breakouts, mostly in the form of albums, are a theme in this book, that first big breakout—*2112*—received next-to-no airplay. It broke through word of mouth, fueled in large part by all that touring. That tour was captured on Rush's first live album, 1976's *All the World's a Stage*.

All the World's a Stage was recorded over three back-to-back shows at Massey Hall in Toronto, Canada, in 1976. This was an era when live albums, especially double live albums, were becoming a force in record sales. Kiss *Alive!*, Thin Lizzy *Live and Dangerous*, UFO *Strangers in the Night*, Deep Purple *Made in Europe*, Queen *Live Killers*, and, of course, the ubiquitous Peter Frampton *Frampton Comes Alive* all came out sometime around the release of *All the World's a Stage*. Part of the success of live albums during this time was due to concerts being a rare treat, with simply no other media (like YouTube) where fans could experience a live rock show of their favorite band. Live albums captured that, and it was something to be cherished. Rush's first live album was certainly no exception.

All the World's a Stage succeeds at every level required for the maximum Rush experience, capturing for the first time the musical intensity of a Rush show. This was not an album like Kiss *Alive!*, where the singer polls the audience on their favorite kind of alcohol. In fact, Lee rarely speaks (the same can be said for today's Rush shows). Nor is this the kind of show where every other song contains extended jams (that would be interesting, but it simply is not who Rush is). It is merely four album sides of face-melting Rush classics, starting with the

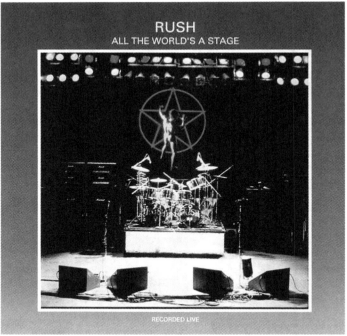

RUSH
ALL THE WORLD'S A STAGE

RECORDED LIVE

Rush's first live album, *All the World's a Stage*, introduced fans to the intensity of the live Rush concert experience.   *Courtesy of Max Mobley*

opener from *Caress of Steel*, "Bastille Day" and closing with "What You're Doing," from the band's first album.

The album reveals the band playing as tight as ever to a hometown crowd, and enjoying the newfound, hard-won success and independence that *2112* had brought them. It features a collection of great songs which the band has not played live in decades, and probably won't ever play live again. One notable exception to this is the full version of "By-Tor and the Snow Dog," which is nearly four minutes longer than the studio version. A slimmed-down version of "By-Tor and the Snow Dog" remained a live gem for a few more tours, including the video and album versions of *Exit . . . Stage Left*. The tune also made a crowd-pleasing appearance on 2003's *Rush in Rio*, recorded off the *Vapor Trails* tour.

Intense touring and word-of-mouth is how Rush became an iconic rock band. This ticket stub is from the *All the World's a Stage* tour, which started just a week after the *2112* tour ended.

Courtesy of Donald Gadziola

ROW (12)   SEAT
No Exchange — No Refund
MM 20
FLOOR
Retain Stub — Good Only
CONCERT BOWL
FRI. DEC. 31
8:30 P.M.   1976
Davis Printing Limited
"RUSH"

Given that Rush had only four studio records to their name during the *2112* tour, the songs on *All the World's a Stage* are, by modern Rush standards, drawn deep from the Rush playbook.

Highlights include "Anthem" and "Bastille Day," two prototypical early Rush classics from *Fly by Night* and *Caress of Steel*, respectively (they are also two of Rush's heaviest tracks ever), the pop-esque (for Rush, anyway) "Lakeside Park" (also from *Caress of Steel*), the moody "In the End" (*Fly by Night*), a rather intense version of *2112*'s B-side "Something for Nothing," and the previously mentioned full version of a true Rush gem—"By-Tor and the Snow Dog," complete with Part III's "Of the Battle." This hard-rock saga represents Rush's first exploration into the depths of fantasy-inspired progdom, and is worth the album price alone. Due to the song's length and the limitations of space on vinyl records, "By-Tor and the Snow Dog" comes right after "2112" (the full song minus "The Oracle" and "The Dream") on the live album, and nearly steals that epic prog masterpiece's thunder. During the actual *2112* tour, "By-Tor'" and "2112" were spaced apart by three or four songs (depending on the leg of the tour), and the song was omitted on shorter sets when Rush was the opening act.

All the World's a Stage works so well as a live album because of its rawness. Live albums, especially in the seventies, were used as substitutes for being there. Rock concerts were commonplace at this time, but they still held a bit of sacredness left over from Woodstock and the pervasive youth revolution. They were supposed to be loud and sweaty, and sound reinforcement, while greatly improved from the tinny "mounted bullhorns" that bands like the Beatles and Rolling Stones had endured, still had a long way to go. In 1976, concerts sounded a bit raw and rough, and Marshall and Ampeg stacks were requirements. And that is exactly how *All the World's a Stage* sounds: like you are at a concert, circa 1976, gratefully sweating and rocking amid the drugsmoke with a few thousand like-minded friends. The album reveals an intense, three-night homecoming

Lifeson shredding on his ES-335 during the *All the World's a Stage* tour. The guitar would soon be supplanted by his white ES-355, the instrument he is most associated with.　　　*Courtesy of Scott Burgan*

for the band. Luckily, they had hired Terry Brown, their producer at the time, to capture it in all its stained and loud glory.

Meet the Band Behind the Band

Reading a vinyl album's liner notes (nee, every word printed on them) had become part of the rock music–listening experience (often accompanied by a wizard bong). Luckily for Rush fans, the band made good use of liner notes by including, along with credits and gear (usually due to endorsement obligations), messages and insights into what was going on at the time, and sometimes even small little jokes or random phrases.

In the liner notes for *All the World's a Stage*, for instance, fans are introduced to some names that are part of the Rush fan lexicon, most notably Howard Ungerleider and Liam Birt, two techs (they were called roadies back then) still working for the band today. Ungerleider (nicknamed Herns in *All the World's a Stage* liner notes) was one of the band's first official roadies and tour managers. He is also credited with teaching the band how to survive on the road (he seems to have taught them well). According to *All the World's a Stage*, he was both "Stagemaster" and the lighting director, the latter being his role throughout Rush's decades of touring. That's a big role for the band, given how the band's lights and visuals are some of the best in the industry.

Liam Birt started as a stage right tech (translation: Lifeson's roadie). He became the band's stage manager in 1984 (during the *Grace Under Pressure* tour), and, in 1994, (during the *Roll the Bones* tour), he took over tour manager duties.

Other names that have come and gone (and a few that have stayed) are remembered well by early Rush fans who read every word of every tour book and liner note: Skip (the Detroit Slider) Gildersleeve, the stage left technician and stage manager when Birt stepped into the tour manager role; Tony Geranios (aka Jack Secret), who made his first appearance on *Exit . . . Stage Left* as a synth and guitar tech, and has been Lee's keyboard tech ever since; and the one and only "Broon"—Terry Brown, Rush's producer through the band's first nine albums, and mixer and producer for *All the World's a Stage* and *Exit . . . Stage Left*.

Peart Speaks—Through Rhythm

The seventies were definitely the heyday of the live album, especially the double live album, which really is its own thing—so much so that live albums on a single disc were seen as lesser efforts, though the reason could have been label influence (interference?) as much as anything else. After all, double albums cost more to make and took up more room in boxes and record store shelves. Pursuant to that meme, live albums introduced the drum solo to millions of rock fans who were unable to attend concerts. Drum solos were so prevalent on double live records that if the album did not contain one, buyers felt cheated. While the drum fills on *2112* turned rock fans on to the power and glory of Neil

Neil Peart behind "Chromey," his Slingerland double-bass kit, heard prominently on *All the World's a Stage*.   *Courtesy of Scott Burgan*

Peart behind the kit, *All the World's a Stage* turned the rock world on to what a
drum solo could be. There was no drum solo even close to what Peart was doing
prior to the album's release in 1976, and very few thereafter. Peart's drum solo
on *All the World's a Stage* bursts from the power riffing of the next-to-last track
on the record, side four's (in vinyl-speak) medley, "Working Man / Finding My
Way." He opens the solo with a "round the kit fill," followed by a blitzkrieg of
snare paradiddles and rolls played at a tempo nearly double that of "Working
Man," which then ritards toward a natural and proper ending. Lee, in one of
his rare speaking moments on the record, introduces Peart as "the Professor on
the drum kit," a name which subsequently stuck. By the end of the solo, it was
clear that drumming in rock and roll could be so much more than a rhythmic
entity; it could also be a melodic device. To thank Neil Peart for this singular
moment when the masses heard a new kind of drum solo is appropriate only if
you thank those who inspired him, and who, long before *All the World's a Stage*,
had beat melodies and new structures and territories out of their kits: namely,
Keith Moon (the Who), John Bonham (Led Zeppelin), and Bill Bruford (Yes,
King Crimson, Genesis). While Moon was somewhat infamous for never doing
a drum solo (though you can find them on YouTube), one could argue that an
entire Who set was one long drum solo with power chords and ripping bass and
vocals on top. And the massive break in "Won't Get Fooled Again" certainly
sounds like a drum solo. Bonham, on the other hand, had no qualms about
laying down intense drum solos on his spartan kit. His solo from Led Zeppelin's
double live album *The Song Remains the Same*, released just weeks after *All the
World's a Stage*, holds up to this day, though it is much more about rhythm and
timing (Bonham's rests were as meaningful as his beats) and comes in at around
eight minutes compared to Peart's, which is slightly over three minutes.

Geddy Lee, wailing on vocals and bass (his trusty Rickenbacker), during the *All the World's a Stage* tour.   *Courtesy of Scott Burgan*

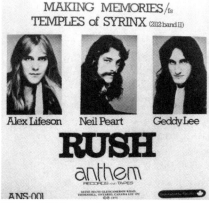

While *2112* may have been an album Rush's label did not at first get or want, as exemplified by this promo release, they changed their tune once they saw the fans' reaction to the record in the way of concert attendance and sales.   *Courtesy of Joe Pesch*

Man, Oh, Man

All the World's a Stage fades out (actually it plays on the run-out groove of the vinyl record) to Lee, Lifeson, and Peart walking (floating?) off-stage, breathing hard, whooping and yawping under the influence of the post-gig euphoria that every rock musician who has ever played live knows well. Then we hear the sound of a huge heavy door slamming shut. As the liner notes put it (written by Peart on behalf of the band): "This album, to us, signifies the end of the beginning, a milestone to mark the close of chapter one, in the annals of Rush."

And it was.

Setlist

Two setlists were used on the *2112* tour, which was the basis of *All the World's a Stage* album. Make that three, if you count the setlist Rush used when opening for other bands. The only differences were the encore number ("Best I Can" vs. "What You're Doing") and song order. Here is the setlist used for the Massey Hall shows recorded for the album:

1. "Bastille Day"
2. "Anthem"
3. "Lakeside Park"
4. "2112" (excludes "Oracle: The Dream")
5. "Fly by Night"
6. "In The Mood"
7. "Something For Nothing"
8. "By-Tor and the Snow Dog"
9. "In The End"
10. "Working Man"
11. "Finding My Way"
12. "Drum Solo"
13. Encore: "What You're Doing"

Exit . . . Stage Left— Enter "Xanadu"

Stellar Live Performances and a Bit Too Much Polish

Rush's second double live album, 1981's *Exit . . . Stage Left*, revealed to fans that a new chapter in the band's musical adventure was underway. And this new chapter seemed all about change. The four albums preceding *All the World's a Stage* had a definite sonic connection, a story arc, so to speak. The biggest changes from the period that culminated with Rush's first live album were both personnel (the departure of John Rutsey and the entrance of the Professor), and content, (the shift from Zeppelin-ish blues rockers to true prog masters). The four studio albums preceding *Exit . . . Stage Left*, however, marked two huge shifts in Rush's sonic space-time continuum. The first two of the four, *A Farewell to Kings* and *Hemispheres*, had obvious evolutionary ties to the monster that was *2112*, but they also had something more—more synthesizers, more textures, more variety—especially with Lifeson often going to the acoustic guitar on these records, and Peart's drum kit growing into a Rube Goldberg–like contraption full of all sorts of things one could hit with a stick and still call it musical. And within those textures, Rush's sound had evolved. A nutshell example of this would be looking at Rush's two biggest hits up to this period: big, plodding, and heavy "Working Man," and lilting, flighty, and pretty "Closer to the Heart."

The next two of the four (in the new pattern of releasing four studio albums followed by a live album) were *Permanent Waves* and the almighty Rush sonic godhead, *Moving Pictures*. Peart has stated in interviews that *Permanent Waves* was a bridge album, and that without it, the band would not have been able to artistically travel from the long-format progginess of *Hemispheres*, to the tidily packaged numbers (for prog) that made up *Moving Pictures*. Where *Permanent Waves* had one foot in long-form prog, it had its face in the winds of sophisticated prog-pop. And so these four albums, and the sonic egress they marked, made *Exit . . . Stage Left* a very different live album. It is still remarkable for the Rush gems it contains (just like its predecessor), but is somehow more stoic. *Exit . . . Stage Left* was also somewhat more scattered—instead of having a mere four albums' worth of material to cover, the band now had eight whoppers to

Despite being a bit too polished for a live release, *Exit . . . Stage Left* remains a fan favorite.

Courtesy of Max Mobley

draw from to make a set (and a live album), one that would make all fans happy. They mostly succeeded, but at this stage (pun intended), and with two distinct groups of fans (original and second-generation fans who discovered the band via *Moving Pictures*), Lee, Lifeson, and Peart's setlist drew some level of controversy from those who discovered their music from different points of entry. This is a trend that would continue.

A UK and Canada Mix

In 1981, the live album was losing some of its allure, as were drum solos. This was due in part due to fan fickleness. It was also part of rock's evolution into punk (perhaps more of a de-evolution?) that didn't make for a great live recording, and New Wave, which didn't translate well live due to being heavily processed, synth-laden, and lacking the guitar hero / rock star swagger that live albums more or less celebrated. In addition, both forms of music rebelled against the trappings of its predecessor, including live albums.

Luckily, Rush didn't give a damn; they just wanted to put out another record of their live work. The band was very open about having a hard time listening to *All the World's a Stage*. They believed it suffered from its rawness instead of being rewarded for it. In attempt not to repeat what bothered them about their last live album, they over-corrected in making *Exit . . . Stage Left*. The audience mics were quite low in the final mix, dimming some of the "live-ness" of the album (which, generally, lives in the domain of the raw). And the mix and performances selected were a bit *too* perfect, even for Rush. In interviews after the album was released, the band agreed it was too pristine to be a rocking, throw-down live album. *Exit . . . Stage Left* also employed fade-ins and fade-outs between each cut, which jarred the listener out of a concert experience. Perhaps this was an attempt to convey honesty about the recordings that comprised the album. Where *All the World's a Stage* feels like one amazing concert (it was actually recorded over three nights at the same venue), the songs from *Exit . . . Stage Left* don't. And rightfully so: the album was comprised of recordings from two totally different tours. Obviously, this was done to release a live record that covered all the bases—old, new, and neither old nor new. Some fans feel this added to the disconnected (though polished) sound of the album. While most of the songs were recorded during the Canadian leg of 1981's *Moving Pictures* tour, "A Passage to Bangkok" (not available on the early CD version), "Closer to the Heart," "Beneath, Between, Behind," and "Jacob's Ladder" were recorded in the UK during the 1980 *Permanent Waves* tour.

Yeah, but It Has "Xanadu"

When *Exit . . . Stage Left* was released on October 29, 1981 (just two months after the debut of MTV), it was an instant fan favorite for second-generation Rush fans. They ignored the individual track fades, and appreciated it for what it was—a great representation of songs like "Tom Sawyer," "Red Barchetta," and "YYZ." It was a somewhat different story for first-generation Rush fans, who had either seen the band live or worn the grooves out of their copy of *All the World's a Stage*. There were a few head scratches and minor outbursts about those fade-outs and the overt polishing of the mix. But forgiveness was found underneath the pleasure dome, so to speak. That is, *Exit . . . Stage Left* contains power trio prog finery in a truly exceptional version of "Xanadu" from 1977's *A Farewell to Kings*. The song just plain delivers, from each tubular bell hit to one of Lifeson's best solos. The song, as it appears on the album, is Rush at its finest to date. And it would be nearly twenty years until the song graced another live Rush album (*Different Stages*).

Over the years, *Exit . . . Stage Left* has become a Rush fan favorite, and in 2004 it was voted the ninth-best live album by the readers of *Classic Rock* magazine.

Exit . . . Stage Left is an important archive as it reveals Rush in the throes of transition. From the album's opener, "The Spirit of Radio" (hard not to love that live, and, by the way, for the two tours the album draws from, the show opener was the "2112 Overture"), to Rush showing they can nail FM hits like "Tom Sawyer" and "Closer to the Heart," the album also serves as a sort of live retrospective (the best kind of retrospective, some would say). And its two instrumentals, "YYZ" and the closing number "La Villa Strangiato," scratch an itch Rush fans know all too well—an itch that especially afflicts those first-generationers. Overall, the record makes good on the expectations of a live Rush album, including a percussion clinic in the form of a drum solo.

The Professor at the Front of the Class

Drum solos are usually saved for the end of the night, a sort of signal to mark the end of the intensity, by its peaking in true rock fashion—with lots and lots of drums! This was not the case with *Exit . . . Stage Left*. Here, the drum solo comes in the middle of "YYZ," the third track on the album. It's good to keep in mind that album length was still a consideration (something CDs would thankfully bring to an end) when *Exit . . . Stage Left* was initially released in 1981. The band had to figure out how best to fill four sides of vinyl, each containing a maximum of twenty-two minutes. But, even on the *Moving Pictures* tour setlist, where "YYZ" was drawn for the recording, it comes in at track seven of twenty-three.

That the band decided to put Peart's solo early on a live album, as well as a live set, speaks to his status as a drummer despite it still being early in his career. Thanks to *All the World's a Stage*, the solo was expected to be amazing, and it was. It may have lacked the wow factor of the *All the World's a Stage* solo simply because that record marked the first time the masses were able to hear what Peart was capable of in solo form. But the *Exit . . . Stage Left* solo is still mighty impressive. It does not pick up from where *All the World's a Stage* leaves off, but improves upon it. Following the *Exit . . . Stage Left* theme of being polished and rather precise, Peart's solo coming in the middle of "YYZ" is faster, tighter, and cleaner than the one from five albums earlier. It's also a bit shorter. But it works like magic, though coming in so early on the track list does take some getting used to. Of the things it does better than its predecessor, key among them is how Lee and Lifeson drop out with precision, and return on a difficult transition, truly nailing it in the Rush tradition.

Enter . . . Stage Artsy

All the World's a Stage had the prototypical live album art of killer concert shots, and fans dug it because as they listened to the album, they could look at the many pictures and imagine the band jamming on their instruments. Sounds primitive, and it was—there was no YouTube then, no MTV /

1. THE SPIRIT OF RADIO 5:11   2. RED BARCHETTA 6:46
3. YYZ 7:43   4. A PASSAGE TO BANGKOK 3:45
5. CLOSER TO THE HEART 3:08
6. BENEATH, BETWEEN & BEHIND 2:34
7. JACOB'S LADDER 8:46   8. BROON'S BANE 1:57
9. THE TREES 4:50   10. XANADU 12:09
11. FREEWILL 5:31   12. TOM SAWYER 4:59
13. LA VILLA STRANGIATO 9:37

Produced by Terry Brown

Hugh Syme's album art work for *Exit . . . Stage Left* features a montage of symbols and icons from previous Rush albums.

Courtesy of Max Mobley

VH1, no band or fan websites—hell, no web! Therefore, it was up to the listener's imagination and the album's photos and art to help create visuals that matched the music.

Exit . . . Stage Left took that standard live album packaging in a different direction by having key elements of Rush's album artwork embedded or, this being the pre-Photoshop era, tastefully clipped and pasted into a live shot with a backstage focus. The cover features model Paula Turnbull, from the *Permanent Waves* album cover, pulling back the curtains from stage left to reveal a familiar scene for Rush concert attendees—a smoky arena packed with happy fans. Geddy Lee's keyboard rig is barely visible in the shot, and that's about it for band gear. To Turnbull's right is the dapper gentleman (representing Apollo), from the *Hemispheres* album cover, and a flying white owl denoting the *Fly by Night* record.

The back of the cover has the requisite liner notes and song titles, along with an expanded version of the front-cover photo. Seen here are the red nude (representing Dionysus) from *Hemispheres*, the puppet king from *A Farewell to Kings* sitting atop a road case with the logo from Rush's debut album, a *2112* red star poster, and two movers from *Moving Pictures*. The picture they are moving this time is that of the Necromancer from the *Caress of Steel* album cover. The very talented Hugh Syme created that cover art. (What Rush is to prog rock, Hugh Syme is to album artwork—more on that later in this book.)

Inside the double fold jacket are three live pictures of the band—all tasteful works from photographer Deborah Samuel—and that's it. The photos are beautiful, and how they captured what Rush does to make all that sound was unique. Fans hoping for a bigger or better visual glimpse into what a Rush concert was like weren't quite satiated, but the music, as always, made up for it.

Exit . . . Stage Left on VHS

A year later, in 1982, Rush released *Exit . . . Stage Left*, their first live concert video on VHS tape and LaserDisc. It boasted the same artwork and only some of the songs found from the album version. However, these songs were captured from an entirely different performance. The songs were recorded on March 27, 1981, during the *Moving Pictures* tour in Montreal, Canada. *Exit . . . Stage Left*, the video, was re-released in 2006 as part of the DVD box set entitled, *Replay X 3*. The set also includes a DVD and CD of the *Grace Under Pressure* tour, and a DVD of the live album and video *A Show of Hands*.

There are definitely some gems to be found here. And for fans of Rush in 1982 (again, *lonnnng* before the Internet), it was quite the treat to see the band in action. Like all Rush projects, the band wanted to make the best product they could. So *Exit . . . Stage Left*, the video, was shot with five 16mm cameras, some hand mounted, and some strategically mounted around the stage. Like the album of the same name (but with different recordings), Terry "Broon" Brown was at the helm of recording, and later mixing. While the VHS version sounded

Exit . . . Stage Left was the first live Rush release available to watch as well as listen to, including the Laser Disc version, shown here.   *Courtesy of Joe Pesch*

about as good as VHS audio could, the re-released DVD version contains remastered audio in 5.1 surround and stereo. And it sounds simply brilliant.

At different times during the video, Lee, Lifeson, and Peart discuss their craft, including one remembrance over a very short excerpt of "YYZ" (the end credits also roll over a segment of "YYZ"). The video opens with Rush's crew setting up for the show, while a two-minute excerpt of a live version of "The Camera Eye" teases viewers. The video contains no drum solo, which is surprising and somewhat disappointing for some fans. However, it does feature a barn-burning version of "By-Tor and the Snow Dog," featuring Peart's solo-esque drum work that brings the song to a close.

As great as the video version of *Exit . . . Stage Left* is, especially in feeding fans the concert experience they were craving, a few gems are missed, like "La Villa Strangiato" (the encore number for the tour, and a track on the album version), "The Spirit of Radio," and full versions of "YYZ" and "The Camera Eye." And, of course, it would have been great to see Neil Peart do what we've been hearing him do on two live albums.

Make no mistake, despite these absences (glaring only through the lens of missed opportunities), the video version of *Exit . . . Stage Left*, like its album cousin, reveals Rush in a very cool, albeit transitory place. They were already under the influence of new music while still embracing their roots. They were becoming a "big act." And best of all, they were Rush, happily on the road.

Oh, Is It "Xanadu"?

Hearing "Xanadu" played live is a memorable experience for any Rush fan. Rush fans can queue up based on if they've ever heard the song live, and if so, how many times. The *Exit . . . Stage Left* video offers fans an excellent live-Rush experience with the full version of "Xanadu," coming fifth in the set (not counting the "The Camera Eye" intro). Focusing on what this video contains instead of what it lacks, "Xanadu" helps make *Exit . . . Stage Left* the video a must-have, as does the eternal champion and foe of Rush's lyrical fantasy fiction, "By-Tor and the Snow Dog" (albeit in a condensed medley version). Watching Rush on this video is essentially watching Rush history. It is also the last time fans can catch Lee and

Lifeson both playing double-neck guitars. Lifeson's is a double-neck Gibson with a twelve-string on the top, and a six-string on the bottom, and Lee's is a custom Rickenbacker with four-string bass on top and six-string guitar on the bottom.

Exit . . . Stage Left (Video) Track Listing

1. Intro (includes narration, with segments of "The Camera Eye" live version)
2. "Limelight"
3. "Tom Sawyer"
4. "The Trees"
5. "Xanadu"
6. "Red Barchetta"
7. "Freewill"
8. "Closer to the Heart"
9. "YYZ" (segments of the live version, with interview audio)
10. "By-Tor and the Snow Dog"
11. "In the End"
12. "In the Mood"
13. "2112: Grand Finale"
14. End Credits ("YYZ")

"Xanadu" is considered a prog masterpiece. Hearing Rush play it live is a huge treat for fans. The song was so popular upon its release that it was featured on bootlegs and promo releases, like the one show here.
Courtesy of Joe Pesch

9

A Show of Hands— and Technology

Pastels, Shoulder Pads, and Mullets, Oh My!

our studio albums after *Exit . . . Stage Left* (the pattern entrenched now), Rush's 1989 live album *A Show of Hands* was also originally released on CD. Technology had become a mainstay in the intervening years between the two live releases, and the format fit the album's sound—synthy, processed, digital. Where *Exit . . . Stage Left* showed Rush in transition, *A Show of Hands* shows Rush swimming with the current of new music technologies and sounds, and occasionally being swept away. The eighties were wrapping up, and Lee, Lifeson, and Peart were celebrating the cheery (and sometimes cheesy) decade with a live album that did not draw from their entire catalog, but from Rush's own early digital period. Outside of the encore tune, "Closer to the Heart," and *Moving Pictures*' "Witch Hunt," the entire album focuses on material from the band's four previous studio releases. That's right—*A Show of Hands* is all about Rush's controversial "synth period."

As an archive, the album is, of course, important. As a live Rush album, it's, well, interesting. This time, the mix fits the music and the evolution of what live albums had become on the eve of the nineties. As Neil Peart put it in a note to fans in *Rush Backstage*: "There are [songs] we had to leave off which we would like to have included, and no doubt some of you will be disappointed not to find one or two you would have liked too, but we had to be ruthless. (And now we have no more ruths.)"

Sound-wise, *A Show of Hands* has that digital sheen common to both early CDs and early digital synths and samplers. And so there is a conundrum here (and heard) in that this is a live album of heavily processed, digital samples whose existence is in a virtual vacuum. It's similar (though in reverse) to playing a vinyl record onstage in front of thousands. The concert noises are appropriately there, but the music is missing something. That is not to say the songs on *A Show of Hands* are not right, because they are, especially for their time. In fact, some of Rush's best songwriting happened during this period: "The Big Money," "Mystic Rhythms," "Red Sector A," and "Marathon" are truly amazing creations—complex, lush, complicated, and tight as hell—with the majority clocking in at around five minutes long. That was the band's goal when they left *Hemispheres* behind, and *A Show of Hands* proved they had reached their goal.

Many albums from this period have a distinct eighties sound to them, and *A Show of Hands* is no exception. But at the same time, the album features live Rush at their most gear-laden, and yet they really pull it off—with aplomb and a mullet. Just listen to "The Big Money" or "Marathon" to get a taste of what Rush was able to accomplish during this era—in songwriting and musicianship. *A Show of Hands* really lives up to its name—a live album featuring artists spinning more musical plates than previously thought possible. And damn if they didn't pull it off.

The Live Laboratory

Bands like Rush, who have no qualms about pushing the envelope either personally or categorically, must be able to live with their experiments being released out into the wild, both the good ones and the, well, interesting ones. As a live album, *A Show of Hands* is a record of some of the band's boldest experiments. And while the album is probably the least-popular live Rush album, it has, over time, earned the respect it originally sought. Case in point: as this book is being written, Rush is currently on tour in support of *Clockwork Angels*. That set contains many of the same songs found in *A Show of Hands*, and the crowds (and the critics) are loving it. Weird.

Multiple Songs, Shows, and Tours

Like *Exit . . . Stage Left*, *A Show of Hands* is really a live compilation album comprised of songs recorded in the UK and the US, across two separate tours: the 1987–88 *Hold Your Fire* tour, and the 1985–86 *Power Windows* tour. Part of the reason for this is that the band owed their label, Mercury Records, one more album before they could flee to Atlantic Records (like bands do). Given the constraints of time and their desire for the switch, they decided the last album on Mercury would either be a greatest hits compilation, or a

The look of the live release, *A Show of Hands*, says it all about this period in Rush's music.   *Courtesy of Max Mobley*

live album. It turned out to be both—well, except for the hits part. A few things that make *A Show of Hands* remarkable are that it contains "Witch Hunt," which had never been recorded live before; "Mystic Rhythms," one of Rush's prettiest eighties songs; and a collection of the band's best synth and sampler-heavy tracks, including one their biggest hits to date, "The Big Money."

The Professor of Electronica

A Show of Hands is also the first live Rush album to feature Neil Peart's drum solo as a separate track, though it is a bit of a cheat. On the *Hold Your Fire* tour, from which this portion of the album was taken, Peart was still taking his solo from the middle of "YYZ," which is not on the album. On *A Show of Hands*, Peart's solo, assigned the apropos track name "The Rhythm Method," employs a fade-in.

In keeping with the high-tech push of this era, and the sound of this album, Peart's solo, once again, takes the listener places a drum solo has never gone before—thanks to samplers and trigger pads. "The Rhythm Method" isn't just a separate track on the album so Peart fans can find it quickly; it is a fully fledged piece of music that goes well beyond percussion and rhythm. Sampled brass sections, marimbas, and sampled percussion a notch above the eighties Simmons drum sound make "The Rhythm Method" a one-man Rush composition. And it smokes—digitally—but still smokes.

The Weapons of Rush's New Sound

Geddy Lee, shown here on the cover of an interview CD, had a different look and a different bass (Wal) for *A Show of Hands*.   *Courtesy of Joe Pesch*

The new-school, polished, plasticine sounds mixed with prog power chords, riffs and rhythms that is *A Show of Hands* is not just about all those boxes regurgitating synth and orchestral sounds and a dozen different kinds of reverb. It is also about the stringed (real strings this time) instrument choices of Alex Lifeson and Geddy Lee. Pursuant to the sound and style Rush had aimed for and hit with typical deadly accuracy were new guitar and bass sounds. Gone was Lifeson's fat, creamy, sound dominated by Gibson Les Pauls, the semi-hollow-body snarl of his Gibson ES-355, and the unique crunch of his Howard Roberts Fusion (the guitar used in the studio recording of

A Show of Hands, from 1989, marked an end to the double-necks, like the ones shown here from the *2112* tour, in exchange for synths and samplers and modern (for the eighties) technology. It was a controversial decision as far as many fans were concerned.

Courtesy of Donald Gadziola

"Tom Sawyer"). In its place were the Fenderish Strat-like Auroras made by the now-defunct Canadian guitar company Signature Guitars. Lifeson had a hand in the development of these instruments. They were one of the new "Super-Strats" to come out of the eighties.

Super-Strats were guitars that resembled the famous Stratocaster, but incorporated modern guitar modifications, such as the powerful and stable Floyd Rose "tremolo" bridge (think early Eddie Van Halen or Joe Satriani dive bombs) replacing the original Fender "tremolo" bridge, which was known for tuning instability and its limitations in vibrato and pitch range. (Quick point of clarity: guitar inventor Leo Fender named the bridge on his Stratocaster a tremolo, though it actually creates vibrato effects—think early Adrian Belew or Hendrix at his wildest.) Super Strats, like Lifeson's Signature Auroras, also used more advanced electronics. The ones used on *A Show of Hands* featured active single-coil pickups, meaning the pickups were the thin Strat-like style (as opposed to the double-coil humbucker-style pickups associated with Gibson Les Pauls), but were charged with a battery. Most guitar pickups are passive, with no electrical source on the instrument beyond the tiny voltage from the wavering eddies of magnetic fields. Powering the Aurora's pickups with a battery made them hotter and fatter and more prone to overdrive (all good things), while still retaining the cut and brightness of a traditional Strat. These guitars are sometimes confused with Lifeson's Hentor Sportscasters seen on the *Grace Under Pressure* tour

Alex Lifeson playing his rare, Canadian-made Signature Aurora "Super-Strat-style" guitar.
Courtesy of Thomas Pashkevich

video, and used as far back as *Moving Pictures*. A black Hentor can be seen on the official "Limelight" video. It is also the guitar Lifeson chose for the song, including the beautiful "Limelight" solo, which is dripping with Floyd Rose whammy.

The Signatures offered a guitar sound that had more bite and cut than what Lifeson and Rush were known for, and more flexibility than Lifeson's previous guitars (except for the Hentors and that mighty double neck). Previously, Lifeson filled the void with chunky fat sounds smothered in natural distortion from his amps. Now, with the synths filling that void sixty-four or more voices at a time, Lifeson went for a guitar that sliced and bit through the fat provided by Lee's army of samplers and synths. It was a smart choice, a necessary choice, and one that altered the Rush soundscape. While some Rush fans criticize Lifeson's tone during this time, it was what the guitars needed to do, and it wholly fit the style and the era. And regardless of that criticism, that line of Signature guitars Lifeson used on *A Show of Hands* are now highly sought after, and they hold their place as one of several high points in the history of guitar-making. Sadly, Lifeson's Signature Aurora was permanently damaged during a guitar handoff between songs during the *Presto* tour.

The Wal of Lee

While Lifeson was riding the customized Super-Strat train of sonic pulchritude, Lee had strapped on a British boutique Wal bass that some bassists argue delivered the best tone he's ever had. These basses complemented Lifeson's new less-is-more tone, while delivering the bottom needed to anchor a synth-based sound. Thanks to how Lee plays any bass, while the bottom was omnipresent, it was also incredibly well defined, with just the right amount of brightness to make sure Lee's fastest and most melodic riffs weren't lost in a sea of synths sharing the same sonic space. There are many successful experiments and accomplishments found on *A Show of Hands*, and sound is chief among them, though it may not be a sound all Rush fans embrace. However, the band's ability to deliver a sound that served their newly mulleted muse in the pastel sport coat, their lust for technology, and their ever-growing musicianship is nothing short of remarkable.

A Show of Video

Well, they sounded good. Like the two *Exit . . . Stage Left* projects (video and album), which offered some of the same songs from the same era, but with different recordings, so were the album and video for *A Show of Hands.*

Sonically they are very similar, and the band, thankfully, lets the music do the talking, which makes it a highly listenable DVD. Watching it, however, is another matter. If the *Exit . . . Stage Left* video shows Rush in transition, *A Show of Hands,* shows the band in need of one. It also reveals, at times, the band with an extreme case of eighties dork-itis. Hard to admit, but at times the video is difficult to watch. As if Lee and Lifeson did not have enough on their plates just trying to simultaneously play the multiple instruments required to accurately perform what was some of their most complex and highly orchestrated music, they also had to follow some rudimentary choreography and seem to intentionally mug for the camera. Whether it was their own idea, their label's, or their management, Lee and Lifeson made an awkward attempt at being camera friendly, eighties style. (Thankfully, Peart was parked behind his kit—a pink one, no less—where he was busy being rock's greatest living drummer.) At times during the video, Lee and Lifeson sort of dance together, separate, and then rejoin like male wallflowers hopelessly dancing in a dark corner at their prom. They actually come dangerously close to bonking heads as they failed to sync up properly during an attempt at some "Let's rock back and forth in unison for a while" moments. They seemingly had forgotten who they were and why fans wanted to see them (certainly not for their skipping and prancing skills), but couldn't ignore either the camera's unblinking eye, or eighties zeitgeist as they did someone else's (certainly not Rush's) shtick. Make no mistake, I do not loathe them for this video, I actually feel bad for them. There appears to be a level of awkward self-awareness that is palpable during some parts of the show. Thankfully these scenes do not make up the meat of the video, but they are the salt, and they appear at intervals too frequent to forget. But in between this dorkiness, Rush was again caught on camera being Rush, playing difficult parts, amazing riffs, and intense transitions with ease. And this, to some extent, redeems the video.

A Show of Hands for *A Show of Hands*

Recorded at the National Exhibition Centre in Birmingham, England, on April 21, 23, and 24 of 1988 during the *Hold Your Fire* tour, *A Show of Hands,* the video, was released in 1989 on VHS and LaserDisc, the same year as the album version. In 2007, a remastered version was released as part of the *Replay X3* DVD box set.

Despite the controversies surrounding Rush's synth period, fans stayed true to their band. This 1988 issue of the *Spirit of Rush* fanzine reveals fans celebrating the band during the holidays.

Courtesy of John Patuto and cygnus-x1.net

Despite the issues with Lee and Lifeson's ill-conceived shtick, the video does what it should: it represents the band, their sound, and their musical equipment during that era. Unlike *Exit . . . Stage Left*, the video, which contains a set even shorter than *Exit . . . Stage Left*, the album; *A Show of Hands*, the video, contains more songs than its album cousin (five more songs, to be exact). The addition rounds off a nice collection, which, unlike the album version, takes viewers back to Rush's early days. "The Spirit of Radio" is clearly a standout. And the perennial fave "YYZ," has a wonderful tonality, thanks to Lee and Lifeson's aforementioned choices in guitar and bass. The inclusion of "La Villa Strangiato" makes any of the video's flaws fall by the wayside. It's also worth mentioning that on the *A Show of Hands* album and video, the tracks "Mission" and "Marathon" demonstrate that Rush knew well what they were doing during this controversial era, and they did it masterfully, at least musically speaking.

A Show of Hands Video Setlist

1. Intro
2. "The Big Money"
3. "Marathon"
4. "Turn the Page"
5. "Prime Mover"
6. "Manhattan Project"
7. "Closer to the Heart"

8. "Red Sector A"
9. "Force Ten"
10. "Lock and Key" (LaserDisc only)
11. "Mission"
12. "Territories"
13. "YYZ"
14. "The Rhythm Method" (Drum Solo)
15. "The Spirit of Radio"
16. "Tom Sawyer"
17. "2112 Overture" / "The Temples of Syrinx" / "La Villa Strangiato" / "In the Mood"

Different Stages Amid Darkness

A Gift from the Past with an Uncertain Future

F our studio albums later, right on schedule, Rush released their fourth live album—*Different Stages*, in 1998. This three-disc set remains one of Rush's best live releases. Discs one and two largely consist of material taken from a Chicago stop of the 1997 *Test for Echo* tour. They also include material taken from various stops on the band's 1994 *Counterparts* tour. Interestingly, *Different Stages* would also be the last live album consisting of material taken from multiple shows and tours. Disc three of the album is what many Rush fans find to be the ultimate gem—an excellent recording by Terry Brown of a single Rush concert (February 20, 1978) at London's Hammersmith Odeon during their *A Farewell to Kings* tour.

Prior to the *Test for Echo* tour, the band had gone on record that they had a live recording from the *A Farewell to Kings* tour that they wanted to release, but it was not evident that another "current era" live album was scheduled. However, circumstances surrounding the band at the time made it a sensible choice.

Different Stages is remarkable for several reasons, including the aforementioned 1978 live set inclusion. Many of these reasons are wonderful. Two are tragic. The album was released shortly after Mr. Peart lost his daughter, Selena, in an automobile accident, and his wife, Jacqueline, to cancer, less than a year later. Because of that, *Different Stages* is an inescapable reminder of what Neil Peart had to endure. It is also a reminder of how this could have easily been Rush's last album outside of material pulled from what seems to be a rather sparsely filled vault.

Hugh Syme's album cover for *Different Stages*, either intentionally or inadvertently, symbolizes the tragedy. The cover depicts three Tinkertoys on a dowel, with one separated from the other two. Clearly this denotes the third disc being separated by twenty years from discs one and two. But it can also be taken as one of Rush's three cogs being separate from the other two. It could also signify one man being separated from his wife and daughter. The album was produced during a time when Peart considered himself retired and was largely (and understandably) lost to the world, let alone his muse and his mates.

The artwork for disc three continues the symbolism, albeit in a very different manner. It depicts the front of the Hammersmith Odeon as it was in 1978. In the picture of Rush fans milling about, waiting for doors to open, a straight-jacketed Lifeson can be seen being carted off, presumably to the nuthouse. (Coincidentally, Lifeson makes a straightjacket reference in the *A Farewell to Kings* tour book.) Lee can also be seen in the image, looking over his shoulder as he scalps some tickets. And if you look very closely, peaking out, as if in hiding, as if unable to deal with fans and the mania and adoration of humanity eager to experience a Rush concert, you can find Neil Peart, alone.

Returning to the Remarkable

Okay, enough with the sadness. *Different Stages* is, as stated previously, also remarkable for some wonderful reasons that greatly satisfy Rush fan's appetite for live performances. Perhaps most notable is the inclusion of "2112," played in its entirety (all seven parts!). From the overture's swirly Arp sounds to the finale's explosions and everything in between, the band actually seems to improve on what is arguably the second-most important song in the Rush cannon. (It may have been "2112" which put Rush into a self-sustaining orbit, but "Working Man" launched the Rush rocket.)

Lifeson is simply brilliant portraying Megadon's anonymous discoverer of music via a guitar, conveyed by curious pluckings and frettings that result in a simple but eloquent open chord progression up and down the neck. It is one of those rare moments in rock and roll where the music becomes the voice and the story. Not bad for a high school dropout on a guitar. This live version of "2112" was recorded on June 23, 1997, at the Great Woods Performing Arts Center in Mansfield, Massachusetts. Outside of bootlegs, it is the only live recording of the full version of "2112."

Another wonder of this album is the recording of "Bravado" (taken from a 1994 show at the Spectrum in Philadelphia), a song that not all Rush fans love, but one that most Rush fans who happen to be songwriters

R U S H

different stages · live

Different Stages features live material from the *Counterparts* and *Test for Echo* tours from the nineties, and a third disc featuring a show from the London stop of the *A Farewell to Kings* tour.

Courtesy of Max Mobley

and musicians adore, especially live. "Bravado" is one of the few songs the band extends live—giving Lifeson space for one of his best (and rare) improvisational solos—a lovely piece with plenty of open spaces that builds in intensity in the way only he can.

Underneath Lifeson's free-form emoting is Peart playing one of his most complicated yet beautiful rhythms. This is not the drum fill-o-rama stuff that he is capable of. It is a beat that builds right along with Lifeson's lead. Peart's students may correct that description and claim that it is actually two beats. One could argue that they are right since he is technically playing two contrapuntal rhythms at the same time. One of the beauties about this moment on *Different Stages* is that, despite the complexities in Peart's and Lee's rhythmic duet (while Lee actually lays back—steady, but back), the song flows exceptionally well. All of this makes "Bravado" one of Rush's best songs, live. Peart's lyrics (inspired by novelist John Barth) also happen to be some of his most poetic.

Different Things Not Alone

Along with the heavily syncopated riff-rock songs, "Driven" (*Test for Echo*) and "Stick It Out" (*Counterparts*), are two instrumentals not counting the drum solo. The perennial favorite fans never tire of—"YYZ" and the modern groove sound of "Leave That Thing Alone" from *Counterparts*, also recorded in 1997 at Great Woods Amphitheatre in Mansfield, Massachusetts. This is a new breed of instrumental for Rush, with a techno groove and laid-back approach.

Different Stages is also aptly named because discs one and two's "main concert" (the packaging and content make disc three seem like a bonus disc) contains rare live cuts from the many Rush eras. Two worth mentioning here are "Natural Science" from *Permanent Waves* (perhaps the last Rush song with one foot in long-form prog) and "The Analog Kid" from *Signals*.

The Professor of the Drum Kit Meets Yoda of the Beat

Once again, every four years Peart's recorded drum solos reveal a virtuoso in progress. At an extended time of over eight minutes, Peart's "The Rhythm Method—1997" is the second-longest cut from discs one and two (the longest being "2112"). It is a tight kitchen sink that both backtracks over some of Peart's previous solos and uncovers new ground. Technology is involved to a greater degree in the form of samples and triggers. Like the solo from *Exit . . . Stage Left* expanded on the solo from *All the World's a Stage*, "The Rhythm Method - 1997," from *Different Stages*, expands on an earlier version from *A Show of Hands*. In doing so, once again Peart takes the drum solo (which, by 1997, had become strictly verboten) to entirely new areas melodically, rhythmically, and, if you happened to be at one of the many concerts, visually.

Different Stages was recorded after Peart had decided to return to "drum school" under the tutelage of Freddie Gruber. Many casual rock fans around the planet are unfamiliar with Gruber's work. The best way to understand his importance in the world of drumming (and, specifically, in the music of Rush) is to look at the legendary teacher's more famous students in addition to Peart: Steve Smith, Dave Weckl, and Vinnie Coliauta—three drummers considered to be in Peart's league.

What Neil Peart is to drummers, Freddie Gruber is to drummers like Neil Peart. Peart and his master Gruber became very close, as shown in this picture.　　*Courtesy of Cindy Kucik*

Gruber was not the kind of teacher from whom you learned patterns and fills, though he could certainly teach it. If you weren't great (or showed a potential for greatness) to begin with, you weren't eligible to be his student. In this regard, he was more of a Yoda (in fact, Peart referred to him as such) than a coach who made sure you could play paradiddles at any tempo with your eyes closed. He taught Peart about the spaces between the hits. The rests and the timing and, most important of all, he taught the prog master how to swing. Swing is indefinable, really. Some say it's playing behind the beat slightly; others say it's a subtle tuplet in the groove that is more felt than heard. But both of those definitions attempt to create a measurable explanation to something that can't be measured the way a great piece of art cannot be measured. Swing (or groove) is a form of musical breath. One cannot try to swing, one merely swings. And Peart (and Rush's) lack of swing was rarely, if ever, evident in their music because, with few exceptions, their music lived off momentum and complexity. It was all about the drive and the breaks, which were often so complex that it was satisfying enough just to keep up and enjoy the surprises in timing and meter.

But then, in 1991, the daughter of the legendary jazz drummer Buddy Rich asked Peart to play with Rich's band at a tribute concert for her late father. *Burning for Buddy Volume 1* featured the best drummers around playing some of Rich's classics. They were all amazing (and included several of Gruber's master students, including Weckl and Smith). Buddy Rich played big band jazz, and it was all about swing and not about the things Rush (and Peart) did so well. So when Peart played the Rich classic "Cotton Tail" with Rich's band, something was clearly off. The band was swinging, and Peart was not. It almost sounded like the band and he were playing at slightly different tempos, or as if the band was chasing Peart, who played like he had to get somewhere and was running late. In his defense, he states he had learned a different version than the one the band played, and that from his position, the rock drummer could barely hear the jazz band. Regardless, this made Peart realize that if anything could be lacking in his stellar musicianship, it was that ephemeral thing called swing. Yoda Gruber was the man to teach it, and the difference in Peart's playing pre-Guber and post-Gruber is both subtle and dramatic. It was a bit like teaching Picasso to also paint like Van Gogh, with the result being the birth of a new level of artistry. "The Rhythm Method—1997" exemplifies this perfectly, as do the first two discs of *Different Stages*. It seems plausible that this is why the end section of the live version of "Bravado" is so powerful yet lean (for Rush), and why "Leave That Thing Alone" has an entirely new feel for a Rush instrumental. And if anyone need wonder if Peart "blew it" during the 1991 *Burning for Buddy* performance, just watch and listen to his drum solo from that concert, and the reaction it drew from the crowd.

Different Stages Disc Three Is a Magic Number

No doubt about it, *Different Stages*' discs one and two are remarkable in sound and substance. They have a great live-album sound, and though they were compiled from different shows and different tours, the music feels like one typically amazing night at a Rush show. It's about as perfect as a Rush live album can be in terms of song selection and feel. If the album contained only those two discs, fans would feel that they got their money's worth. But Rush tends to be generous to their fans (as their fans are to them), and so, tucked inside the trifold packaging, falling into lucky laps during the unfolding is that marvelous *Different Stages* disc three.

As previously stated, this disc contains a recording of a 1978 Rush show at London's Hammersmith Odeon. It is Rush at the peak of their adolescence, so to speak. Though "2112" and the drum solo were cut out (they appeared, after all, on the other *Different Stages* discs), the album contains long, epic, prog tunes, Geddy Lee at his high-pitched best, and the band playing their asses off because they still had something to prove, and still had something to honor: the success and freedom earned from *2112*. Given that this was taped in 1978, the production aspect of the show was really just about three young men playing some of the most intense rock and roll ever recorded. No lasers, no props, no inflatable bunnies, no cheeky videos. And that's how it sounds. There are no laid-back moments; it is Rush rock, played with a fresh intensity and the authority of young Turks in their prime. The album sums up better than any prior recording—live or studio, and better than any interview or media piece, how Rush earned their place in the rock pantheon—one show at a time, one riff at a time.

Different Kings

Disc three of *Different Stages* is not just amazing for the Rush era it captured, but also for its setlist. Being the *A Farewell to Kings* tour, the setlist is really a live prog masterpiece. It is a set so strong that "Xanadu"—the song many feel best sums up Rush at the height of long form prog—doesn't stand out, but rather just fits in with the other big prog pieces: "A Farewell to Kings," "Cygnus-X-1," and "By-Tor and the Snow Dog." Here, "Xanadu" is still new, and the band plays it like they do the rest of the set—feverishly. The album also reminds listeners that the tune "A Farewell to Kings" is right up there with "Xanadu" as an early Rush masterpiece (if their fifth studio album could indeed be considered early in Rush's *oeuvre*).

The enthusiasm barely contained in the performance leaps from the speakers when playing this disc. It is arguably the most intense of the official live Rush recordings, and like a top-shelf single-malt scotch, cannot be consumed casually.

The Brown Sound

It had been seven albums (excluding compilations) since Terry Brown's name had appeared in the liner notes of a Rush album. And it was great to see it again. Brown engineered the live recording of the show that would end up on disc three of *Different Stages*, and it sounds like it. Justified or not, first- and

The heavy *Counterparts* material featured on *Different Stages* heralds Peart's drumming after learning how to swing from drum master Freddie Gruber. *Courtesy of Max Mobley*

second-generation Rush fans tend to be partial to Brown's engineering and production styles. He just seems to be able to unobtrusively capture Lee, Lifeson, and Peart at their intense best. There truly is a chemistry that Brown was able to manifest, and he deserves credit for the aforementioned accolades of the 1978 recording on *Different Stages*. It is enough to make fans wonder what would happen if Brown returned to work with the band again (which is a bit like wondering what Pink Floyd would be like had Syd Barrett not gone bonkers . . .).

If Rush had wanted, they could have released disc three on its own and, like all things Rush, it would have been gobbled up by their fans. *Different Stages* disc three is only three songs and one drum solo shy from the concert's full setlist (though about ten seconds of Peart's solo can be heard in the album's closer, "In the Mood"). The missing songs include "Lakeside Park," "Closer to the Heart," and an abbreviated version of "2112" (minus "The Oracle"). An album containing the full setlist would make a great release for the band and SRO-Anthem.

Unfortunately, unlike the previous two live Rush albums, video / DVD versions of the shows do not exist (or, if they do, they have not been released). The availability of a filmed performance of the 1978 Hammersmith Odeon tour could possibly give Rush fans the vapors—it surely is the stuff of dreams. And a filmed version of either the *Counterparts* tour or the *Test for Echo* tour, which comprise the music on *Different Stages* discs one and two, would be a real treat for fans as well. It would show Rush breathing a bit more easily, exuding the grace of maturity (it happens to us all), and the confidence of well-loved kings who need not ever worry about revolutions, poison, or backstabbers.

According to Lee, the first of two Toronto shows from the *Test for Echo* tour (1997) was filmed for subsequent release. However, problems with the audio recording portion forced the band to shelve the idea (too expensive, too broken). Technologies for fixing those kinds of problems have become both cheaper and more effective in the intervening years, so perhaps it is something that may see the light of day before too long.

Different Stages of Technology

Driving home the technology-pushing themes of Rush, the original CD of *Different Stages* contained a video-art program called "Clusterworks." By today's standards the "app" seems quaint at best, antiquated at worst—like an old Atari video game (oh, how far and how fast we have traveled during the past twenty years, technologically speaking).

Clusterworks is an application designed by the Japanese computer artist Hisashi Hoda. It is reminiscent of the early visuals of iTunes—sort of a 3D-ish rendering of light in motion that grows and flows like a fountain in sync with the music. Well, sort of. Lee joked that it would be interesting to fans who smoke a lot of, um, herbs.

The app probably will not work on modern computers (*Different Stages* was released when the operating system Windows 98 was considered "awesome"), but that may not matter since, as of this writing, the album is only available as a download. Hard copies (CDs or vinyl) are mostly available used, and you should expect to pay big bucks if you stumble across a new one.

The Artwork of *Different Stages*

Different Stages' album booklet and interior art, thanks to Hugh Syme and Rush's official photographer, the late Andrew MacNaughtan, is likewise noteworthy. The included booklet is, on one side, a compendium, of sorts, of Rush paraphernalia covering the twenty years between discs one and two, and disc three. These were compiled by MacNaughtan, who spent weeks on the project. The other side features a collection of excellent live photographs, including an amazing audience shot with storm clouds and the Tinkertoy totem— this time devoid of color. Unlike the previous live albums, the *Different Stages* CD booklet is an ersatz tour book in itself. Speaking of tour books, first-run pressings of the Japanese version of the album contained two mini tour books of *A Farewell to Kings* and *Test for Echo*, and an additional track—"Force Ten."

The Sound of *Different Stages*

All the World's a Stage is raw and a tad rough; the rock and roll sound jostles the listener like someone standing in the festival-seating

Different Stages also included music from 1991's *Roll the Bones* album, including the setlist mainstay "Dreamline," the poignant and beautiful "Bravado," and the controversial (due to its rap section) title track.
Courtesy of Max Mobley

floor section of a Rush concert (the album was recorded back when that was common). *Exit . . . Stage Left* is polished, so much so that the live-ness was almost polished right off the record. *A Show of Hands* is pristinely digital, yet maintains its live-concert appeal. All those ones and zeroes line up nicely to deliver some amazing music during an amazing (and occasionally misunderstood) period during the height of Rush's digital age. *Different Stages* sounds, well, different yet again, in part because it's two distinct eras and multiple venues, tours, and recordings. The sound of disc three has been aptly described at the time of its release as arguably Rush's best-sounding live album. Discs one and two sound great as well, especially in the bass, drums, and vocal departments. However, sometimes Lifeson's guitar gets a bit muddy in the mix. (*Terry Brown, where are you? Oh, yeah, you're on disc three.*) Lifeson's energy and what he's playing largely compensate for any loss of clarity, which is sometimes overrated (and underappreciated) in rock and roll. This is probably due largely to the combination of guitars, amps, and pedals rather than the mix or production (the album was mixed by the talented Paul Northfield, who engineered several Rush albums, including *Moving Pictures, Permanent Waves*, and the previous live album *A Show of Hands*). Lifeson used creamy-sounding Marshall amps during these tours, along with the controversial choice of Gallien Krueger (popular with bassists and as an acoustic guitar amp—not so much for rock and roll guitar). But for the *A Farewell to Kings* tour, it was the classic Marshall stack accompanied by fat analog effects, and the mighty semi-hollow body Gibson ES-355, which, due to it not being a solid body guitar, has a lot of cut and snarl when played through an overdriven tube amp (i.e., a Marshall). For the *Counterparts* and *Test for Echo* tours, Lifeson primarily used compressed and lush-sounding solid-bodies (Gibson Les Pauls and Paul Reed Smiths) into Marshall combo amps (small but powerful amps with the amplifier, controls, and speakers in a single cabinet). Sonically speaking, combo amps can be a bit spongy compared to their tower of power Marshall stack counterparts. These rigs were, of course, augmented by Lifeson's arsenal of effects. There was some expansion in this department over previous tours, thanks to the evolution of digital signal processors. Digital effects are precise and powerful as far as parameters and functionality go, but they are devoid of rock grit and often lack the punch associated with analog. So while the guitar rigs for *Counterparts* and *Test for Echo* tours, as heard on *Different Stages*, sound good, they just don't quite have the attack and chunk that best serves Lifeson's playing (as heard on disc three with his glorious seventies-era Marshall amp stack sound).

Different Stages is superb at summing up the two Rush eras it covers, as well as eras covered by the band's previous live records. Despite the incredible collection of songs spanning three discs (and over two decades), and the popularity of the record (especially that disc three), it seems odd that the album remains available only via download.

You Forgot the *Grace Under Pressure Tour*

No I didn't, but it's key to remember that the *Grace Under Pressure Tour* was released first as a live concert video on VHS and LaserDisc, and that the live album version (this time from the exact same show—how about that!) wasn't released until 2006, as part of the Rush *Replay X 3* box set, which also contained a remastered version of the concert video. Given that order of releases, it's placed here after *Different Stages*, following the live-album release order.

Grace Under Pressure: Tour 1984

Rush Get the Eighties (in a Good Way . . .)

This tight live album sparkles with Rush diving headlong into eighties pastel silliness, though steers clear of the dorkiness found on *A Show of Hands*. Though the album (and video) were, as the title suggests, from the 1984 *Grace Under Pressure* tour (specifically, a September stop at Toronto's Maple Leaf Gardens), only five of the fourteen tracks are from *Grace Under Pressure* or the album before it, *Signals*. For the most part, the rest of the set features songs Rush fans have been hearing live on previous albums and tours—"Finding My Way" / "In the Mood," "The Temples of Syrinx," "Closer to the Heart," a super-medley of "YYZ" / "2112 Overture" / "The Temples of Syrinx," and "Tom Sawyer." The album sounds live—*very* live, in fact, though the drums are perhaps a tad flat-sounding (which may be due to Peart's use of that eighties percussion phenomenon: the Simmons electric drum set). The album and video also contains two standouts, covered below.

Grace's "Vital Signs"

"Vital Signs," a song cherished by fans who discovered Rush from the *Moving Pictures* album, is arguably the gem of this record. It makes the most out of the synth technology of the day, with MIDI technology simplifying Lee's chore of playing sequenced keyboard parts, non-sequenced parts, and bass (and don't forget vocals!). Though "Vital Signs" was released in 1981, its prog-reggae vibe and super tight, Stewart Copeland–esque drum parts make the tune really sound "of the time" on this record. This was 1984, and the eighties sound was in full swing. Both the *Grace Under Pressure* studio album and the subsequent tour captured live proves that Rush had really owned their place in the era. Unlike the video version of *A Show of Hands*, the *Grace Under Pressure: Tour 1984* is an example of the whole package working, which, while being the norm for the band, was not easy to do during such an odd (and technically swift) decade in rock and roll music.

Though the *Grace Under Pressure* video was briefly available on VHS, it was not until the release of the four-disc box set, *Replay X 3*, that Rush fans en masse could add it to their collection. The set also included a CD version.   *Courtesy of Max Mobley*

Live Fear

Another thing that makes *Grace Under Pressure: Tour 1984* a must-have live album (released as a standalone in 2009, and available as part of the *Replay X 3* box set) is the inclusion of Rush's Fear Trilogy (part one: "The Enemy Within," from *Grace Under Pressure*, part two: "The Weapon," from *Signals*, and part three: "Witch Hunt," from *Moving Pictures*). The Fear Trilogy is played in order on the album, and *Grace Under Pressure: Tour 1984* is the only recording where fans can find it. The Fear Trilogy concept came to Peart from a conversation he had with an "older man" who believed life was ruled by fear, not love. Peart disagreed, but upon studying those around him, he realized that the man had a point. Peart's lyrics of the Fear Trilogy explore how fear works inside of us ("The Enemy Within"), how it is used against us ("The Weapon"), and how it fuels the mob mentality ("Witch Hunt").

Count Floyd Under Pressure

The Fear Trilogy covered dark themes, though the decade in which they were written (the eighties) was a happy time, artistically speaking anyway. Similarly, members of Rush were considered overtly serious, though they were, in truth, lovable goofballs. How to reconcile this disparity? Why Count Floyd, of course! Count Floyd was a recurring character from Second City TV (SCTV), a Chicago-based improv group that is home to some of the best comedians and comedy writers on the planet, including Tina Fey, Bill Murray, and Stephen Colbert. SCTV's recurring Count Floyd skit featured actor / comedian Joe Flaherty as a horror movie host who dressed as a cheap vampire (Count Floyd). The "show," dubbed *Monster Chiller Horror Theatre*, consisted of Floyd introducing lame horror flicks (or just lame movies hyped as horror). The show satirized syndicated horror movie shows like *Creature Feature* from the sixties and seventies. Many of these sketches pushed oddball film technologies, like horror-vision and 3D glasses.

In a prelude to Rush playing "The Weapon" during the Fear Series, Count Floyd appears on the giant video screen behind Rush's backline. He emerges from his vertically placed coffin, howling like a werewolf (yeah, he was a vampire . . .), touting the need for 3D glasses for the song "The Weapon" ("If you don't have your 3D glasses you'll only be watching in one-half D!") and letting fans know that they were about to experience something scary (pronounced "scaddy," à la Bela Lugosi). Incidentally, Rush gave out 3D glasses to fans at their Toronto shows, including the show filmed and recorded for the *Grace Under Pressure: Tour 1984* album and video. SCTV fans and Rush fans definitely cross over, and the short comedic segment was very well received by both sets. It was also a sign of things to come for Rush live.

A video of Second City Television's *Monster Chiller Horror Theatre* host, Count Floyd (shown here on the album cover of his comedy EP), introduced "The Weapon," to great comedic effect, during the *Grace Under Pressure* tour.

Courtesy of Joe Pesch

Trilogy Plus One

The 2002 album, *Vapor Trails*, extended The Fear trilogy to a tetralogy through the addition of "Freeze, Part IV of Fear." "Freeze" explores how one behaves while under the influence of fear—fight or flight, surrender or defend. It's about fear being in control to a paralyzing degree. The timing of *Vapor Trails* can't help but give the song an added poignancy. It is the only song of the Fear Series that has never been performed live.

The Sound of *Grace Under Pressure: Tour 1984*

Unlike the albums and related videos of *Exit . . . Stage Left* and *A Show of Hands*, the album version of *Grace Under Pressure: Tour 1984* really is the soundtrack to the video—same recording, same everything except format. Whether that has any bearing or not on the sound of the *Grace Under Pressure: Tour 1984* album is unknown, but given the slightly lo-fi sound of the record (for its era), it's

The *Grace Under Pressure Tour* DVD jacket, within the *Replay X 3* set, features some of Hugh Syme's more haunting work.   *Courtesy of Max Mobley*

possible. It's as if the album version was lifted from audio tracks built for video production. Lo-fi is really an overstatement. *Grace Under Pressure: Tour 1984* contains better fidelity than the awesomely raw *All the World's a Stage*. But, given the music and the year, the sonic expectations of the two albums are different. The eighties had a sound, of that there is no question. Most of Rush's recorded music during this time likewise had an eighties vibe—prog style, but eighties nonetheless (most notably the live sound of *A Show of Hands* and the studio albums *Power Windows* and *Hold Your Fire*). *Grace Under Pressure: Tour 1984* (which, by the way, is also remarkable for being the only official live Rush album NOT containing a drum solo) has a rather classic live-album sound, yet with modern (for its day) material. One of the benefits of this is that, for a synthy period, the guitar is well up in the mix (where most fans believe it

belongs). It's redundant to say that the band's playing was top notch—though it was, and Lifeson's solo on "The Weapon" is one of his best solos from any official live recording. As mentioned earlier, Lifeson played his custom Hentor Sportscasters (one white, one black) on the tour (and on the studio recording of *Grace Under Pressure*). They had the bite to cut through the synth stacks and matched the edgy guitar sounds that were common to the decade. Lee played a Steinberger bass on the recording and tour—a popular instrument for the time. The Steinberger's claim to fame was its ability to deliver a solid bass sound despite being about as small as a bass guitar could be. The strings were mounted in reverse, which removed the need for a bulky bass headstock with fat tuners. These were replaced instead with small thumbscrew tuners down on the instrument's bridge and tailpiece section (where the strings stop on the body-side of the guitar). The body just barely fit the electronics and hardware required for an electric bass. This made the bass quite small and funky-looking in a total eighties high-tech way. They were lightweight, comfortable, and easy to play. Some feel the lack of wood made the instrument sound a bit lifeless. Given the prodigious use of signal processing during the eighties, this was rarely an issue at the time. Arguably, the bass did not quite fit Lee's tonal palette, previously defined by bright and bold Rickenbacker basses that had plenty of high end while still owning bottom-end rock and roll frequencies.

Peart was still in the midst of his Tama drum era (the snare was still his trusty Slingerland used from his earliest days). This time it was a glorious (and slightly gory) blood red. The toms were oversized, and their big fat resonance can be heard quite well on the recording. Peart still employed double-kick drums and the classic (well, modern for the eighties) Simmons drum modules that were part of the back-kit surrounding Peart.

What Is a Hentor, Anyway?

Never heard of a Hentor Sportscaster guitar? Never seen one at the music store? You're in good company, and here's why. These guitars, used on the *Grace Under Pressure: Tour 1984* video and the albums *Permanent Waves*, *Moving Pictures*, *Signals*, and, of course, *Grace Under Pressure*, were custom-built for Lifeson and the music Rush was playing during this era. The name of the guitar was Lifeson's idea. Hentor was the nickname of Peter Henderson (Hentor the Barbarian), who co-produced the *Grace Under Pressure* album. Sportscaster was obviously a riff on the name Stratocaster.

Lifeson's heavily modified Stratocasters—dubbed Hentor Sportscasters—are considered part of his legendary sound, from *Moving Pictures* through *Grace Under Pressure*. The guitar is used heavily on the *Grace Under Pressure Tour*. Lifeson gave permission to luthier Fred Gabrsek to make exacting replicas of the instruments, with the profits going to charity.

Courtesy of Fred Gabrsek

For those unfamiliar with guitar brands or names—Fender Stratocaster is the guitar most associated with Jimi Hendrix, Jeff Beck, and Eric Clapton. Gibson Les Pauls are most associated with Jimmy Page, Slash, Pete Townshend (up through the nineties), and Zakk Wylde. The aforementioned Super-Strats (like Lifeson's Signature Aurora) are most associated with Steve Vai and Joe Satriani. The Hentor Sportscasters could safely be classified as a Super-Strat. Lifeson started with a Strat body, and then customized pretty much everything else, including the neck and pickups. Unlike the Signature Auroras Lifeson played on *A Show of Hands*, the Hentor Sportscaster featured a humbucker pickup in the bridge, and two single coils in the neck and middle positions. This has since become a common pickup set for Super-Strats. The Hentor Sportscaster's unique combination of materials and electronics makes them a one-of-a-kind sounding instrument. An upgraded version of the Hentors has recently been reissued, with the approval of Alex Lifeson, by Canadian luthier Fred Gabrsek. Gabrsek was also chosen by Lifeson to rebuild his original ES-355, which was damaged during a tour by a speaker cabinet falling onto it. The reissued Hentors sound amazing, and replicate Lifeson's "Limelight" sound to a tee.

The Look of *Grace Under Pressure: Tour 1984* (Smiling's My Favorite)

Prior to the eighties, rock concerts were often intense affairs, not for the faint of heart. That all changed during this decade of mullets and headbands, and those who used to be afraid of the loud, smoky, sweaty rituals that were seventies-era rock concerts started going to them and having a nice time. And it was no different for Rush during this happy, fun, pastel era. Make no bones about it, the above is not meant as an insult or a negative in any way. It was progress, for fans and the industry at large. For bands, the only difference was the wardrobe, the style, and the lights. The *Grace Under Pressure: Tour 1984* video exemplifies this nicely. Rush's lighting, which really began to take on a life of its own during the eighties, was heavy on the pastel pinks and purples. And the video was recorded pretty hot, meaning those bright lights wash out the image in quite a few instances. *Exit . . . Stage Left* has a dark look to it, due to the lights (lighting live concerts for videotaping is never easy), and, by extension, a sort of "old school" concert vibe, despite it being recorded just three years earlier. *Grace Under Pressure: Tour 1984*, on the other hand, had lights so bright they burned into the video, creating a sort of video distortion effect that became redolent of the era. Considering that Lifeson positively glows in his white eighties jacket, this lighting burn-in phenomenon must have been intentional.

Speaking of a glowing Lerxst, throughout much of the video, he steals the show. Normally this is done with his playing, and of course, he sounds great and, as previously mentioned, is well up in the mix. But this time he captivates

The back of the *Grace Under Pressure Tour* soundtrack features Syme's iconic egg-in-a-vice image, symbolizing grace under pressure.

Courtesy of Max Mobley

through an awesome asymmetrical haircut, and a smile that is constant and wholly infectious. His presence is the epitome of joy expressed through art.

Grace Under Pressure: Tour 1984 is a tight one-hour set (again—no drum solo!) of music, visuals, and gear mostly inspired by the times. Somehow, Rush manages to keep the sound organic and raw enough to feel like a rock concert, with emphasis on the word *rock*. Where *A Show of Hands* reveals some of the more contentious elements of Rush's explorations during a controversial musical era, *Grace Under Pressure: Tour 1984* reveals what totally worked for the band during that time.

12

Rush in Rio—The Boys Are Back Onstage

A Prog-Rock *Carnival*

Vapor Trails, released in 2002, was not a breakout like some albums before it (and *Snakes and Arrows* after it). It was something equally important, however—it was a comeback. Not just any comeback, but one from seemingly insurmountable heartbreak. The subsequent tour kicked off with a whiff of trepidation. It was still a sensitive time—serious years and events had passed since the last tour. And fans, either well meaning or sometimes just plain selfish, could easily rub salt in wounds whose true healing were questionable at best. To make matters worse, everyone involved knew the story, and they'd all be studying the very private guy behind the drums on a very public stage—seeing how he was holding up, seeing what (if anything) had changed, on any level. They would be looking for smiles, or grimaces. A focus renewed, or one that was tenebrous.

Most fans were just grateful that the amazing musical odyssey was not yet over, and they were just happy to see and hear the band, as a band, again. But even they could not help but wonder about the Professor of the drum kit who just wanted to be left alone to make his music, play his best, and get on his bike and ride. And he did. And that the *Vapor Trails* tour was great was not borne out of these things (with the lone exception of a heightened gratitude for all involved to be able to do this some more). It was, instead, borne out of what makes a Rush tour exceptional. And that starts with a setlist that was impressive in length as well as selection. The *Vapor Trails* setlist was one for the ages. Gems for all, including "La Villa Strangiato," "By-Tor and the Snow Dog," and "Natural Science." The show also featured a wholly revamped live style. Lifeson played an impressive and large collection of guitars, old and new; Lee had eschewed typical bass amplification for amp simulation technology, replacing the big boxes of speakers and amps with three industrial dryers (oh, the comedy . . .), and Peart had reached (again) a new level of percussion instrumentation on his custom Drum Workshop kit with tarot-themed artwork.

As the tour marched across North America, it was clear that Rush was back, and better than ever. Their spirit, their sound, their love of progressive music, their virtuosity—were all front and center. And so it seemed entirely fitting that they would wrap up this important tour in Brazil, playing to huge and hungry crowds upwards of sixty thousand each night.

Fun with Rain and Electricity—Brazilian Style

Rush headed to South America mostly because they had never played there. It sounded like fun and they would most likely not lose money on the deal. Little did they know that they were absolutely huge in Brazil. This was due, in large part, to the country's rampant black market, which made album sales figures meaningless. In addition, the country was hungry for rock and roll from North America, which explains why so many fans had shown up to meet the band at the airport—a Rush first. (Luckily, Peart rode his bike in from another country, and was therefore able to wheel in under the radar.) Rush playing Brazil turned out to be an epic event for the country and its huge Rush fan base. It was likewise epic for Rush, and a humbling honor. It would be hard to think of a better way to end such an important tour.

Rush in Rio celebrated Rush's return to the limelight. This is the band's first concert film released on DVD. It included special features DVD's random-access technology accommodated, including Easter eggs, and the ability to watch the same song from different camera angles—each focusing on one member of the band.   *Courtesy of Max Mobley*

The band's three stops in Brazil were the major cities of Port Alegre, Sao Paolo, and Rio de Janeiro. It was the Rio show, at the Maracana Stadium on November 23, 2002, that was the source for the *Rush in Rio* DVD and CD.

Rush in Rio is not the band's best-sounding live album or DVD by any stretch. The DVD and album sound about the same, with the album version pushing the crowd up higher in the mix. And, at times, the DVD suffers from a slew of fast edits that intrude on the viewer's ability to study the performance—something Rush fans tend to do. The reason *Rush in Rio* sounds the way it does is because the Brazil shows were plagued with gear and weather problems, including a torrential downpour during the Sao Paolo show. It was one helluva a combination for the band and crew to deal with. Casualties included the *Vapor Trails* stage carpet that was so rain soaked it became too heavy to move (it eventually sold on eBay after it dried out) and Peart's rotating drum riser that was smashed by a fork-lift driver underestimating its size as he tried to load it onto a truck.

Traveling so far from America meant that the band would be using a lot of local equipment for their sound-reinforcement system (aka PA). Unfortunately, they discovered a bit late that much of the local equipment employed was in poor shape and long in the tooth. This included power cables that fried their insulation and some of the gear attached to it when a load was applied, as well as the breaking down of local sound truck used to record the audio of the Rio show. But the tour (and these last three stops) were so important in the story of Rush that it had to be to be captured for posterity. Along with the gear and weather issues, there was also a good dose of magic happening. It was palpable in the massive venues, among the massive crowds, and, more importantly, onstage. This is also readily apparent on the DVD.

Once the show was over and things had settled back down to post-tour normalcy, Jimbo Barton, who had recorded the show in a sound truck full of technical gremlins, got together with Alex Lifeson to make the songs sound as best as they possibly could for release on CD and DVD. And it's not bad, although considering where audio recording technology was in 2002 it certainly could have been better. But the bootleg sound of *Rush in Rio* actually helps tell the story of a tour that almost never was, and its final stop in a colorful, music-loving land teeming with beautiful Rush fans.

The amazing Brazilian crowd was such a huge part of the *Rush in Rio* video that they are featured on the back cover of both the album (shown here) and the DVD.
Courtesy of Max Mobley

The 125,000 Other Members of Rush

Yep, Rush fans are a unique brand of rock and roller. And any band throughout the history of rock music would be lucky to have such a large, faithful, and enthusiastic following. It's been that way almost since the beginning, and fans—as well as the band members themselves—are proud of this component of the Rush story.

And then Rush played to over 125,000 Brazilians over three nights, and, well, the Rush fans we've all come to know and love suddenly looked like amateurs. Seriously. This is not meant as an insult to the Rush fans of North America or Europe, who genuinely are amazing rock fans. It's just that the Brazilian fans were *beyond* amazing. They arrived early, handled the long rain delays patiently, and left late. They sang and air-played and rocked out on every single song, even the instrumentals. As revealed on the *Rush in Rio* DVD and album, they were a significant part of the show. This is due in part to their sheer number. A typical Rush show usually peaks around twelve thousand seriously stoked fans. In Rio, they played for forty thousand. In Sao Paolo, they played for over sixty thousand (the largest crowd ever for a Rush concert), and in Port Alegre, they played for twenty-five thousand. As the *Rush in Rio* DVD proves, forty thousand people rocking out and singing in unison (especially to a complicated instrumental like "YYZ"!) does command attention—even when musicians the caliber of Lee, Lifeson and Peart are on stage. This new level of enthusiasm, their eagerness to bond with fellow Rush fans, and their heartfelt appreciation for the music and the moment, changed the game for all Rush concerts that followed.

Nice job, Brazilian Rush fans!

Enter the Dragon

The *Rush in Rio* DVD showed the band at their absolute best thus far. This extends to the stage production of the *Vapor Trails* show. Howard Ungerleider, one of Rush's earliest techs, had been delivering the goods for several prior tours. But, in the five years since Rush's last tour, stage lighting techniques had advanced, and bathing a band in light and shadow had become an art form more easily achieved. This was evident in the subtle effects employed as much as the big lighting tricks. Whether due to the location or not, the *Rush in Rio* DVD has a very clean look, lighting-wise. All members are easily seen and yet the lighting is not muted or overemphasized. The colors are beautiful, and separate, and it really is a matter of quality over quantity. It must be mentioned, however, that, during the late and manic setup for the show, the camera and video production crew had placed lights and cables around the stage without the band's permission. While this no doubt helped the cleanly bright (but not brash) look of the *Rush in Rio* DVD, it totally impinged on the band's freedom. The front of the stage was a tripping hazard, so Lee and Lifeson avoided it. Instead of running freely wherever and whenever the band wanted to, they had to be conscious of their surroundings. This made focusing on the job of playing their instruments a bit harder. In addition, setup issues, including the gear arriving late from the last stop, forced them to forgo a sound check. That would be considered sacrilege at any rock concert, and potential suicide at a concert slated to be filmed. Lee has gone on record saying the Rio de Janeiro concert was a difficult one during which to remain cool, calm, and collected. That's totally understandable. Viewers would never know that based on the look of the show, the vibe from the crowd, and how the band carried themselves.

The large rear-projection screen behind Rush's backline also matched the show's aesthetic to a tee. The animation on "Bravado" is but one example; one of Rush's most poetic songs gets a fully poetic treatment. And more intense numbers, like "Natural Science" and "Driven" (relying on its music video—one of Rush's best), get intense visual treatments that reflect the musicianship. Hell, even the dryers look awesome! (More on that later.)

The rear-screen productions for *Rush in Rio* and the *Vapor Trails* tour were far from heavy-handed, especially during the first set. But when the band returns from intermission for set two, they return afire.

Vapor Trails, being "an evening with" tour, meant Rush played all night, and there was no opening act (1994's *Counterparts* was the last tour to include an opening band, and it was the mighty Primus). In the States, intermission meant a reasonably orderly dash to the bathroom, followed by a restocking of beer for the next set. In Rio, fans weren't going anywhere. They were too in love with the show to do anything but wait for their band to return to the stage.

And, boy, did they return.

The end of intermission was signaled by the faint but growing sounds of nature, occasionally interrupted by an ominous low tone. The rear-screen was subtly coming to life—dawn in an alien desert landscape, the sound and the video began to make sense. It all fit—not sure how—but at least the sound and the image aligned. And more importantly, it seized the attention of the forty thousand Rush fans in attendance. Suddenly, there was a flame in the distance. And then another. And another. "Dragons. It had to be dragons," you could almost hear some lost man of Willowdale uttering sardonically. For a prog band who cut their teeth on fantasy, dragons seemed both fitting and serious. And

Rush in Rio gave fans a chance to hear some stellar *Vapor Trails* material, such as "One Little Victory," without the digital muck that hurt the studio release.   *Courtesy of Max Mobley*

then one flew to the foreground, seemingly breaking out of the screen, even without fans having Count Floyd's 3d glasses (Dragonvision!). The beast sized up the crowd. It was all so legit, especially for prog-rock animation coupled with a foreboding soundtrack. And then—it pulled out a cigar. A cigar! Indeed, there was much to celebrate. Seems like a simple set up, but it was pulled off perfectly by the digital animation team Spin Productions. The cigar is lit, the dragon enjoys a deep inhalation, and then does what dragons do best—it started a fire—onstage!

The fire onstage was real and controlled, in large red columns across the entire backline, just a few feet behind Neil Peart. Fans in the first fifteen rows could feel its impressive heat (making us wonder how it felt onstage). Its ignition was perfectly timed with the cigar-smoking dragon's exhalations. That first exhalation also ignited Peart's blazing snare and double-kick intro for "One Little Victory," the first song marking Rush's return from darkness.

"By-Tor and the Snow Dog" Live!

The triumphant return of Rush, as announced by the delighted Brazilian audience, featured some of the band's best live cuts—songs strong enough to cut through gear problems and the constant roar of forty thousand of Rush's best friends. Chief among them was "By-Tor and the Snow Dog," which hadn't been played live in over twenty years, during the *Exit . . . Stage Left* tour of 1982. Wow. No doubt the song is a special one. It's sort of a test (and testament) of what Lee and Lifeson could do with their new drummer Peart, back on 1975's *Fly by Night*. As if listening to the band playing "By-Tor and the Snow Dog" was not enough, during the condensed version of "The Battle," the song's main instrumental section, the band brought back there flair for oddball comedy with a cartoon played on the rear screen. It featured Lee and Peart in various duels as bodybuilders, dogs, and Macarena-dancing robots. Peart is seen sitting in a comfy chair, superciliously looking up from his book at his bandmates' antics (until the final scene, which will not be spoiled here). The entire animation sequence is available as an Easter egg on the *Rush in Rio* DVD (during the disc-two documentary, *The Boys in Brazil*, press the enter key on the DVD remote when Lifeson talks about the song). "By-Tor and the Snow Dog" was featured during the encore of *Rush in Rio* and the *Vapor Trails* tour. It was reduced in length (minus a verse, the epilogue, and some subsections from "The Battle"). It segued into the intro to "Cygnus X-1," followed by "Working Man."

Rush Live and on Camera

At a show of forty-thousand fans in a hundred-thousand–seat stadium built for soccer, not music, one fan is unlucky enough to have the worst seat (but still lucky enough to be there, witnessing and helping make history). The forty-thousandth seat belonged to someone, after all. Luckily for that guy or gal (Brazil was also remarkable for having a large number of female fans at the show, and they seemed to be glad to be there, too!), the best use of this rear-screen tour were the ample close-ups of Lee, Lifeson and Peart rocking their asses off—prog style. An astounding twenty cameras were employed to capture this high point in Rush's triumphant return. And to think that, because of difficulties in set up (including getting the gear from São Paulo to Rio De Janeiro, where some key pieces were replaced out of safety and fears they would not last through the show) and due to the crowd filing in during the hugely late setup, none of those cameras were able to do any pre-checks. Thankfully they all worked, and the only issue was that a cameraman inadvertently interfered with Alex Lifeson during the show, causing the guitar player to lose his happy thoughts. It was enough of an issue that Lee had to settle Lifeson down in between sets, helping him let go of the issue and return to having a good time "because there's just no sense looking pissed off on tape," Lee pointed out in an interview about the DVD.

Return of the Dragon

The dragon featured in the *Vapor Trails* tour, and on the box art of the *Rush in Rio* DVD (and the DVD menu and homescreen) was inspired by Hugh Syme. One of Syme's art concepts for *Vapor Trails* featured a rendering of a tiny dragon as the source of the vapor trail. When Lee was looking for production ideas for the tour, he remembered that dragon and thought it would make an interesting character. He was right. The crowd loved it at each stop on the tour, including those in Brazil. The dragon has since become an icon for the band at this stage of their arc, which seems completely apropos. And it wouldn't be the last time Rush fans would see the beast.

Rush in Rio's Twenty-Nine Tracks

The *Rush in Rio* live album contains the full set of twenty-nine songs from the Rio de Janeiro show, as well as additional "board mixes." A board mix is simply a stereo output of the mix as it is coming from the sound console. These are usually reserved for the band and techs—the equivalent of watching film of last week's game to learn what worked and what didn't, and to relive choice moments.

The *Vapor Trails* show, as played in Rio de Janeiro, was so lengthy it required a third CD in order to hold all that music. This disc contains only four songs from the Rio show: "Limelight," "La Villa Strangiato," "The Spirit of Radio," and "By-Tor and the Snow Dog" married with the "Cygnus X-1" intro and "Working Man." To fill out the disc, the band added two songs recorded earlier in the tour: "Between Sun and Moon" (recorded in Phoenix, Arizona) and "Vital Signs" (recorded in Quebec City, Canada).

Special Features Galore!

Rush in Rio was the first live video to be released on DVD. Rush and SRO-Anthem took advantage of that medium by including a second disc full of special features, Easter eggs, and the first official Rush documentary, *The Boys in Brazil.*

The Boys in Brazil

It's not surprising to read on the different Rush forums that disc two is watched by Rush fans more often that disc one. The reason is the late Andrew MacNaughtan's mini-rock doc, *The Boys in Brazil,* which gives fans something they have been waiting for since they discovered Rush—an inside look at the band. Fans know them for their music. Their personalities on stage lurk mostly behind their performances (with a few exceptions, like Lee and Lifeson cutting up a bit, and Peart's occasional smile). *The Boys in Brazil* shows Lee and Lifeson (and occasional glimpses of Peart, sometimes with his nose in a book) living their lives as highly successful touring musicians. Lifeson cuts up incessantly, and his impression of Ozzy Osborne lends credence to the notion that he could have a great career in comedy if he wanted to.

MacNaughtan, a close friend of the band and their official photographer from the eighties to his passing in 2012 (while on tour with Rush, no less) was somebody Lee, Lifeson, and Peart could be comfortable around, and it shows in the documentary. The interview portions show the members at their most relaxed, maybe ever. The fly-on-the-wall bits, including Lee on his way to the venue (where he infamously misplaces his shoes and grows a bit tense), Lifeson chilling onstage during sound check, and Peart's pre-show warm-up (which is essentially a stunning drum solo) give fans insight into watching these men at work—where they are their most comfortable. Better still, the doc shows how Lee, Lifeson and Peart relate to one another outside of performance. From Lifeson helping Peart with his shoes before they run onto a rain-soaked stage, putting plastic bags around them to keep them dry so they won't slip on his pedals, to Lee and Lifeson cracking each other up in the way only lifelong friends can, MacNaughtan's film (which won him a Juno award), helps Rush fans confirm much of what they love about their band—that its three members are close friends who are unabashedly normal and down to earth (even the guy with the big brain). They are rock's answer to Clark Kent. No, better than Clark Kent who never rose above being uncomfortable in his skin as a regular Joe, the members of Rush *are* regular Joes. They just happen to make some of the most incredible rock music in the history of the medium—because they are driven to do so.

Also, when on the road—soup matters!

Three Video Clinics

As mentioned previously, the fast-edit style of *Rush in Rio* is a bit jarring at times. As if to compensate, disc two contains multi-angle views of "YYZ," "La Villa Strangiato," and Peart's Grammy-nominated drum solo, "O Baterista." For "YYZ" and "La Villa Strangiato," the multi-angle feature allows the viewer to focus (mostly) on a specific band member. For "O Baterista," viewers can choose different angles of Peart throwing it down, including an overhead view (great for drummers wanting to study Peart at his best).

A Well-Hidden Anthem

Hard to believe, but in 2002 DVD video was still a fairly new technology: the US standard for DVD production came out five years prior, in 1997. As such, "Easter eggs" were a popular treat for DVD video buyers. Easter eggs on DVDs are essentially hidden material accessed by clicking the right button on the remote control, or selecting the right items on the DVD menu. Doing so would result in previously hidden material being available in the random access world of DVD technology. In the linear modality of video tape, such tricks were simply not possible.

Disc two of the *Rush in Rio* DVD contains two Easter eggs, the aforementioned "By-Tor and the Snow Dog" cartoon, and the 1975 "Church Session" of "Anthem," mentioned elsewhere in this book. For most fans, *Rush in Rio* was the first time they got to see a very young Rush perform that song. To access the "Anthem" Easter egg, fans have to select "O Baterista" (video 2), then return to the menu and select "YYZ" (video 1), return to the menu again, select "YYZ" again, and then return to the menu and select "O Baterista" one more time. Returning to the menu again, and lo and behold, a new item is available: "Anthem 1975." Sheesh! Notice that the selection spells out (by menu order) 2-1-1-2. Oh, those funny guys! In order to not drive certain fans crazy, "Anthem 1975" would also appear after watching all of the listed content on disc two (thank God!).

And the 2002 Grammy for Best Rock Instrumental Goes to ...

Not Neil Peart. But his drum solo from the *Vapor Trails* tour was nominated for one. Think about that for just a moment. A drum solo, once considered wankery or a pox on rock concerts during the eighties and nineties, was being singled out as an important musical endeavor by the National Academy of Recording Arts and Sciences. Dubbed "O Baterista," in honor of the Mexico City stops of the tour (the term is Spanish for "the drummer"), Peart's nearly nine-minute solo piece contains melody and harmony and simultaneous multiple rhythms galore. So much so that calling it a drum solo is a bit like calling Mozart a melody maker.

While fans are accustomed to Peart taking the drum solo to new places, "O Baterista" is by far the largest leap. And at the same time, it contains pieces from every Peart drum solo ever recorded. Cool.

Watching Peart perform "O Baterista" is like watching the world's most impressive stupid human trick. People just aren't supposed to be able to do that with such aplomb. And, at least outwardly, Peart always seems to be in a sort of Zen state during his solos, though he has reported that he has a lot going on inside his head. That Zen-like outward vibe is present during "O Baterista," which is pretty amazing since Peart dove into the solo unsure if his electronic pieces (most notably the MIDI marimba controller) were going to work properly, given that they had been soaked by the previous show's rain storm. But, working those angels overtime once again, everything worked like it was supposed to.

Speaking of Gear

Despite the tragic reasons behind Rush's five-year break, something good seemed to have come out of it. The band appeared to have a new appreciation for what they get to do (it had never been taken for granted, but heavy life events often remind us how privileged we are to do what we do, even if it's just being able to walk outside and breath clean air, let alone be in that "thing" known as Rush). This comes across in the *Vapor Trails* tour's performances, the quality of its production, and the bounty of material in the show itself, including what was put out in the form of the album and DVD. It also translated into Rush's choice in gear. As always, the band did not shy away from new technologies (such as Lee's Palmer bass cabinet simulators instead of physical bass speaker cabinets). But mixed in with the new were old technologies that have been part of the rock and roll gear pantheon for over forty years. This is especially evident in Lifeson's tube-amp stacks, and his use of one of his early Rush axes, the Gibson ES-355.

Over his long career, Alex Lifeson has freely explored different kinds of guitar amps. He's toured with nearly every amp technology imaginable, except for digital-simulation amps. He started with classic all-tube stacks from Marshall and Hiwatt, combo amps (amp and speaker in the same relatively small box), solid state amps (transistors instead of tubes, which are still verboten in many rock guitar circles), and then finally came full circle with his German-made Hughes and Kettner all-tube, full-stack rigs. He used four of these on the *Vapor Trails* tour: one for clean sounds, one for distortion sounds, one to drive his FX package, and one for backup ('cause it's a tour and things happen!). As a result, *Rush in Rio*, despite flaws in the audio, boasts one of Lifeson's fattest and heaviest tones, perhaps his heaviest ever.

In the guitar department, Lifeson traveled with a slew of beautiful instruments. Some standouts from this mobile guitar museum include that rebuilt and gorgeous ES-355, several Gibson Les Pauls, including a Black Beauty Custom (a heavy guitar both literally and figuratively that will sustain for days),

Not only did *Rush in Rio* mark the triumphant return of a true rock-and-roll phenomenon (the multi-faceted live Rush experience), it also marked the return of an important instrument, Alex Lifeson's fully restored Gibson ES-355. The painstaking restoration was performed by luthier Fred Gabrsek.

Courtesy of Fred Gabrsek

a Gibson SG used on "Roll the Bones" (think Angus Young and Frank Zappa), several PRS (Paul Reed Smith is a boutique company that makes stunning instruments in sound, playability, and looks) including the Les Paul-ish PRS Singlecut, and several PRS CE24s.

Perhaps the strangest guitar in Lifeson's arsenal was also one of the most traditional: a blonde Fender Telecaster. The Tele (for short) is an American classic, as popular in country as it is in rock, a fave of Bruce Springsteen, the late Joe Strummer from the Clash, and Radiohead's Johnny Greenwood. That list does not scream prog rock, or even hard rock, and yet the bright, chimey Tele sound contrasts nicely with the heavy cream Les Paul sound for which Lifeson is best known. His Tele gets a fair amount of usage, and its magic in Lifeson's hands, as heard on *Rush in Rio*'s fabulous version of "Bravado."

That Tumble-Dry Sound Minus the Static Electricity

Geddy Lee's gear list featured dryers; three, to be exact. They were coin-operated and boasted clean, toasty T-shirts that he and Lifeson threw to lucky fans in the crowd. Why the dryers? Well, bass player are generally a fastidious lot, and doing laundry on a tour is always a pain in the butt, so doing it onstage kind of made sense. Okay, while that may be true, or at least sound good, that's not why Lee had three massive dryers on his backline. The reason was simple—having embraced digital-simulation technology, Lee opted for a Palmer speaker simulator instead of actual speaker cabinets. A speaker simulator is basically a box that takes a signal (Lee's bass guitar, in this instance) and processes it through an algorithm designed to simulate the sound of audio being pushed through the wood, speakers, and air of an actual speaker cabinet. The technology is sophisticated, moderately popular, and quite controversial among musicians and audiophiles (as is Lee's bass tone on *Rush in Rio*). At least some of this controversy is due to Lee breaking tradition. For most musicians, especially virtuosos like Lee (and Lifeson and Peart), their tone comes from how the musician plays the instrument far more so than the electronic boxes processing it. Lee's tone comes from his right hand as much as anywhere else, which explains why, despite the new digital gear and large changes such as a lack of speaker cabinets and wholly different basses (more on that in a bit), Lee's tone on the *Vapor Trails* tour is reminiscent of Lee's tone on *All The World's a Stage*. It's not the boxes; it's what goes into them, and the alchemy of performance. If the *Rush in Rio* bass tone is lacking, it's likely due to the technical challenges surrounding the concert and its recording. After all, Lee's setup is one of the most complicated in rock bass history.

Lee actually sends three different bass signals to the mixing desk: one dirty (a bit of overdrive), one clean (a direct-to-board signal common in early studio recordings of bass), and one that is low-end focused. These three signals are mixed and controlled by the sound engineer (talk about trust!). Any one of those three channels failing at any point between source and recording devices, in whole or in part, will dramatically alter the sound he's been developing for most of his life.

Big Times Four

Geddy Lee will forever be associated with Rickenbacker basses. It's the sound of the thing in his hands, and the look of it against his kimono, or (these days) his black T-shirt. And whenever he breaks one out, the crowd goes wild(er). But, on *Vapor Trails* as on previous outings, Lee was all Fender, all the time—four different Fender Jazz Basses, to be specific. The primary Fender Jazz is from 1972 (vintage, baby!); another is a Geddy Lee Signature Jazz Bass; and the remaining two were built in Fender's Custom shop in the nineties.

Bass players rarely change their instruments live. It's a foundation instrument, and a certain level of tonal consistency is called for. Lee's bass guitar changes have more to do with the tunings. One of his Jazz Basses is tuned a half-step down (which helps with singing those high notes), and one uses an alternate tuning for some of the *Vapor Trails* numbers (from low to high D, A, D, G. Traditional tuning is, from low to high E, A, D, G). The alternate tuning is, in part, what gives *Vapor Trails* its complex sound.

Folk Prog

After Peart and the air-drumming crowd's workout on "O Baterista," Lee and Lifeson re-emerge bearing wood—acoustic guitars, to be exact. Now that the MTV unplugged era was officially over a decade ago, it was safe to break out an acoustic ditty without the risk of being trite. Lee and Lifeson chose "Resist," from *Test for Echo*, which Lee had described previously as "just a folk song." The acoustic duo approach works quite well on the Oscar Wilde–inspired number.

Lerxst Speaks

In case it's not obvious, *Rush in Rio* DVD and album (and the *Vapor Trails* tour), are gifts that keep on giving to all Rush fans, especially ones holding the red star proudly since the 1970s. The last gift worth mentioning here is Alex Lifeson's amusing and, at times, hilarious rants during the instrumental "La Villa Strangiato." Remember that the tour happened before any fans could see Lifeson as a cutup during the accompanying documentary, and glimpses into his lunacy and comedic improv skills were few and far between. And though his appearance on the wildly funny *Trailer Park Boys* series aired five months earlier, he played a good-natured straight man in that. So, when he took the mic during a breakdown in the instrumental tune, fans weren't quite sure what to expect, but were riveted nonetheless. Thanks to the Internet, fans had learned that each night during the *Vapor Trails* tour he would say something different. Usually it was some off-the-wall stream of consciousness rant. In *Rush in Rio*, Lifeson introduces jazz music by saying "jazz is weird," and then scats and sings like an untalented Martian jazz musician searching for a lost pet. Chuckling, he moves on to introduce his "back-up band," with Milton Banana on drums, and "the guy from Ipanema" on bass (and Lerxst himself as Stan Getz). It is this sense of humor that his bandmates know and love about the guy, and probably the secret behind Rush's ability to stay together all these years. For Rush fans, it was something new they learned about their favorite guitarist.

The *Vapor Trails* tour, which was the basis for *Rush in Rio*, was an important milestone for the band and their fans. This custom-designed poster by famed artist Bob Masse commemorated the event. *Courtesy of Max Mobley*

The *Rush in Rio* DVD, due in part to its timing in the Rush story, is one of the best Rush "products" ever released. It is also the first instance of a new, well-received trend of a live album and concert DVD from a single show (or stop) after every tour. It makes sense, given the fact that Rush earned their place in the rock pantheon by touring. As great as Rush studio albums can be, nothing beats Rush *live*.

13

R30: Rush Celebrates Thirty Years the Only Way They Know How

Anniversary Anthems and a Well-Stocked Automat

wo short years after the success of *Rush in Rio* the band hit the road again with (almost) nothing to promote, except for the fact that they have survived (in a huge way) for thirty years. Yeah, the Stones have been around longer, but they stopped being relevant decades ago, and when was the last time someone hurried out to buy the newest Stones album? Conversely, as Rush winds along their long, loud path, the band only grows more and more relevant.

Any "important" rock band lasting more than a full decade is a headline-worthy feat. Led Zeppelin lasted twelve years, if you consider their demise commencing with the tragic death of their legendary drummer (and Peart influence) John Bonham. But, actually, there was a three-year gap between their last amazing album, *Presence*, and the last album, *In Through the Out Door*, released when Bonham was still alive. The Beatles, arguably the most influential band of all time, lasted exactly one decade, if you count their earliest days as a cover band playing clubs in Liverpool and Hamburg, Germany, and mark their demise with Paul McCartney's 1970 press release announcing what the Fab Four had known for months.

In light of this, that Rush has been comprised of the same three guys since 1974 is nothing short of remarkable. Lee, Lifeson, and Peart, as well as the fans, understood this, and the *R30* tour was the party that celebrated it, and the *R30* Deluxe Set (two DVDs and two audio CDs) was one helluva party favor.

Something Old, and Something Older

R30 was released as a DVD package only, with the Deluxe Edition also containing a double CD, souvenir backstage passes, and souvenir guitar picks from Lee and Lifeson (even though Lee does not use a pick).

RUSH

R30

30th Anniversary World Tour

The *R30* DVD featured some of Rush's best live material, though it was slimmed down from the show's actual setlist.   *Courtesy of Max Mobley*

Where *Rush in Rio* revealed a band rising from the ashes of tragedy and near-demise, *R30* reveals a band on a much-earned victory lap. They had nothing to promote (other than a thrown-together EP called *Feedback*, featuring a rather ho-hum collection of classic tunes the band covered back when they were learning to play together), but the R30 tour, as captured on DVD and CD, is teeming with the lighter side of being in a heavy band for thirty years.

The *R30* DVD and audio CD captures the Frankfurt, Germany, stop of the R30 tour, on September 24, 2004. The video production featured sixteen cameras, all shooting in 1080p High Definition. While the German crowd certainly cannot compete with the Brazilian audiences, the sound and image quality of *R30* is superior to any of the band's prior live videos / DVDs. The fast-editing approach of *Rush in Rio* was replaced with more thoughtful pacing. At times, the *Rush in Rio* editing made it feel like post-production was trying to be the show (especially on the dizzying edits that accompany "YYZ"). In *R30*, the music is the star, followed by the comedy and the visuals.

Rush's first song in the concert is an instrumental medley of some early Rush faves—including music the band hadn't recorded live since 1976's *All the World's a Stage* (that's twenty-eight years, if you're keeping score). Dubbed the "R30 Overture," fans who had been with the band for thirty years or so practically wept openly at what it contained. The *R30* Medley starts with Lifeson's instantly recognizable opening riff from "Finding My Way." It then moves on to excerpts from "Anthem" and "Bastille Day," "Passage to Bangkok," "Cygnus X-1 Book I: The Voyage," and, finally, a truly rare gem: "Cygnus X-1 Book II: Hemispheres." This powerhouse opener clocks in at nearly seven minutes, and is followed immediately by "The Spirit of Radio." The combination is celebratory in nature, and the perfect way to kick off a celebratory show.

A Band That Needs No Introduction Gets a Big One

Once again, rear-screen projection plays a large part in the proceedings. This is evident from the show's cleverly animated opening montage featuring imagery of Rush album covers over the thirty years celebrated. They are not shown in sequence, but presented based on how they best transition from one to the next. The opening montage starts with "The Necromancer" from *Caress of Steel* perched above his smoky, waterfall-filled mountain (part Mount Doom, part Rivendell), followed by the binocular-wielding kid from *Power Windows*, then the owl from *Fly by Night* carrying a top hat in which a bunny from *Presto* tries to emerge. This is followed by a fleet of Dalmatians from *Signals*, one of whom spies the red fire hydrant from the same album cover. A nut from the hydrant spins off into space, where it is joined by a bolt to symbolize the *Counterparts* album cover. Mixed with this image are the red, yellow, and blue Tinkertoys of *Different Stages*. The bolt and nut fall back to earth, landing in the rubble next to the puppet king of *A Farewell to Kings*. The king turns to dust and is swept up by one of the movers from *Moving Pictures*, who sweeps past framed pictures of *Permanent Waves*, *Moving Pictures* (moving, no less), and *2112*. The naked red man rebelling against conformity in the *2112* picture ends up in the *Hemispheres* "brain-scape," where the *Fly by Night* owl returns, this time dropping the top hat where it can be used to cover his, umm, stuff. Mr. Red Nude (technically he's Dionysus from the "Cygnus X-1 Book II: Hemispheres" story) tosses his hat to Apollo from the same album and story (he's the dapper gent in the suit). Here, the transition more or less breaks and starts anew (hey, they had a good run!) with the stone sculpture of *Test for Echo* being smashed by the skull from *Roll the Bones* like an errant baseball through a window. One stone from the *Test for Echo* sculpture lands in the vice of *Grace Under Pressure* and under pressure, it turns into the three red balls of *Hold Your Fire*. These turn into the fireballs (*Vapor Trails?*), and, finally (phew), out from these red orbs pop three baby dragons, looking like offspring from the dragon featured in *Rush in Rio*. This creative montage (by Toronto's Spin Productions) takes place in the span of a couple of minutes, before the band takes to the stage.

Did you notice which studio album is not represented? That's right: the eponymously titled debut album is not covered in the montage for obvious reasons (Peart's not on it, and it's his thirtieth anniversary too!).

R30's Comedy Legend

The montage does a fine job of setting the stage for why all are gathered—to celebrate thirty years of one of rock's best loved bands, and the reason for that admiration (notice the word used is *best*, not *most*). And then, perhaps just to keep perspectives in check, and perhaps as a means to remind all involved not to take things too seriously, the montage ends with a shot of American comedy legend Jerry Stiller (father of actor Ben Stiller) in a Rush T-shirt loudly waking up (like only Stiller can) on a cheap recliner. It was a dream by an old geezer, get it? Stiller has a classic "old fart" look about him, which he knows how to play up. He calls the band members to the stage, using the well-worn nicknames serious Rush fans know well: Lerxst (Alex Lifeson), Dirk (Geddy Lee), and the Professor (Neil Peart).

Great Concerts Are All About the Setlist

R30's setlist rivals the *Vapor Trails* tour captured in the *Rush in Rio* releases. Hearing even just a few bars of very early Rush songs was truly momentous. Given the band's knack for arranging tight medleys, it's a wonder why they have not gone back to this idea.

The tour's actual setlist included eight songs not heard on either the DVD or the CD (but available on the Blu-ray version). The missing songs are some of Rush's most popular: "Bravado," "One Little Victory," "By-Tor And The Snow Dog," "La Villa Strangiato," "YYZ," "Red Sector A," "The Trees," and "Secret Touch." According to Lee, in an interview with the European metal rag *Aardschok* magazine, the songs were omitted for technical reasons, and because they felt it was too redundant to include material that had been featured on *Rush in Rio*. In the article, Lee admits to a "what were we thinking?" moment, and has since made good on a promise that the songs would see the light of day. Hopefully, the band now realizes that the fans don't care how many times a live version of a song has been released, or the time span between releases. Being live, each performance has something unique about it. And, subtle though it may be, the fans appreciate that.

Knowing the difference between what was released on the *R30* and what was played at the actual concert leads one to feel that an opportunity was missed, especially regarding the two instrumentals which feature Rush at their blistering best. Of the *R30* songs played but not included on CD or DVD, "Red Sector A" was released as a bonus video on the *Snakes & Arrows Live* DVD and Blu-ray; "Secret Touch" can be found on the CD and DVD of the 1989–2008 hits compilation *Retrospective 3*, and "One Little Victory" is on the CD and DVD version of the live hits compilation *Working Men*. Best of all, the Blu-ray release of *R30* includes all eight songs in their rightful place in the set. Unfortunately (and perhaps again—what were they thinking . . .), the Blu-ray version does not contain any of the special features found on the DVD version.

Really?

Great Concerts Are All About the Musicianship

Despite the glaring absence of those eight wonderful tracks, the *R30* DVD and CD contain music that gives the band a workout. "Animate" features one of Rush's most driving riffs, and an excellent break full of mood and tension that evolves into an innovative whammy-bar–filled solo by Lifeson. And, what had to be one of the more memorable highlights for fans attending one of fifty-eight *R30* shows, one that really translates on the R30 video and CD is the epic prog number "Xanadu." The band appeared to love playing this fan favorite again; the last time it had been played was on the *Counterparts* tour. It is a shortened version, reduced to seven minutes from its usual eleven-plus. Some of what's missing is the lengthy ambient section from the intro, but it's also missing a verse. What's definitely *not* missing is Lifeson's Gibson double-neck guitar. That's an instrument that hasn't had much attention for decades. It's such a bombastic-looking thing that just its appearance onstage is an event in itself, as if announcing that whatever song is about to be played is going to be a big one, one so big it requires an enormous guitar with eighteen strings. (In my 2009 interview with Mr. Lifeson for *Premier Guitar*, he commented that once you allow yourself to be photographed playing a double-neck, those are the only pictures magazines want to run. While he was somewhat joking about this, he does have a point [including in the *Premier Guitar* piece]. A quick image search of Alex Lifeson on the web once illustrated his point. But, given the fact that the man is also synonymous with the white ES-355 and now has his own line of Gibson Les Paul guitars, images of him on double-neck have receded to two or three out of every dozen.)

Overall, the vibe of this particular Rush show is that of a band quite comfortable with where they are in life and in music (perhaps that is one and the same in this instance). They play as intensely as they always have, but in *R30* (and all the shows thereafter) they do so in a way that seems more laid-back, if that's possible. A bit like an athlete who is so good and so experienced that he makes circus touchdown catches look effortless. Rush followed their muse, and it paid off. They played what they wanted and needed to satisfy themselves and the fans came and spent their money. And when darkness descended, and all seemed lost, they tried again and kept trying until they succeeded—again. What's left but to smile with the wisdom of true perspective? To walk with the gait of a survivor, and play, like they always have—for the fans and for the absolute JOY of playing, spelled now and forever in all caps.

In *All the World's a Stage*, Rush was testing themselves by touching the boundaries of rock and roll, and then pushing it to see what happened. They were at the foot of a mountain and eager to climb. With *Exit . . . Stage Left*, the climb had begun, and through the songs they were now capable of writing, they assured onlookers (fans) that they knew what they were doing, while doubters hoped for a fall. In *Grace Under Pressure*, they had reached a plateau and were adjusting to the giddy atmosphere that was the eighties. In *A Show of Hands*, they seemed to want to make sure that everyone knew that, whereas they have yet to reach the peak, they were having a good time (which they undoubtedly were) and that they deserved to be there right alongside their fellow successful musical brethren. Nearing the summit, tragedy strikes with two punishing blows. And having suffered a great fall, with *Different Stages* they planted a flag in the hopes of not being forgotten, reminding anyone who cared that they once were there. From the bottom of the crevasse where they had landed, rescue seemed dubious—like something greater than music had swallowed them whole like Jonah to the whale. *Different Stages* was also the call for compassion—the only thing that mattered at the time (Absalom! Absalom!). With *Rush in Rio*, they had climbed out of that chasm (both privately and publicly) under their own power—music. They were different, now and forever. But they were also, in some ways, better. Looking around, during those last minutes of the *Vapor Trails* tour in Rio, they realized they were looking down from the summit. They had made it, but their stance there was somewhat tenuous, because it almost never happened. But it did, and thousands of Brazilians helped them realize not only had they made it, but the climb was over—they could relax. As if . . .

And then came *R30*.

With the mountain conquered, it was time to take in the view all around them. Time to allow themselves a pat on the back. There was nothing left but to celebrate. And they did—with thirty-one songs and thousands of their best friends from Europe and North America. Thank God.

A band that never gave a damn about fame or acceptance now had masses lining up as if ready to give an overdue apology, admitting that Rush and Rush fans were right all along. (*What were we thinking* . . .) The power of their music need not be measured in riffs or the number of complicated time changes. It need not be measured at all anymore. The word *Rush* itself was all that need be said. The music on *R30* was as serious as always for the band, and seriously played and devoured. And, at the same time, Lee, Lifeson and Peart, and the fantastic (and at times fantastically funny) stage show made sure we knew such things should never be taken too seriously. True.

Never Forget Where You Came From

So from this refreshed perspective, with only the JOY of live music at stake, and all the money, baseballs, wine, motorcycle tours, guitars, and golf clubs three Canadians could ever want, they humbly added a few cover songs to the set. As an homage to those earliest days when they discovered rock and roll was a mountain they had no choice but to climb, the band chose covers nearly as old as the mountain itself. Famous songs, some perhaps already played to death that were their very first steps on that thirty-year trek. The cover songs in *R30*, taken from the *Feedback* EP Rush turned out faster than a cricket match, were sort of the opposite of what Rush's music is all about. The historic "Crossroads," for example, is a simple, repetitious blues number that any beginner rock musician could master (well, except perhaps for the solo). And "Heart Full of Soul" (played acoustically during the band's second and last unplugged moment) was little more than a catchy hippie-folk tune. At least "The Seeker" was a Who song borne out of three other amazing musicians (Pete Townshend, John Entwistle, Keith Moon) and one ballsy singer (Roger Daltry). Let's be honest here, when each of these songs started on the tour (or their titles were spotted on the DVD and CD), many fans could not help but think of all the other Rush-penned tunes that could have been played instead. It was like an arithmetic word problem—three songs adding up to about ten minutes equals one "A Farewell to Kings" plus "Cinderella Man," or one "Cygnus X-1 Book I," or five-eighths of one "Cygnus X-1 Book II," or one "Natural Science" with a remainder of forty-seven seconds. But a funny thing happened while Rush plowed through these songs (at least the electric ones, "The Seeker" and "Crossroads"), the band made them Rush-y. These well-worn tracks had a bombast and heaviness to them that made these old early steps sound significant, or at least more original than anyone had been expecting. And so fans could close their eyes during these numbers and think: *So this is what it sounded like in the beginning. No wonder they kept getting gigs early on. No wonder Ray*

Rush released *Feedback*, an EP of songs the band (and Peart separately) had covered during some of their earliest days as musicians.   *Courtesy of Max Mobley*

Danniels wanted to manage them and Terry Brown wanted to mix them. Indeed, Rush playing these covers was its own original thing, a new path. The bombast, the chops, the throw-it-down "play as hard and as much as you want just make it work" mentality was evident. And it gave the fans insight. It was the sound of the Rush star exploding from nothingness into illumination all those years and songs ago. It was Rush feeding back onto itself. And it was awesome.

Special Anniversary Gifts

Where the *Rush in Rio* DVD's special features were all about performance and MacNaughtan's wonderful documentary, the *R30* DVD special features were all about history. This makes sense given the theme of the tour. Disc two of *R30* contains five interviews, spanning 1979 through 2002. It's a nice compendium of Rush speaking—something fans were still getting accustomed to. Lee's 1979 Wynne Stadium tour interview is available here, as is the 1980 Le Studio interview with what appears to be a very stoned band (well, at least Lifeson appears to have wished he had waited for the bong hit until after the interview). Both of these are covered in detail in the chapter, "Rush Milestones on TV and in Film." The interview: "Rush speaks" section also includes footage from the 1990 "Artist of the Decade" special (the eighties, Rush's most controversial decade, and also rock and roll's), and their 1994 induction into the Juno Hall of Fame. Notice these features are all very Canadian—a great reminder that Rush is a homeland band, and despite it taking the US (thank you, Cleveland) to break the band, home is where the heart is, and in this case it's north of the forty-ninth parallel.

The second section of *R30* disc two is dubbed the "Anthem Vault." It contains a treasure trove of Rush performances rarely, if ever, seen or heard prior to the *R30* release. Ten different performances can be found here, covering twenty-nine years of Rush on stage. "Fly by Night" from the "church sessions" is here, so are grainy-but-precious versions of Rush blowing camermen's hair back on *Don Kirshner's Rock Concert*, circa 1974 (also covered in "Rush Milestones on TV and in Film"). The "Anthem Vault" also features the music videos for "Circumstances," "La Villa Strangiato," "Xanadu," and "A Farewell to Kings," with the band performing live, but the studio recordings dubbed in. Much of this footage is now taken for granted, thanks to YouTube, but in 2005, it was as rare as a Bigfoot sighting. Rush forums and fan websites lit up about it. And despite hearing the recorded versions of "Xanadu" and "La Villa Strangiato," just seeing them rock their prog in kimonos, hair, and vintage gear was something to behold.

The *R30* album was only available within the deluxe version of the *R30* DVD.   *Courtesy of Max Mobley*

The "Anthem Vault" section also includes some interesting fly-on-the-wall footage of that mystical ritual commonly known as sound check. The venue is Wynne Stadium in Hamilton, Ontario; it was the *Permanent Waves* warm-up tour, and it features a working band and crew going through pieces of setlist to dial things in and work out the nuances of the night's performance as demanded by the state of the road worn gear and the venue itself. Sound checks are interesting things for both musician and non-musician Rush fans. It's a bit like seeing the mortals behind the curtain operating the levers and switches that animate the wizard. From a musician point of view, it's a time to exercise wanton gear lust.

Rounding out the "Anthem Vault" assortment are two recent performances by the band—"Freewill" at the 2003 Toronto Rocks "SARS-stock" benefit concert, and a 2005 (the same year the *R30* DVD was released) studio capture of "Closer to the Heart" for the "Canada for Asia" Asian Tsunami Relief fund. These two videos show Rush at their philanthropic best. While the band has had a philanthropic side once their finances allowed for it, and have always been generous to their fans regarding music and product (length of show, etc.), they rarely play benefits due to their uncomfortableness with the rigor, hassles and logistics common

The *R30* Deluxe edition also included a souvenir backstage pass.   *Courtesy of Max Mobley*

to large-scale events with multiple acts and huge crowds. But SARS-stock was an important event for Canada. In 2003, a SARS (Severe Acute Respiratory Syndrome) outbreak crippled the Toronto area, which, like many cities, relied in part on tourist dollars to thrive. The disease originated in China, but migrated via humans to the Toronto area, where it was responsible for forty-four deaths. While in China and Hong Kong thousands of people contracted the disease, in Toronto, less than three hundred had, so it seemed unnecessary for the World Health Organization to warn against traveling to the region. But they did, and way too many people stayed away, hence the need for the benefit concert.

SARS-stock boasted a crowd of a half million, the largest crowd Rush had ever played. The Rolling Stones headlined the event, and they were clearly more comfortable with the situation than Rush. Rush's SARS-stock performance of "Freewill" is not their best, and their discomfort with such mass-scale events seems evident. Nonetheless, it's interesting to see how the band looked and played under the stresses and noise of such a huge event. It's a bit like watching your favorite sports team play in a hurricane.

Moments before Rush went onstage, Peart met up with Stones drummer Charlie Watts. Peart has retold the story in his book, *Traveling Music.* In short, an old gent struck up a conversation with Peart just moments before Rush was to go onstage. In the deep focus of performance mode, and against the backdrop of the chaos of the massive event, he did not recognize Watts and saw nothing more than some old guy who wanted to chat moments before Rush was to go on. Watts, in fact, had to introduce himself twice. With that second introduction, Peart was taken aback by the honor of meeting the legendary drummer. And as if Peart didn't have enough to deal with, Watts remarked that he would be watching Rush's performance.

Rush played an eight-song set for the event, including a very short (but none-theless interesting) instrumental version of the Stones' "Paint it Black." The core set consisted of "Tom Sawyer," "Limelight," "Dreamline," "YYZ," "Freewill" (as shown in *R30*), "Closer to the Heart," and "The Spirit of Radio." They had planned to play "Working Man" as an encore, but, due to a miscommunication amid the chaotic event, it never happened.

The "Anthem Vault"'s "Closer to the Heart" was recorded in the studio and featured two very special guests: Ed Robertson from the popular (and funny) Canadian group Barenaked Ladies, and the loveable Bubbles (actor Mike Smith) from *Trailer Park Boys*, the Canadian television series and films. Robertson and Bubbles play acoustic guitar throughout the track. The triple-acoustic treatment makes things sound quite lush and yet delicate in keeping with the tone of the early part of the song. Lifeson jumps over to electric when the song requires it, and Bubbles and Robertson add some interesting harmonies and screams to the number.

Anniversary Hardware

The gear for *R30* wasn't much different than that of the previous tour. The most notable difference can be found atop Peart's rotating riser. With the exception of the early tours, the Professor of the Drum Kit took a new, artfully crafted drum kit on the road for every tour. He had tried out different manufacturers over the years, like his infamous, hint-of-pink Ludwig kit used during 1988's *Hold Your Fire* tour, as seen on the "A Show of Hands" video. Prior to going Ludwig, Peart had used Tama kits which replaced the early Slingerland kits he used when first joining Rush and up through the 1978 Tour of the *Hemispheres*. But since 1997 (*Test for Echo*), Peart had become a tried-and-true DW (Drum Workshop) man. And each DW creation seemed to surpass the previous one in artisanship. The *R30* kit remains one of Peart's most impressive-looking kits (it was even available as a re-issue for purchase for a mere thirty thousand dollars—hey, cymbals were included). The look of the kit was inspired by the *Pictures of Lily* kit belonging to one of Peart's greatest influences, Keith Moon of the Who. That kit was renowned for its remarkable look, which featured panels of the Who's logo and the burlesque-styled picture of Lily, the song's inspiration, on the shells. (It's a matter of debate as to the actual identity of Moon's Lily. Townshend says it is Lilian Mary Baylis [1874–1937], a British performer and producer; others believe it is Lillie Langtry [1853–1929], a legendary British actress known as "Jersey Lily.") Peart's version of this artistic treatment is to have similar panels on the shell, featuring various icons and

Neil Peart's custom *R30* kit was such a sensation that it went on tour after the *R30* tour, without a drummer to play it. *The S.S. Professor* tour allowed fans to get a close look at one of Peart's most amazing kits. It sounded good, too. *Courtesy of Andrew Olson*

logos from past Rush albums, including the Starman logo, the p/g fraction from *Grace Under Pressure*, and the bolt and nut from *Counterparts*. The logos have a holographic look to them. They are printed on black shells with red trim. The hardware is all gold-plated. The kit is worthy of an art museum, but, as Peart would likely point out: it's meant to be played, not studied.

Alex Lifeson's and Geddy Lee's rigs for the *R30* tour were virtually indistinguishable from the *Vapor Trails* tour, right down to the Maytag dryers. Lee had also added an automat vending machine to his back line (convenient if the band or crew get hungry during the show). He relied on his favorite Fender Jazz Basses again, and Palmer speaker s imulations and Avalon pre-amps for his amplification. Lifeson's amp rig featured the huge-sounding Hughes and Kettner amplifiers. His guitar assortment included a couple of Fender Teles to round out the Les Pauls and PRSs. He also used his signature ES-355 on "Working Man."

Canadian Pirates Have a Great Sense of Humor

Maybe it was because the Johnny Depp–Disney film *Pirates of the Caribbean* was a huge hit the year before the *R30* tour, or maybe it was an inside joke. Either way, Rush was clearly struggling to hide their inner-pirate during the entire *R30* tour. This is mostly evident in *2112*'s "The Temples of Syrinx," in which Lee can be heard doing his best "talk like a pirate" shtick ("We are the pirates of the Temples of Syrinx—all the gifts of life are down below!"). Regardless of the reasons, it was not uncommon to hear savvy (and perhaps swarthy) fans talking like pirates at intermission. It was also an interesting contrast for humor to be injected into one of Rush's all-time heaviest tunes, a song with dark themes. On "La Villa Strangiato," which was played on the tour but not included on the DVD, Lifeson went into one of his rants similar to what fans saw and heard on the *Rush in Rio* recordings. This time it was often pirate themed. On the San Francisco stop of the *R30* tour, Lifeson pointed out that the hardest part of being a pirate was making sandwiches for all the other pirates.

Funny!

"Der Trommler"

Though not Grammy nominated like Peart's *Rush in Rio* solo, his solo master-piece on *R30*, dubbed "Der Trommler" (literally "the drummer" in German—fitting since the *R30* material was recorded in Frankfurt), is very close in style and substance to "O Baterista." One key difference is a rather obvious departure in tone, thanks to that impressive *R30* kit (the smaller toms are especially tight and punchy, and the floor toms sound like contained thunder). Another is that Peart's pacing seems to be a bit more relaxed. While "O Baterista" from *Rush in Rio* sounds amazing (and probably would have won the Grammy had sentimental favorite Brian Wilson of Beach Boys fame not released an instrumental on his album *Smile* the same year), compared to *R30*'s "Der Trommler," it sounds a bit, well, hasty. Perhaps this is due to the stress of going on without the ritual and validation of a sound check. Professional performers tend to have their pre-show routines, and there was nothing routine about the Brazil shows—not that the crowd could ever tell. It could also have simply been the adrenaline of the night: the final performance of an almost-yearlong comeback tour in front of forty thousand maniacal fans, with cameras and cameramen invading Rush's space. Regardless, by contrast, "Der Trommler" exudes a laid-back confidence. Once again, Peart had nothing to prove—he was just a man with an amazing sense of rhythm and timing, and four limbs put to use in a way that would surely embarrass an octopus. And that tone. Yeah, the *R30* kit looks stunning, but the sound of those drums throughout the entire show—not just the drum solo—may be one of Peart's best, sonically speaking. Both drum solos have much in common otherwise, and both end with an excerpt from Count Basie's big-band number "One O'clock Jump," undoubtedly an *homage* to that other great drummer, the late Buddy Rich, who helped make the song famous.

"Between the Wheels"

Every Rush show, let alone tour, has that magical standout moment. At least one. Several moments in *R30* vie for this: the comedic intro video with Jerry

Stiller, the "R30 Overture," pirate jokes, the list goes on. But perhaps the one great surprise was a song that had been hiding in plain sight since 1984. It is the last song on the *Grace Under Pressure* album—"Between the Wheels." The last slot on any rock album is an interesting place. Sometimes a song is placed there because it doesn't fit in the flow of the rest of the album. Sometimes a song is dropped in to up the track count, and sometimes a song is placed there so that the listener ends the record on a powerful note—a memorable ending. When *Grace Under Pressure* came out, all anyone seemed to talk about were the synths, the Police and ska influences, the heavy lyrics of "Red Sector A," the new Fear song ("The Enemy Within"), and Lifeson's brilliant solo on "Kid Gloves." "Between the Wheels," the moody but powerful closer, was not brought up much. And then it was played live on the *R30* tour. Live, the song had a heaviness that was not apparent on the synthy mix of the studio version. Lifeson's power chords and the crying main guitar riff behind the dark lyrics were about as ominous-sounding as Rush ever gets (which is saying something). The timing of the verse synth stabs in this tune can really get under one's skin. The song has one of Rush's darkest, heaviest vibes, and the animated lavender-and-blue spotlights and ceaseless gear animation on the rear screen blended with the music, culminating in a live single work of art. It remains one of Rush's best live moments—period.

Return of That Darned Dragon

The rear-screen animation featuring a CGI dragon lighting the stage on fire was a highlight of *Rush in Rio*, blending the best elements of any rock concert—visuals, performance, and music. During the intermission of *R30*, the opening of that dragon sequence started up again, and fans seemed happy to experience it again—live. And then, once again, the comedy took over.

Just as the video got cooking (pun intended), fans were treated to the sight of the dragon channel surfing, eventually parking on a parody of the popular yet low-budget kids' puppet show, *Thunderbirds*. The parody, entitled "Darn That Dragon," has bobblehead versions of Lee, Lifeson, and Peart as the heroes out to vanquish a cheesy marionette version of the dragon. It works due to the handful of gags only Rush fans would get, including a heavily sweating Lerxst. The fans loved it, despite it lacking the atmosphere of the previous tour's dragon-themed intro. Its lightness, however, was in good keeping with the celebratory mood of the *R30* tour.

14

The Ssss—Zing of Snakes and Arrows Live

A Clean Shot at Being Hard, Heavy, and Happy

A mere three years after the victory lap that was the *R30* Tour, a truly high point in the band's career arc and in the eyes and ears of Rush fans, the band reached even higher, and somehow they met their own lofty and ever-rising expectations. The result was their nineteenth studio album, *Snakes and Arrows*, released in 2007. It boasts a bruising sound, and a return to the massive yet sophisticated arrangements that had been an all-but-forgotten Rush hallmark. Under the stewardship of producer Nick Rasculinecz, Lee, Lifeson and Peart were encouraged to embrace the bombastic and heavy tendencies of their muse. Rasculinecz made sure everyone in the studio, including the band, remembered that Rush taking chances, throwing it down as hard as possible and playing as much as possible while making it work, was far preferable than Rush playing it safe. For example, *2112* was Rush throwing down hard; *Test for Echo* was not. And in many ways the sound of *Snakes and Arrows* has more in common with *2112* than it does any other Rush album. In the Rush pantheon, *Snakes and Arrows* was a big deal. Fans had satisfied their jonesing for the sound of early Rush via *R30* (especially the special feature–laden *R30* DVD), and they were now ready to join the band in doing something they do well: looking forward. And that meant—with the sound of *Snakes and Arrows* straining the drivers of earbuds and the woofers and tweeters of good-old-fashioned stereos—a new tour.

Snakes and Arrows Live

Unlike *R30*, which was recorded at a single stop on the *R30* Tour, *Snakes and Arrows Live* was culled from a two-night stand. Again it was captured in Europe, though this time in beautiful Rotterdam, in swinging Holland, at the Ahoy

Arena. It was considered by many to be Rush's best-recorded performance to date with regards to picture and sound quality.

27 x 3

Starting with the setlist, *Snakes and Arrows Live* shines simply because it is the *full* setlist played on the tour. No omissions like *R30* which cut out premium material, most of which has since been released in compilations and as bonus material. So much stellar Rush material is available just from the *Snakes and Arrows Live* concert that it takes two DVDs to hold it. All in all, there are twenty-seven songs from the main concert on disc 1 (set 1) and disc 2 (set 2). And, as if that was not enough Rush in a single package, disc three contains an additional four songs that were swapped into the massive setlist during the 2008 US leg of the tour: "Ghost of a Chance," "Red Barchetta," "The Trees," and "2112 Overture / The Temples of Syrinx." Together, these four songs make up the "Oh, Atlanta," "official bootleg" recordings. And they are pretty remarkable for bootlegs. The videography is as good as the Rotterdam show, and the audio mix (although a tad rough and uneven) is remarkably clean sounding. The rawness in sound mixed with the clarity of picture makes for an "as if you were there" kind of experience.

Snakes and Arrows Live remains one of Rush's best-sounding and best-looking live recordings.　*Courtesy of Max Mobley*

Fingers and Toes and Chicken

For fans who have been gathering Rush live footage since *Exit . . . Stage Left*, and accustomed to the standard video quality while appreciating its slow evolution to the 1080p HD world we now take for granted, *Snakes and Arrows Live* is a rich concert film experience. As is the case with most concert film experiences, and especially the best Rush concert film experiences, the production of the show plays an important role.

The true HD quality of videography employed on *Snakes and Arrows Live* is truly stunning from first note to last. This becomes quite obvious during the opening moments of the show. After the now-obligatory comedic introduction video (more on that later), Lifeson, dressed in various shades of black (including skinny jeans, no less—well, tight jeans, anyway . . .) walks onstage while playing the opening riff to a song the band had yet to use as an opener— "Limelight." But there's a rare catch in the riffing. Instead of repeating the iconic opening riff the way fans are accustomed to hearing it, Lifeson lets the last chord of the riff ring out, on a custom Les Paul that has enough sustain to reach the moon. As that chord plays out, Geddy Lee strolls out (stage left), the two joke around a bit like they are prone to do, and then Lifeson repeats, this time closing the riff just like it was played in the studio. During this elongated intro, the crowd is roaring and Lifeson and Lee look great on an otherwise dark stage. (You can almost see their pores, despite the fact that the lighting is nothing more than follow spots—those spotlights that follow Lee and Lifeson around the whole show.) At the point when Peart comes in with the floor tom fill that brings in the rhythm and bass, there is a well-placed video edit. The dark shadows of drums and hardware flash under the bright whites, glaringly illuminating Peart and his red-and-gold *Snakes and Arrow*s kit at the very moment he first hits them. It's a moderately quick edit, and in it you see the high-definition quality of the image, you hear the sound of one of the most well-known Rush drum fills ever, and you gain insight into the Rush concert experience from the drummer's point of view.

It's all very effective, and the mostly white follow spots are a trend through the early part of the set. In fact, that's what makes *Snakes and Arrows Live* such a beautiful concert film—the unflinching view of something normally associated with color, smoke, fog, and props, reduced to little more than black and white. This nearly monochromatic view of the concert environment allows viewers to get a sense of the expanse of the stage and the venue. Such a big place, and a big sound, and yet only three normal-sized humans wandering about a big stage making all that music. Longtime Rush fans can sometimes lose sight of the fact that one of things Rush is known for, especially when performing live, is creating so much sound despite being just three guys and some gear. The colorless setting lit mostly in transparent white does a great job of illuminating that Rush formula.

Admittedly, color does arrive quickly to the show; it is, after all, a rock concert. In fact, it comes as early as the second song: "Digital Man" from *Signals*. But the timing and the spacing, thankfully, retain the contrast and openness. Indeed, even when lighting director Howard Ungerleider cranks up the hues, it is Lifeson's beautiful sunburst Les Paul, Peart's gorgeous (and gorgeously clean, especially compared to the sensational-styled *R30* drum set) kit, and, Lee's, um . . . roasting chickens that are highlighted. (Yep.)

In support of this clean, open, style, the video cuts are likewise well spaced. There are long lingering shots of fingers on strings and feet on pedals. This makes *Snakes and Arrows Live* the ultimate live show for musos and fans wanting to study the musicianship of Lee, Lifeson, and Peart. More than any video of the band, official or otherwise, *Snakes and Arrows Live* has many wonderfully long and lingering money shots of Lee and Lifeson's hands making the music of Rush on their instruments. Peart is equally featured, of course. Being the kind of drummer he is, including his showmanship and what he manages to pull off on his beautiful mega-kits, he has never lacked for camera time.

With twenty-seven songs available, *Snakes and Arrows Live* contains a host of juicy Rush riffs. And kudos to the camera crew and director, for many of them are accompanied with these musicians-at-work close-ups.

Go Toward the Light

As *Snakes and Arrows Live* builds, and as one great Rush song is played out and then replaced by another, the lighting and the mood intensify slowly, steadily, in no hurry to show off its best tricks, which are revealed in set two. The openness of the early moments of the show is reflected not only in the jaw-dropping arc of the production and lighting but in the attitude of the band itself. There is an almost a Zen-like serenity beneath all that intense music-making. The two extremes—a deep cool mixed with the throw-down intensity required to play songs like the instrumental "The Main Monkey Business"—work well together and are palpable throughout the show.

The clean, dark look of the stage, and Lee, Lifeson, and Peart wearing various shades of black (Lee is sporting a black T-shirt with the words "Blah, Blah Blah" emblazoned on it—as if a precursor to Lifeson's Rock and Roll Hall of Fame speech) help sell this atmosphere. What? Their T-shirts help with the look and the feel? This does seem odd, certainly. But it does keep the look of the show super clean—clearly a production theme. Indeed, the absence of color on the guys and the stage means the drums, the guitar, the chicken roasters (it's true), and the huge hovering lighting system (much like an alien thing slowly coming to life) own all color in a landscape otherwise devoid of it, and that means it Pops with a capital "P."

After intermission, set two of the *Snakes and Arrows Live* has a somewhat different feel and look. It's almost as if set one was Rush at their most insouciant, and set two was Rush with a lot on their minds.

Exploding Snakes and Fiery Arrows

Set two kicks off like a snake going for the throat. The end of intermission is signaled by an effective video featuring Alex Lifeson being darkly funny. The video is essentially Rush's humorous take on the Hindu self-discovery game Leela (the album title *Snakes and Arrows* is loosely based on the game). The viewer is presented with a black-and-white version of the game board, full of spiritual planes—squares with terms relating to one's spiritual path. There are terms like Plane of Balance and Astral Plane. Arrows land on these squares, and on one (The Plane of Cosmic Consciousness), the square opens like a trap door, revealing a ladder, upon which a mystical Alex Lifeson climbs, talking about spiritual planes and complaining about stupid, stuck doors. Once again, the band's use of contrast has great impact—a clean, dark and serious atmosphere, mixed with Lifeson's lunacy (and fans are once again reminded that he could have been one helluva comedian had he not chosen rock and roll). He appears behind a few other spiritual planes—the Plane of Primal Vibrations (genuinely creepy, yet totally odd), Envy (the same detached genie head that accompanies the menu on the DVD), and the Plane of Dharma (Do the right thing!). From there, the camera shifts focus to another square: The Birth of Man, at which point the pounding, odd-cadenced intro riff of "Far Cry" blasts from the stage below the screen. The lightness of the video (albeit with dark undertones), followed by the heaviness of the opening track from the *Snakes and Arrows* album, makes these moments of the tour a true high point. In regards to those memorable opening riffs, they were so iconic of Rush returning to what they do best, that shortly after "Far Cry" was recorded in the studio, the band released it as a tease on their website—just that intro piece, ending with the "Alex chord" (an Fmaj7add4, if you're keeping score). That is something they had never done before, and it speaks to the energy and enthusiasm surrounding the making of the *Snakes and Arrows* album.

In keeping with the new dark vibe of set two, Rush uses pyrotechnics to shock the senses of fans, both visually and aurally, at the onset of "Far Cry's" middle chorus. The dark vibe of set two (especially the early part) also comes from the band running through some of the best cuts from the *Snakes and Arrows* studio release. Following "Far Cry" (in chronological order) is: "Workin' Them Angels," "Armor and Sword," "Spindrift," and "The Way the Wind Blows." Add

The dark *Snakes and Arrows* symbol, designed by Hugh Syme, is indicative of the show and the record.
Courtesy of Rob Silverberg

"Malignant Narcissism" and "Hope" from later in the set, and the "Main Monkey Business" and "The Larger Bowl" from set one, and you have the most songs from a single album ever played on tour to date. That's nine of the album's thirteen tracks.

Peart's lyrics from *Snakes and Arrows* studio album have some of his best turns of phrase, and are rich with imagery. They are words from someone wise enough to know that hope has its enemies. And that, despite hope, despite being on a good spiritual plane or a bad one, the unavoidable curses on the innocent of fear and alienation delivered via religion, socioeconomic conditions, and culture, and the seeming randomness of beauty and wretchedness are hurdles on the way to heaven.

Haunting imagery, some of it real, some of it invented, fill the rear screens during the *Snakes and Arrows* material. It would almost be depressing if the music wasn't so soaring. The band seems to sense the heaviness of this part of the show, and they bring back that comedy to help soften the blow. Case in point: prior to "Tom Sawyer," a short video plays, featuring characters from *South Park*, one of America's most subversive and popular animated programs. In the video, the obnoxious Cartman pretends he is Geddy Lee, and, with his band attempts to play "Tom Sawyer." It's funny stuff, and classic *South Park*.

Meanwhile, throughout the lovely arc of mood and production that is *Snakes and Arrows Live*, Rush's best-lit live production to date continues its steady rise in intensity that began with those dry, white opening moments of the show. By now, fans have been treated to more color, more smoke and fog, a dash of pyro, and lasers (the green laser show that accompanies "Dreamline"—something fans have seen repeatedly over the years but never seem to tire of). It all works incredibly well, thanks, in part, to its slow bloom. And then, the "one from the archive," last heard on *R30*—"Between the Wheels," kicks in, and the lights seem to come to life. The fixtures are suddenly animated, as if some sort of alien artificial intelligence has awakened to find life in motion on the stage beneath it. The lights hover and shift just feet over the heads of Lifeson and Lee as they play their instruments, studying them with dumb wonder. It is truly arresting.

The roughly three hours of music that make up the *Snakes and Arrows Live* sets also includes three rarities previously unavailable on any official live Rush release. Those songs are: "Digital Man" (this excellent track from *Signals* has a much more guitar-oriented mix on *Snakes and Arrows Live*), the sentimental (for Rush) cautionary love song "Entre Nous" from *Permanent Waves*, and "Circumstances" from side two of the vaunted *Hemispheres* album. Lee breaks out his red Fender Jazz Bass for this track, indicating the song has been detuned a half step so that Lee can hit the high notes on the *Hemispheres* album. (According to Lee, the keys chosen for *Hemispheres* worked okay in the studio, where there is time for rest and plenty of warm lemon water between takes. But, live, the *Hemispheres* vocals proved rather difficult to sing.) These three rare cuts smoke on the recording, and add value to one of Rush's best live products.

Snakes and Comedy

Snakes. Arrows. Hindu imagery, ethereal music wending its way between fog and smoke. (Yuck. What a dream!) These are the opening scenes from the *Snakes and Arrows* tour's opening video. It's not quite chilling, but it seems serious. Until, that is, it cuts to the next scene—Lifeson, in his jammies, sitting up, suddenly awakened from a dream. "Why did I dream about *snakes*?" he asks. Lifeson is inside what looks like a Winnebago that has seen too many tours. Lightning flashes in through the window. At this point, he does what all good boyfriends and husbands do: he wakes his partner to report on his nightmare. Rush fans know of Lifeson's wife, Charlene; they've been married forever. She was last seen in the *Boys from Brazil* rock doc. She's also the long-suffering band-wife saluted (and mockingly denigrated) in Lifeson's solo record, *Victor*. Lifeson incessantly taps the shoulder next to his, only it doesn't belong to Charlene Lifeson—it's Peart! Neil "Pratt" Peart, who apparently sleeps in his stage clothes with drum sticks in lieu of a teddy bear.

This is truly hilarious stuff. Fans always dig Peart, the brainiac professor, getting in on the comedy. And here he has done so in a huge way. The scene (but not the video) ends with them staring into the camera, screaming. What Lifeson and Peart are actually freaking out over lies at the other end of the motorhome relic—a baby stroller—the old-fashioned kind; not something hip and modern, but the kind Rosemary would be forced to use for her baby—and from it you can hear cries. A baby's cries, and that storm on the other side of the thin walls—it lashes and flashes and seems to grow in intensity. The comedy is gone again, and maybe it's from the fragrant smoke filling the venues (for those of us lucky enough to experience the show in person), but this is not what an intro Rush concert video is supposed to be like—let's get back to the jokes, please. The video has gone from a wonderful gag to truly uncomfortable imagery. It seems more like a visual from Pink Floyd after going off their medication. This is not prog fantasy, this is chilling stuff. And then BAM! We see Geddy Lee in his own Winnebago, with a bit of chicken grease on his howler.

"What the hell did I eat last night?" he asks.

He is awakened by the one and only Harry Satchel—Lee in Scottish garb doing a passable, though stereotypical, impression of an angry Scotsman. When Lee's face fills the screen, the crowd erupts. He is Geddy effing Lee, after all. No one looks like him, plays like him, sings like him, or sounds like him.

Pause the video for just a moment, if you would.

Comedy and analysis of the video aside, it is a moment when one realizes that the face of prog, the face of mad-musician skills, and the face of Rush, is *that* guy. The guy with the funny but awesome name. The guy with the big nose and the small glasses and the bigger voice and even bigger bass skills with the Canadian version of the "aw shucks, eh?" attitude about being a rock star. Geddy Lee has become an icon.

Weird.

Unpause.

Turns out the whole thing, including Lifeson's nightmare and the eerie pram, was actually Lee's dream (à la Inception). And now, some Scottish bastard is demanding that he get his arse out on that stage and earn his keep.

And he does.

And they do.

For nearly three glorious hours.

The creepy baby carriage returns to great effect during "Far Cry." This time it's accompanied by a stormy night. Rain falls violently from dark skies, with thunder for screams. The pram, sitting at the end of an otherwise empty dock jutting out over an angry sea, looks as if it, and worse, its contents, could be blown into the water at any moment. And the pounding riffs, like prize-fighter jabs delivered in a kung-fu rhythm, seem to beckon the looming tragedy or blessing—one can't be too sure.

This is just a sampling of the quality of visuals that fill the rear screen throughout much of *Snakes and Arrow Live*. Like the lighting, the sound, the live production and the DVD production with those long, lingering looks of the hands of prog-rock gods and demons in the midst of alchemy, a new, sophisticated level of artisanship and craftsmanship has been reached. And looking back over the tours—both officially captured and some just passing through time—this arrival, this new plateau, seemed inevitable. Once again, Rush hit the high mark they were aiming for. And, once again, they did it for the fans as much as they did it for their collective muse. And once again, there was nothing left to do but aim higher.

That is the only constant in the Rush universe.

Damn straight.

"Der Werkslager"

Just like "O Baterista" (*Rush in Rio*) is Spanish for "the drummer," and "Der Trommler" its German counterpart, "Der Werkslager" is the Dutch version, and it is the name given to Peart in his latest foray into the sound and rhythms that drums, technology, and a solitary human can accomplish. And, man, that combination can accomplish an awful lot.

"Der Werkslager" has much in common with Peart's previous solo, R30's "Der Trommler," with a few notable exceptions. The solo is a bit tighter on the arrangement side of things, and is one of the few times when a Peart solo is shorter than those of previous tours. The difference is less than thirty seconds, and may be nothing more than fluctuations due to Peart routinely incorporating improvisation into what was previously methodically composed material. The difference in time is felt, however, as "Der Werkslager" zooms at a significant pace, where "Der Trommler" breathed a bit more.

The other key difference lies in Peart's choice for the big-band jazz ending. Previously, the Professor had been kicking the daylights out of Count Basie's "One O'clock Jump," while keeping the swing (thanks to Freddie "Yoda" Gruber). For *Snakes and Arrows*, while the main body of the solo had not changed dramatically, the Basie piece had been replaced by "Cotton Tail," one of Buddy Rich's signature pieces. It was also one Peart struggled with pre-Gruber (the same could be said for "One O'clock Jump"). Post-Gruber, Peart swings with authority on the number, and the accompanying video montage has some nice shots of the late Rich being his awesome self.

"Hope"

True to the smartly arranged set (never an easy feat; just ask anyone who has ever been in a band), Peart's solo, with its big bombastic ending is followed by Lifeson's poignant acoustic twelve-string solo piece, "Hope," also from *Snakes and Arrows*. "Hope" was written by Lifeson, "all by hisself" according to the album's liner notes. Makes sense, given that it is a solo performance. The beautiful piece uses an alternate tuning that helps create a lush and slightly somber (but nonetheless hope-filled) tune. On the DVD, "Hope" shows Lifeson melding into his instrument, forgetting the crowd and everything else as he creates a mesmerizing combination of rhythm and melody. A live version of "Hope" was included on the awareness- and fund-raising album, *Songs for Tibet: The Art of Peace*, which was released to coincide with the 2008 Beijing Summer Olympics. This version of "Hope" was nominated for a Best Rock Instrumental Grammy in 2009. Naturally, it didn't win, but at least this time Rush lost out to a worthy competitor—*Zappa Plays Zappa*'s "Peaches en Regalia."

Snakes and Chickens and More German Amps

The gear used on *Snakes and Arrows Live* is not very different from that of *R30*. Lifeson was keeping the tubes of his multiple Hughes and Kettner rigs nice and hot, though this time his own signature model was in the mix. Again, he used one amp rig for his main distortion sound, one for amplifying his FX sound, and one for his clean sound. Through this era of Rush (from *Vapor Trails* through the *Time Machine* tour), Lifeson still relied on T. C. Electronics, a high-end Danish effects and signal processing company. This is notable in that many guitar players, after embracing rack-mounted signal processors in the eighties, have since returned to individual stompboxes using analog technologies for their effects processing. Digital rack-mounted devices, like Lifeson's T. C. Electronics ultra-powerful G-Force and TC1210, were borne out of the eighties drive to digital. These devices offered unparalleled sound quality, parameter control, and flexibility. Traditional stompboxes process the signal in a singular way in the analog domain, with limited controls over the sound (a distortion stomper distorts the guitar sound and does nothing more, with the controls only varying the tone and amount of distortion). With a rack-mounted signal processor like Lifeson's multiple G-Forces, he can have multiple effects (mostly delays and modulation, as Lerxst gets his crunch and distortion from those tube-driven Hughes and Kettners), with complex signal chains and a mindboggling level of control over each little component of Lifeson's sound. And, to a significant degree, as much as Lifeson's sound is in his fingers and his wonderful choices of what notes to play and when to play them, it is also in his use of rack-mounted effects and how he programs and employs them. Granted, in the albums preceding the digital age, Lifeson's wonderful tone was purely analog driven, but it is his tone and its myriad complexities in the digital era for which fans know him best. And that modern tone, with its analog amplification, is the best of both—analog heat and grit, and digital polish and complexity. It is the sound of Lerxst.

Lifeson's Wall of Gibson

Lifeson's guitar choices for this tour can be summed up in a word—Gibson. He started as a Gibson player and is mostly known for playing instruments of the brand, like his classic Alpine White ES-355. But, in the two landmark tours preceding *Snakes and Arrows*, Lifeson had really mixed it up. He broke out a very un-proggy Fender Telecaster (which he made smoke on tunes like "Bravado"), and played the modern and tone-ful Paul Reed Smiths. In between, he broke out iconic Gibson Les Pauls and the crowd-pleasing ES-355. For *Snakes and Arrows Live*, it was all Gibson, all the time. Three vintage Les Pauls, from the late fifties, including a classic Gold Top, the Howard Roberts Fusion guitar, along with Lifeson's original 1976 ES-355, which had been wonderfully restored by Fred Gabrsek.

Along with the great-sounding vintage pieces, Lifeson took two prototype Les Pauls on the road. These shouldered much of the tour's workload. They had been modified with Floyd Rose tremolo bridges, and featured electronics not found on traditional Les Pauls. At least one sported piezo electronics. When engaged, the piezo system allowed these solid-body electrics to sound like acoustic guitars—a requirement for the *Snakes and Arrows* tour, given the myriad acoustic tones on the album. If these augmentations to the traditional Les Paul sound familiar, it's because these prototypes were the inspiration for Lifeson's signature Les Paul guitars, which sell for around forty-five hundred dollars.

Speaking of Lifeson's excellent acoustic tones on his very electric, very rock-and-roll, piezo-equipped Les Pauls, the wizard behind the curtain lies in his use of Fishman acoustic guitar models, which take that piezo signal and process through a filter that closely matches the sonic fingerprint of an acoustic guitar. It works remarkably well, as heard on songs like "The Larger Bowl" and "Natural Science" (the intro).

That Finger-Lickin' Rotisserie Chicken Sound

It started with the *Vapor Trails* tour, as seen on *Rush in Rio*. Then it evolved on the *R30* tour to incorporate rotating Vendomatic vending machines, replete with old sandwiches and rubber duckies. It has now evolved into the intriguing and tasty world of poultry in the form a giant rotisserie oven machines stocked with whole chickens. We are referring, of course, to Geddy Lee's backline.

Never one to give a damn about what critics or the mainstream think about pretty much anything, with *Snakes and Arrows Live*, Lee has once again forgone the traditional bigger-is-better bass rig for the world of small-box processors and speaker simulators, sending three bass signals straight into the mixing desk, which the band hears exclusively through in-ear monitors. What is remarkable about all this is that, onstage, the band hears everything they need to hear (i.e., themselves and each other), almost exclusively via in-ear monitors. This makes Rush's concert stage one of the quietest places during a Rush concert. (In my 2009 interview with Alex Lifeson, he stated that the band's onstage level is about that of a home stereo.) Granted, Peart hits his kit very hard, and no doubt that equates to volume. And Lifeson's amp stacks are just loud enough to deliver feedback. But, given the size of the venues they play, and that many of the concerts are held outdoors, where the sound has few surfaces to reflect off, onstage, at least, the band's volume is well managed. It is somewhat incongruous that the sound of one of rock and roll's best bass players is only available through ear buds. Weird. But, clearly, it works.

Red and Gold Rhythms

Like *R30* and *Vapor Trails* / *Rush in Rio*, Neil Peart once again dazzles with a new highly stylized, highly artistic drum kit. Following the fanciful, bling-y and bold *R30* kit, Peart once again goes in an entirely new direction. His *Snakes and Arrows* kit is simple yet elegant. Its clean lines fit the style of the tour. The kit is decidedly red without a hint of brashness. The finish is subtly glossy—almost matte, with a nice hint of sunburst. (Typical guitar finishes, especially Les Pauls, employ a sunburst finish, where the color fades from the edges toward the center.) There are natural shifts to the shade of the dominant red paint on each and every shell, so that each one looks hand-painted, and not machine finished. In gold on each and every drum is the *Snakes and Arrows* logo, repeated around the shells. This is the logo of the snake in a circle eating its tail, and inside the snake's circle is an arrow. The inconsistencies of the hand-drawn (or made to look hand-drawn) lines of the logo have an organic quality, which matches the organic themes of the *Snakes and Arrows* (Leela) inspiration, and the raucous sounds of the material.

The standard fare (for over a decade now) of an electronic kit with matching shells completes the 360-degree kit, including the MIDI marimba and embedded triggers lurking about the rig and firing off samplers when needed.

Tonally speaking, the *R30* kit is hard to beat (no pun intended). The *Snakes and Arrows* kit may not pop as much as the one from *R30* and its respective DVDs, but it sounds incredibly dialed-in, almost as if the drums were recorded in the studio.

The Bonus Quiver

Unlike the riches found on the bonus disc of *R30*, *Snakes and Arrows Live* bonus disc (disc three), is light on content but still worthy of inclusion. The disc consists solely of the previously mentioned "Oh, Atlanta" recordings ("Ghost of a Chance," "Red Barchetta," "The Trees," and "2112 Overture / The Temples of Syrinx") played during the 2008 leg of the *Snakes and Arrows* tour. Though the mix is a tad rough, they are nonetheless fun to watch.

The Secret Snake

Snakes and Arrows Live is the last Rush DVD / Blu-ray to include an Easter egg, at least as of this writing. (In truth, the Easter egg phenomenon has more than run its course. Just give us the stuff without all that clicking—please.) The egg in question is a short vignette of outtakes and interviews in character captured during the filming of the band's interstitial videos for the tour. To find it, let disc one of the DVD sit for a good couple minutes until Lifeson's green genie head, Envy, is replaced with that of the one and only Jerry Stiller. Mr. Stiller gives instructions to "push *Play* already," and then Lifeson returns, encouraging you to do it, and the menu disappears. At this point, pressing *Play* or *Enter* on the DVD remote starts the 5:30 "What's That Smell?" montage. To access this same egg on the Blu-ray version, simply scroll down on the menu page until nothing is highlighted, and then hit *Enter* on the remote control. While it seems like a bit of work, it is actually worth it. The humorous videos that were part of the *Snakes and Arrows* tour are some of Rush's funniest.

#1 Live Snakes

As a complete package—sound, camera work, editing, setlist, performance, and production of both the media and the actual concert—*Snakes and Arrows Live* was Rush's most sophisticated effort at the time of its release. It sold over twenty-five-thousand units during its first week, earning it the number-one spot on *Billboard's* Top Music Video chart. The Blu-ray version also won the 2009 International Digital Media Alliance Excellence Award for Disc Audio. Not too shabby. The music guide service All Music gave it four out of five stars (not bad for a band loathed by critics—case in point, *Rolling Stone's* music guide gave it a mere two stars). It went double platinum in the US, and five times multi-platinum in the band's native Canada.

15

The *Time Machine's* Mean Stride

"Tom Sawyer" Meets Jules Verne

I f there is one constant in the progression of Rush's live shows, and the products created from those shows, it is one of evolution. Albeit sometimes, though rarely, that evolution forks into a branch destined to stub out (*A Show of Hands* is the only example which comes to mind), that evolution can be measured as nothing less than successful. Even when there are unavoidable flaws, like the sound problems of *Rush in Rio*, or avoidable ones, like the overreaching aim for perfection plaguing *Exit . . . Stage Left*, the sum is always net positive. *Time Machine 2011: Live in Cleveland*, fits that description to a tee.

Once again, the video does a remarkable job of capturing Rush live, and for some fans of a certain Rush generation, captures Rush at their finest musical hour—the *Moving Pictures* album, played in its entirety.

For many first-generation Rush fans (those who discovered the band via *2112* or even earlier), *Moving Pictures* is held in somewhat less reverence. This is due in part to *Moving Pictures* allowing the secret Rush clubhouse to be infiltrated by a younger generation (nonetheless, it's considered an important milestone, even by first-generationers). But as these fans have been treated to parts—and sometimes complete versions—of the "2112" opus over many a tour, they embraced the significance of Rush playing their second breakout album from stem to stern along with every other Rush fan big and small, young and old. Plus, all fans wanted to hear them pull off "The Camera Eye"—a truly rare live gem. And if *R30* failed to make first-generation Rush fans feel like they were old, accepting the fact that *Time Machine* celebrated the thirtieth anniversary of Rush's eighth studio album probably did. Thankfully, the Vernian-era steampunk look of the show helped ease that blow.

Again with the Comedy

Upon hindsight, one could say Rush fans should have seen it coming—the comedy, that is. It started as far back as the *Grace Under Pressure* tour, with the nutty Count Floyd from SCTV introducing "The Weapon." It hit a new level of sophistication with the intro video from the *Snakes and Arrows* tour. So what else could they do but to run the concept into the ground with the sheer weight of video intros, outros, and interstitials that were part of the *Time Machine* tour. The intro video alone comes in at nearly six minutes, or the length of one proper Rush song. The outro video is even longer. By comparison, the *Snakes and Arrows* intro video is funnier and well under three minutes—ahh, brevity is key to comedy.

Typically unable to restrain themselves (which plays a big role in why they sound the way they do, and why fans love them), this time the band goes full Monty Python—costumes, story line, sausage jokes, stereotypical accents, accordions, and a band called Rash. Some of this works, some of it doesn't.

To be clear, the extended comedic videos that are part of the *Time Machine 2011: Live in Cleveland* DVD do not ruin the experience, nor do they impede the quality of the product or the concert itself for the thousands who attended. In fact, given that "pushing the envelope" is part of Rush's growth pattern, and having the temerity to experiment and push themselves in front of an audience, the extended stay in the land of comedy is to be expected. Say what you will, and chalk it up to sincere enthusiasm, Rush is never afraid to try, and pushing a tad too far before realizing it is no great sin. Arguably, many fans would agree that the unbridled enthusiasm Rush applies to whatever has caught their fancy is far better than the world-weary *ennui* of some artsy-fartsy critic's darling of the month. This is what they did with the tech- and synth-heavy eighties, the long-form prog-heavy *Hemispheres* era, and the overly polished *Exit . . . Stage Left* material. Hell, even the kimonos were a byproduct of this.

Now, on to the music.

The *Time Machine* tour featured Rush playing what many consider their holy grail: the album *Moving Pictures* live.

Courtesy of Max Mobley

Cleveland Rocks

As Geddy Lee pointed out in an interview with Cleveland.com, Rush had yet to capture an entire show at any US venue in their thirty-plus years of touring. And since they truly launched the Rush rocket in Cleveland, Ohio (thanks in large part to Donna Halper), it made a helluva lot of sense to film the *Time Machine* tour, of all tours, in this Rush-friendly town. And it went over wonderfully (major understatement, indeed). The twenty-six-song show covers Rush in the past, present, and even the future, with the inclusion of two new songs destined to be on Rush's next record: "Caravan" and "BU2B" ("Brought Up to Believe"), from the forthcoming studio record, *Clockwork Angels*.

After the introductory "Don't Be Rash" video, the band rips into "The Spirit of Radio" (made a tad anticlimactic since the intro video plays a healthy segment of the studio version of the song right before Rush (not Rash . . .) walk onstage. Still, "The Spirit of Radio" will probably forever remain Rush's best opener, thanks to its pacing, its mix of bombast and FM-friendly melody, and Alex Lifeson's iconic opening riff. From there, the band blasts through the hit "Time Stands Still" (which reached number three on the *Billboard* charts), followed by "Presto," from the 1989 album of the same name, which was met as a pleasant surprise. The *Presto* album tended to be overlooked by fans, perhaps due to its timing. It was a bridge album, linking the end of the eighties-synth period with the return-to-heavy nineties period. The album contains an eclectic mix of heavy riffs, FM prog-pop, and synth textures. The album happens to have some of Peart's best lyrics as well ("The Pass," "Available Light," and, of course, "Presto"). "Presto" is far from Rush's heaviest material, and the same can be said for *Hold Your Fire*'s "Time Stand Still," yet, with the stage props (more on that soon) and the overall celebratory mood (another anniversary already?) of the *Time Machine* tour, it fits right in. Besides, heavy is just around the corner, courtesy of "Stick It Out," from 1993's *Counterparts*. The signature riff from "Stick It Out" evolves into feedback, a truly wonderful rock guitar phenomenon that Lifeson traditionally uses sparingly. Live, the feedback portion of the "Stick It Out" riff appears to be programmed, and not played by Lifeson via his guitar. This is somewhat controversial given the nature of feedback itself. But given how temperamental it can be, and the physics responsible for generating it, this is understandable. The sound of the electric guitar from its speakers has to be loud enough and close enough to affect the magnetic field of the guitar itself, thus causing the guitar sound to create a feedback loop with the amp; too much, or the wrong kind, and it's an ugly squeal. And when conditions are less than perfect, the swell into the right feedback note may take too long to occur properly in the limited space between notes in the "Stick It Out" riff. If the wind, or the angle, or the reflections (if there are any) are just right, then the feedback may happen, and, if they aren't, then any number of things can happen, including the complete absence of sound. Intentional feedback is an art form, to be sure, and Rush's "Stick It Out" is one of rock's very few songs that requires it to come in at a certain place and a certain pitch every time. Therefore, having it canned instead of live makes sense. It's not like Lifeson's twiddling his thumbs, just hanging around for the solo . . .

Speaking of solos, "Stick It Out" contains one of Lifeson's most aggressive, and he nails it on *Time Machine 2011: Live in Cleveland*. The solo also features Lifeson working the hell out of the Floyd Rose whammy bar, something he does with a great deal of discretion most of the time, but not here. The Floyd Rose on his black Les Paul helps him get some great animated screams and bends on the short but powerful piece.

Like the past several tours, dating back to 1997's *Test for Echo* junket, the *Time Machine* tour had no opening act, and Rush split the show into two separate sets. With set two featuring *Moving Pictures* in its entirety, there was a definite sense of anticipation during set one. This feeling was unique to a Rush concert, as fans often want to hold off the night's end for as long as possible, and every song played is one step closer to that inevitability. This time out there was no new album to support (though there were those two new songs destined for *Clockwork Angels*), and, like *R30*, the show was about legacy. Although *Moving Pictures* was the show's peak and *raison d'être* in many ways, it was about that album as a thing unto itself—what it brought the band in terms of continued freedom, respect, and tribute to the muse. It was also about what it meant to the millions-strong Rush family, but definitely not what it meant for Alex Lifeson, Geddy Lee, and Neil Peart. They just seemed too cursed or blessed with the inability to get cocky about their accomplishments; they prefer to look to the future than to linger in the past. On that note, with *Moving Pictures* on the menu, *Time Machine*'s set one felt like watching an all-star pitcher strike out batter after batter on the way to a coveted no-hitter.

Time Machine featured only three *Snakes and Arrows* songs—two that seemed destined for steady live rotation ("Working Them Angels" and "Far Cry"), and one never heard live before, "Faithless," which features the best solo of the entire *Snakes and Arrows* album. Also included in the set is a stellar version of the melancholy celebration of endurance, "Marathon," from 1985's *Power Windows*, and Rush's grooviest instrumental of all time, "Leave That Thing Alone," from 1993's *Counterparts* album. "Leave That Thing Alone" is yet another Grammy-nominated Rush instrumental destined to lose to a more popular artist; this time it was Pink Floyd, for their track "Marooned" from 1994's *The Division Bell*.

While on the subject of the Grammys, when I asked Alex Lifeson about the nominations for the *Snakes and Arrows* studio release ("Malignant Narcissism" and a live version of "Hope"), he had to be reminded of which two songs were nominated.

Non-Musical Gizmos Galore

The *Time Machine* tour featured the band's most elaborate production to date in the form of steampunk-themed props, gizmos, and sausage makers. The steampunk style really captured Rush's imagination, and was borne out of Peart's appreciation for the works of H. G. Wells and Jules Verne. It was a rather timely choice for the band as well (pun intended). The dryers and chicken roasters that had been Lee's backline the past few years had run their course. And the time-travel theme of the tour dovetailed nicely with the Victorian sci-fi look of the *Time Machine* stage. This time, instead of modern machines invented for the mundane chore of laundry and cooking chicken—humorously out of place on a rock and roll stage—polished wood, fanciful globular shapes promising mystery and adventure filled the space normally relegated to rock-and-roll machinery. Lifeson's guitar rigs were tucked away into large contraptions that looked part-ancient televisions and part-Victorian laboratory generators. There were three lined up where Lifeson's three Hughes and Kettner stacks should be. Each possessed dials and knobs in intriguing locations, and bulbous cathode-ray tubes emitting cloudy light and Lord knows what else.

Lee's backline looked like a cross between a Seussian Whoville band instrument and some Victorian device used for contacting spirits from another dimension. As a byproduct of its use, it made sausage. The rig, evidently an integral part of the time machine on display (both as props and within the setlist) also marked the status of the night's time travel: Real Time, Half Time, Bass Time, and Sausage Time.

Time for *Moving Pictures* Live

"Tom Sawyer" has been played on every tour since its creation (that's sixteen tours, if you count the brief *Power Windows* warm-up tour), "YYZ" has been played on all but one (1991's *Roll the Bones*), and "Limelight" and "Red Barchetta" have remained in respectable setlist rotation. And yet, as the lights

Fans cheers as the time machine counts down to 1981, the year *Moving Pictures* was released.   *Courtesy of John Carretta*

dimmed, signaling the end of intermission, the crowds at every stop could barely contain their enthusiasm for what was about to happen. Such is the power and mystique behind what many consider Rush's greatest album.

But first, there was another slightly overlong video to get through.

Near the end of intermission, Rush's enormous rear screen showed a very analog-looking timer—like an odometer from a very old car, slowly ticking off the years from the beginning of Rush time. It took fans no time to figure the significance of this clock. Ticking off the years signaled the time machine's steady approach to its destination. In many venues, every time the wheel on the timer turned, the crowd cheered. By the time it had ticked over to 1979, the cheer did not dim back into the usual rhubarb of an audience in between sets—the cheering and applause was sustained. And when it turned to 1980, the year *Moving Pictures* was born, the cheers and applause rivaled almost anything heard at any Rush concert (Brazil notwithstanding, for those fans are in a category all their own). The timer had gone off and so had the crowd—to a mere video (albeit a highly suspenseful one) with bells and buzzers slightly reminiscent of Pink Floyd sound effects. It was indeed time, well almost . . .

With the time machine parked at its destination, fans were treated to yet another longish video (nearly four minutes, enough time for one of Rush's shorter numbers). This time, it was *The Brief History of Rash*, starring Lifeson in a fat suit, playing the part of Rush's one and only manager, Ray Danniels. It was a bit of an inside joke perhaps, and the fans seemed to indulge it. The gist of it was that the slovenly Ray Danniels kept hitting the time machine button, causing the members of "Rash" to change ages (from toddlers to hoary wizards) in the midst of a video shoot. Lee played Cecil, the Warhol-esque video director, and Peart played Percy, the cameraman, dressed in jodhpurs. The time-travel joke more or less worked, especially when it cuts to Lee, Lifeson, and Peart, on one another's instruments. An odd choice for the video is that once again, a sizeable segment of "Tom Sawyer" is played by Rash. It's hard not to consider this as somewhat anticlimactic once again, especially as fans have been waiting ever since they landed a ticket for that iconic opening synth growl that kicks off Rush's (not Rash's) best-known song, and most beloved album. And then it happens.

Mean, Mean Pride

Moving Pictures played in its entirety, stands as one of the major moments in the history of rock concerts. For many first-generation Rush fans who have loved *Moving Pictures* but don't consider it the band's best album, its significance was understood. As mentioned previously, *Moving Pictures* had been underappreciated by some first-generation fans, in part because of how it changed the Rush universe forever, and also because it was Rush's "pop" album. As incongruous as that sounds, it's as close as Rush will ever get to mainstream, thanks in part to how that stream was bending at the time. And it is such a different record from *2112*, the album that many "first gens" consider the inaugural door that led into the Rush world. *Moving Pictures* came four albums after *2112* (counting *All the World's a Stage*). It was well into the band's evolution. There is also half a decade between albums, and 1976 and 1981 were very different eras in rock-and-roll and in pop culture. So, from the opening chords of "Tom Sawyer" through the throbbing final notes of "Vital Signs," everyone who witnessed the performance—whether during a night on the *Time Machine* tour, via the *Time Machine 2011: Live in Cleveland* album or video, or the collectible vinyl record *Moving Pictures: Live 2011*—had understood how Rush had truly elevated from the norm.

"The Camera Eye"

There are really only two songs from *Moving Pictures* that have remained largely out of the lineup for most Rush tours since 1981—"Vital Signs" and "The Camera Eye." After "YYZ," "The Camera Eye" is perhaps the most popular song on *Moving Pictures* for diehard Rush fans. It had not been played since the short Tour of the Nadars, in 1982, which was a warm-up for the *Signals* tour.

Just as *Moving Pictures* was unlike any Rush album before or since, "The Camera Eye" is unlike any Rush song before or since. It has a very open sound to it. It also uses sound effects better than any other Rush track. The arc of the song's energy matches the lyrics at times, but also acts as a metaphor for bustling city life. Where "Tom Sawyer," "Limelight," and "YYZ" require a pounding rhythm, "The Camera Eye" is laid-back. Its intensity is derived from repetition and Lifeson's optimistic-sounding melodies. On that note (those notes?), the song's essence is hard to pin down. Like many Rush songs, the lyrics play a big role in the song's popularity. Its title comes from the book of the same name, written by John Dos Passos. The book was part of his USA trilogy about American life in the thirties. Another book from that trilogy, *Newsreels*, also inspired Peart. Dos Passos's story, *The Camera Eye*, was written in a stream-of-consciousness style. The text read like wide-shots of a documentary about life in a city—the voice was similar to that of an unflinching and detached camera eye capturing everything within its scope. *Newsreels*, on the other hand, gave voice to the events that were shaping American city life.

"The Camera Eye," the song, also represents one of Peart's early attempts to write personally in his lyrics ("Limelight" was another). In it, he contrasts memories of his time struggling in London to his present status as a very successful musician walking the streets of Manhattan. In an interview with Canadian talk show host George Stroumboulopoulos, Peart also singles out a line from author John Steinbeck as an inspiration. The line was from the opening of Steinbeck's ode to Monterey—*Cannery Row*. In the book's memorable opening sentence, Steinbeck describes life on the row as a poem, a stink, a quality of light.

Rush's "The Camera Eye," musically and lyrically, incorporates these influences with a great deal of subtlety. Perhaps that's why the song is one of the harder ones to describe—Rush fans, after all, are used to bombast. Rush songs are big meaty things, usually, and "The Camera Eye," while the last Rush song to come in at over ten minutes in length, is, in its own way, one of the band's most delicate and finely detailed tapestries. And on the *Time Machine 2011: Live in Cleveland* DVD, when it's over, there is a palpable sense of accomplishment, as if years of hoping followed by a season of promise, the moment had finally arrived. And it was too precious—too poignant—to mourn its passing. Because fans were just so stoked that it had happened at all. And it did.

And the band was not yet done.

Vital Signs

In some ways, "Vital Signs" is the opposite of "The Camera Eye." Where "The Camera Eye" conveyed in both music and lyrics the bustle and solitude-within-a-crowd vibe of life in a city, "Vital Signs" conveyed the mania of life in the electric. That is, the early days of visiting boulevards, intersections, sidewalks, streets, and all their electron traffic and potential inside a little silicon chip. It was man and machine—part robot, part high-tech bouquet. "Vital Signs" is about human life trying to converse and dance with the animated life of the technology it had created. It is a Rush song with a new kind of pulse, and, as the last song on *Moving Pictures*, it prophesied what was to follow: *Signals* and *Grace Under Pressure*. The song represents Rush stepping off the shore and onto a voyage that would carry them over the next four studio albums. Electronics and gear factor so big in the sound it's as if a robot had joined the band—one the band wasn't quite able to control, at least not at first. Parts of "Vital Signs" seem almost out of place at a Rush concert (almost). There is a thinness in the choruses, and the synths really do drive the band on this one, especially because the drums are all about what happens in between the beat. The song is prophetic in another way as well. If anyone asked Rush in 1981 what the rest of that decade was to be like, their answer would be this song. Lifeson breaks out a Telecaster once again to get that crisp Andy Summers–like tone that the song requires. Neil Peart uses a thin snare sample that is part Stewart Copeland and part eighties electronic drum technology. And Lee's bass line in the verses contains one of his most angular and melodic riffs. (The bass part on "Vital Signs" is a favorite among many rock bass players due, in part, to the chorus-effected bass line during the break.) Where "The Camera Eye," despite its own heavy synth tracks, is a timeless song—it could have been written in any decade—"Vital Signs" is of its time. And that makes it a fitting tune to close *Moving Pictures* live in its entirety.

Hunting Witches

"Witch Hunt" comes between "The Camera Eye" and "Vital Signs," and has little to do with either. It is a dark song. It is a moody song, and it is a heavy song without a happy ending, perhaps Rush's most foreboding number post-*Caress of*

Steel. Despite being released in 1981, "Witch Hunt" hadn't made it into a Rush setlist until 1984's *Grace Under Pressure* tour. It was around for every other tour or so until it was dropped at the end of the eighties, only to make a triumphant return with 2008's *Snakes and Arrows* tour, where, in both mood and message, it fit right in with all those heavy *Snakes and Arrows* songs. In fact, one could argue that "Witch Hunt" fits in better with the songs from *Snakes and Arrows* than it does with *Moving Pictures.*

Placed between the optimistic pulse of "The Camera Eye" and the manically moving "Vital Signs," "Witch Hunt" borders on sounding like a dirge. Electronic drums have remained an intriguing counterpoint to the thick power chords that push the song at the tempo of a lurching pitchfork-wielding mob climbing a tor. With its overt Vonnegutian themes, the song seems incredibly relevant today. Where "Vital Signs" lyrics seem a quaint take on humans and technology, written decades before smart phones, "Witch Hunt," heard live in 2011, makes one wonder how bad could it have been in 1981, given how intolerant and angry we are today. Perhaps Rush feels that way as well, since at the end of the *Moving Pictures* segment of *Time Machine 2011: Live in Cleveland,* Lee admits it's hard to believe that that album, and its diverse content and messages, are a whopping thirty-plus years old.

Back to Before Clockwork

After Rush's truly remarkable trip down memory lane, they immediately jump back to the future with "Caravan," a song destined to open their next studio album, *Clockwork Angels.*

Like "BU2B" from the first set, "Caravan," and its "can't stop thinking big" theme bridges Rush's young muse with the one followed by their wiser, more evolved selves. (In fact, that line from the song—"Can't stop thinking big"— sums up Rush's entire *oeuvre.*)

"Caravan" boasts the bombast of the band's early work, but also has a vibe that is very post-*Snakes and Arrows.* The calliope-like intro to the song is tied to the Time Machine's steampunk theme through the synchronized smoke and fog coming from the fanciful contraptions onstage. It is placed perfectly in the set, allowing fans to leave the live *Moving Pictures* feat squarely behind them as the band energetically breaks new ground ("Caravan" also has one of Lifeson's more intense solos).

In truth, the eight songs played after *Moving Pictures,* which includes Peart's drum solo, dubbed "Momo Perpetuo (featuring "Love for Sale")," and "O'Malley's Break," Lifeson's solo twelve-string acoustic number that segues into "Closer to the Heart," has the feel of an encore—bonus material, if you will, that keeps eyes and ears glued to the *Time Machine* show. Fans witnessing the *Time Machine* tour live just didn't want the concert to end. Watching on DVD and Blu-ray, it's a reminder of the band's stamina and longevity.

Love for Sale

Not to sound like a broken record, but Peart's drum solo featured on the *Time Machine 2011: Live in Cleveland* disc is nothing short of astounding. His name has become synonymous with great drumming—that has been a given for decades. Likewise, his name has become synonymous with epic drum solos (whether one goes for that sort of thing or not, he still gets proper credit for that feat). However, neither makes "Momo Perpetuo" so incredible. This time it's about how dramatically different the piece is. Even the big-band jazz ending—this time beating the snot out of the drums, almost to the point of losing control (almost) to the Buddy Rich standard, "Love for Sale," which Peart played at the 2008 Buddy Rich memorial concert—was different from endings past. "Momo Perpetuo" has none of the linearity to which Peart fans have grown accustomed, dating back to *All the World's a Stage*. Instead, the drums, the rhythms, and even the electronics are layered and integrated. It is by far Peart's most avant-garde work, as well as his most intricate. There are enough dynamics to make an opera fan weep, and enough texture to make one forget that what's being played is the most rudimentary of instruments—drums. The only downside to the eight-minute-plus piece is that fans who had warmed up their air-drum chops in anticipation of attending another Rush concert were caught well off guard, albeit in a good way.

From Just Like the Album Version to Nothing Like the Album Version

For the *Time Machine* tour (and all previous tours), the songs from *Moving Pictures* were not monkeyed with in any way. They were played true to form, right down to the sound effects and instrumentation, wherever reasonably possible. This is not true for the songs that came after the *Moving Pictures* portion of the set. The band incorporated a different kind of swing toward the end of "Closer to the Heart." It was interesting, and nothing suffered, though many fans felt it was not an improvement over the original. This may simply be due to the fact that Rush fans tend to like their music like they've come to know it. After all, jam bands and jam band fans are not really part of the Rush family. A more comedic twist is in store for the encore number "La Villa Strangiato." Its polka-inspired intro borders on sacrilege, and fans would most likely have preferred the song's original intro (Pt. I "Buenos Nochas, Mein Froinds") which has Lifeson on a classical acoustic guitar playing Spanish-influenced arpeggios that culminate in one of helluva run up and down the neck. This intro has not been heard live since 1981's *Exit . . . Stage Left*.

The third twist in these changeups comes in the final encore number, "Working Man." (Okay, technically "2112 Overture / The Temples of Syrinx" incorporate a different swing also, and it works quite well.) This time, Rush goes full Rasta, putting their best reggae flourishes on the classic rocker. Given

"Working Man" has been heard live about a million times, and considering that reggae lends itself to lots of freedom of expression in the bass department, the twist works very well. In fact, *Time Machine 2011: Live in Cleveland*, has one of the best live versions of "Working Man" ever recorded—period. At the point when the band shifts from a Rasta groove to classic Rush hard rock, the song dominates in a way it hasn't in previous live renditions, revealing that Lee, Lifeson, and Peart still have enough in the tank to pull this off after playing Rush music for over two hours. Not that anyone needs a reminder, but it does reflect the fact that Rush has always been a live act first, and a studio band second. And with Rush's most highly regarded studio album in the setlist, *Time Machine 2011: Live in Cleveland* celebrates both sides of a phenomenal and once phenomenally misunderstood band.

While "Working Man" proves the members of Rush still have all the energy and talent required to put on a clinic of a rock concert, it is Alex Lifeson's "Working Man" solos that causes the night to end with jaws dropped. Of the many great solos found on *Time Machine 2011: Live in Cleveland* ("Faithless," "Limelight," "Stick It Out," "Freewill," "Marathon," "YYZ," "Caravan," and "La Villa Strangiato"), Lifeson's leads on the show's final song may possibly be some of his all-time best shredding work. Lerxst is accurately known for being a tasteful soloist—always serving the song, the theme, the message. Many guitarists know that this is something that cannot be taught. And while many guitarists around the world can certainly learn an Alex Lifeson solo, few, if any, can create one. And though the speed and articulation of his chops is nothing to sneeze at, he's not really known as a speed player (think Eddie Van Halen, Steve Vai, and the countless shredders who bludgeon listeners with rapid and emotionless arpeggios). Because of the circus aspect of that type of playing, it seems that ever since the album *Van Halen One* which, compared to today's shredders rarely gets out of third gear, rock guitar players have been judged by speed alone. This is primarily why Lifeson has been under-recognized among mainstream rock glitterati. But among a large number of rock guitarists at all levels, Lifeson earns high praise not just for *how* he plays, but more importantly *what* he plays, and what his playing *says*—how it fits the song, and for possessing the restraint to not just stand up on stage and incessantly wank off. The end solo of "Working Man" on *Time Machine* goes right up to that line. It contains the fastest riffs one will ever hear Lifeson play. It also boasts some seriously hard-to-reach pitches—even so far as playing above where the guitar neck ends and the body begins, using the guitar's hardware and his magic touch to elicit sounds above the guitar's range, at a speed for which he is not really known. It is a fitting end to the night and the show.

Of course, Rush doesn't give a damn about what rock music is supposed to do, what rock music is supposed to sound like, and how rock instruments are supposed to be played. They simply can't stop thinking, and playing, big.

Time Machine Technology

So much of the *Time Machine*'s sound has to do with cutting-edge technologies in the bass and guitar department. In fact, it is these technologies that allowed for the *Time Machine* backline to be filled with steampunk props instead of amps and cabinets. And, of course, at the center of it all is Peart's massive kit.

Cymbals with Symbols

The tools Rush chose to bring on the road had been seen (or at least heard) before. There were also a few new bits. Starting with the drums, Peart had another custom Drum Workshop (DW) kit built for the tour. The design of the kit relied heavily on the steampunk, future-as-viewed-from-the-past aesthetic, right down to the Sabian Paragon cymbals. Peart had a hand in the design of the Paragon cymbals from a tonality perspective, and worked with graphic artist Wendy Cosman Parlee for the steampunk embellishments found on them. Settling on the art was easy—Peart, naturally, was able to describe exactly

Alex Lifeson, playing his viceroy brown sunburst signature Gibson Axcess Les Paul serial number 01, and Geddy Lee, sporting a "Rash" T-shirt and a vintage Fender Jazz Bass.
Courtesy of Max Mobley

Rush spared no expense when it came to miking the steampunk-era sausage maker found on stage during the *Time Machine* tour. *Courtesy of Tina Davey*

what he was thinking, and Parlee was able to interpret that, as she had done in the past in for drummer Joey Jordison (Slipknot) and Jimmy DeGrassi (Alice Cooper). It was clear to both Peart and Parlee that alchemical symbols fit the steampunk theme, as would a clock face on the big twenty-two-inch ride cymbal.

That was easy, and Parlee's work is excellent. The challenge was in imprinting the art onto cymbals that get their sound from the material they are made from. It turned out that the ink from the printing had a negative effect on the sound, and that just would not do. They tried different inks and methods, but the problem remained. In the end, Parlee created stencils for each design, and used a pad printing process to fill the ink into the stencil's shape. This allowed for the thinnest layer of ink to be applied while still meeting the steampunk artistic goal. The process, however, had to be done by hand, holding each cymbal and sliding it in and out of the pad printing machine. Going this route worked—the sound of the cymbals was preserved and they are some of the wildest looking (and best sounding) cymbals ever to grace a rock-and-roll stage. The whole process took about two days. Because of the amount of time involved in applying the artwork, the *Time Machine* Paragon cymbals are not commercially available. In the end, Sabian made fifty cymbals for the first leg of the *Time Machine* tour, plus another thirty-two for the European leg. Why so many? Cymbals do eventually break after getting the snot beat out of them night after night. And Peart has never been one to go easy on his gear. Like many drummers, he is a firm believer that you have to smack hard to get the best sound.

Time Machine Sounds Best in Maple

Peart's choice of maple for the tonewood of his drum shells has nothing to do with his being Canadian. It just so happens that maple tends to be the most popular wood for rock-and-roll drums. Maple is bright yet warm. It has about the same low end as other popular drum tonewoods, such as birch or the somewhat rarer option of African mahogany (though mahogany is the top choice for electric guitars, including Lifeson's Les Pauls). Maple has more mid-range than these other woods, and more than enough highs to make the drum sound really pop and snap when hit (shell thickness also has much to do with drum pitches, but that's another discussion...). Maple's natural color is blonde, which makes it amenable to a variety of paints and finishes. Suffice it to say, dating back at least to Peart's

Peart's *Time Machine* kit had that unmistakable steampunk look and produced a huge sound. This image is from the Bay Area stop of the tour's first leg.   *Courtesy of Max Mobley*

Test for Echo kit from 1996 (also made by DW) and probably much earlier, maple has been Peart's choice of wood. In addition to the maple shells that help deliver Peart's truly stellar tone, DW also covered the outside of each drum with a very thin single ply of walnut. This does not affect tone so much as it delivers on the steampunk look. The walnut on the drums matches the lacquered walnut slats that make up the base of Peart's riser, which, for the *Time Machine* tour was a work of art unto itself. The single-ply walnut-finished outer shell gives the beautiful *Time Machine* kit its Victorian time-traveler look. In a promotional video for DW drums, Peart described the kit as something Jules Verne would have had on his ship, the *Nemo*. More alchemical symbols laid around a clock face complete the fantastic look of these drums. As beautiful as previous Neil Peart DW kits have been, the *Time Machine* kit stands alone. The hardware is copper and built to look like the kind of pipes found on a steampunk submarine or time machine. That's a lot of detail for "just a drum set." After all, arguably the stands have no impact on the sound. But, in terms of aesthetics, and to coincide with the tour's themes, these details are part of the magic of the *Time Machine* tour and subsequent media. This massive kit with all its copper and wood and brass and symbols that strike wonder in most (and fear in a few) sits atop a rotating rise that features sprockets and glass orbs—all there to deliver on the promise Rush offered this time out.

Classic Guitars of the Future

This book has provided ample evidence that Lifeson's guitar sound revolves around the historic Gibson guitar company—Les Pauls, primarily (the archetype of the rock guitar), although his white Gibson ES-355 screams his name, whether he's strapped one on or not. Like the *Snakes and Arrows* tour, Les Pauls were Lifeson's primary weapon for the *Time Machine* tour. But given that Rush never sleeps when it comes to exploring technology—Victorian or otherwise— while Lifeson's two main Les Pauls look traditional, they are anything but. These guitars had more mojo than any Les Paul ever created. When examined closely, they look slightly different as well. For one, they are thinner, which in guitar circles is often considered taboo.

Les Pauls are some of the thickest and, therefore, heaviest solid-body electrics ever made. This is especially noticeable after the instrument has been hanging off a player's shoulders for a few hours. That heft is also considered responsible for their tone and sustain. Early Les Pauls were so heavy, and modern guitarists apparently so wimpy, that for about a decade Gibson added chambers to the Les Paul body. Marketed as "tone chambers," they make the modern Les Paul lighter than the Les Pauls of old—the ones Jimmy Page played, and the vintage ones in Lifeson's collection. Chambered Les Pauls were rather controversial when they came out, though that brouhaha has since died down. Indeed, go to a music store and pick up a Gibson Les Paul made in the past ten years and then a vintage Les Paul from the seventies or before (prepare to ask permission to do this) and notice the obvious difference in weight. And then play them and see if you hear a difference—that part is subjective, though not exclusively, there are, of course, several other differences between vintage guitars and modern ones. The two not-quite-traditional-looking Les Pauls Lifeson favored on the *Time Machine* tour are thinner than both the chambered and non-chambered models, but they are not exactly lightweight. This is because they are truly solid, just like the Les Pauls of old.

Lifeson's New Electronics

As mentioned previously, if the Gibson Les Paul has a limitation, it is its lack of diversity when it comes to tone (but what an amazing tone they have). Granted, this is in comparison to the Les Paul's arch nemesis, the Fender Stratocaster, which boasts three pickups, available in five different combinations (most Les Pauls have a two-pickup, three-combination setup). The two Les Pauls Lifeson had slung on his shoulder during most of *Time Machine 2011: Live in Cleveland* did not suffer from this limitation. Indeed, they were two of the most diverse Les Pauls ever built.

Looking at the hardware on the bodies of these Les Pauls, they don't look much different—yeah, they each have a Floyd Rose bridge more commonly found on Super-Strats and shredder axes. But Lifeson had those on the prototype Les Pauls he used on the *Snakes and Arrows* tour. And Floyd Rose bridges don't offer tonal difference as much as playing differences—serious amounts of vibrato / whammy sounds, both up and down in pitch, and dive-bomber detuning effects on the fly. Again, Lifeson's solo on "Stick It Out" is arguably the best example of what the Floyd Rose system can do in his capable hands. These

Floyd Rose bridges also have something innovative and quite useful that Floyd Rose players are not normally associated with—piezo-electric saddles under each string, which gives these Les Pauls the ability to sound like an acoustic guitar. Similar functionality was covered in this book in regards to the Les Paul prototypes used on *Snakes and Arrows*, but that was a trick exclusive to one guitar. On *Snakes and Arrows*, if Lifeson wanted whammy, he was handed a Floyd Rose–equipped Les Paul. If he wanted to simulate an acoustic sound, he was handed a fixed bridge Les Paul, equipped with piezo electronics. If he wanted both—well, tough—until the *Time Machine* tour, that is.

Lifeson enjoying the hell out of his signature Gibson.   *Courtesy of Max Mobley*

All guitar pickups must do one important thing if the guitar on which they are mounted is to be truly electric: they must create voltage based on the speed of vibration for each string. That speed, and how the different speeds of different notes interact with each other, is why a C major sounds happy and a D minor sounds sad. Guitar pickups "pick up" those frequencies as voltage. That voltage gets passed through a variable resistor (the volume knob), and then gets passed through a capacitor and another variable resistor (the tone knob), and then out the familiar one-quarter-inch jack, through effects and, eventually, through a guitar amp and speaker cabinet, and *voilà!*, you have "The Spirit of Radio." Add a switch to determine which pickups are to be used and you have the elegantly simple circuit for making a guitar electric. As previously stated and repeated to drive the point home, standard guitar pickups use magnets which create a flux field through which the string passes. The string's vibration disturbs that field, and that is how the voltage is created. It is also why swapping out guitar pickups is such a popular modification for electric guitars; there are literally hundreds of different kinds of pickups available today, all of which have a huge impact on tone. Piezos, on the other hand, work on an entirely different principle. Instead of magnets and magnetic fields, piezos detect minute changes in pressure, which they translate into voltages required for outputting sound. So the piezo-electric pickup system on Lifeson's two hot-rodded Les Pauls were part of the Floyd Rose bridge, and for these to work, the string must actually be resting on them, which happens down where the string crosses the bridge before being terminated. Both the piezo's physical position and the method of creating voltage give it the ability to have more of an acoustic sound. But to make it truly acoustic-sounding, that piezo signal gets processed by a system designed to simulate an acoustic guitar sound (like the Fishman system discussed in the *Snakes and Arrows* tour gear section). In order to maximize this while still having those Les Pauls be able to rock as they should, the guitars have two outputs on them: one for the traditional Les Paul electric guitar output; one for the piezo electric signal. This is similar to the way in which the prototype Les Pauls from *Snakes and Arrows Live* also managed the different tones on output. But, in the spirit of adding a ridiculous amount of tonal flexibility to these *Time Machine* Les Pauls, Gibson, with input from Lifeson, removed one of two tone knobs and replaced it with a knob that could blend the "acoustic" signal with the electric one. This feature was dubbed Life-o-Sound, and it was quite effective on the *Time Machine* tour, especially on songs that mixed both electric and acoustic sounds (much of the material from *Snakes and Arrows* and *Clockwork Angels*). And since sonic diversity is part of the Rush trademark, Lifeson and Gibson did not stop here, though if they had, they still would have created one of the most diverse and powerful Les Pauls ever created. But, as if on their way to eleven 'cause it's one more powerful than ten, the *Time Machine* Les Pauls also offered coil-splitting capabilities, meaning both humbucker double coil pickups could, with the pull of a knob, switch to single-coil mode. Remember, Les Pauls, and most Gibsons, including the illustrious ES-355, used two magnetic coils for each pickup, which gave a fatter, warmer tone while eliminating noise (hence the term humbucker). Single-coil guitars have a crisper, brighter tone (again, think Fender Stratocaster and Telecaster). The coil-splitting ability on the *Time Machine* Les Pauls offered both types of pickups, while keeping the traditional double-coil pickup look and base configuration that makes a Les Paul a Les Paul. Whew!

Add it all up and you have a guitar with seven distinct tonal possibilities, with the additional ability to blend acoustic voicings to any of the six different electric tones available. These guitars are now known as the Alex Lifeson Les Paul Axcess. The ones seen on *Time Machine 2011: Live in Cleveland* were production models, neither custom models nor prototypes. The Royal Crimson model is serial number 003, and the Viceroy Brown Sunburst model is serial number 001. They are the ultimate Rush guitars, fittingly premiered on the *Time Machine* tour, having both the latest in guitar technology with superb rock-and-roll tone, and subtle but key physical tweaks to make them not only the most diverse and advanced Les Pauls ever created, but also the most playable.

Lerxst's Tone Lurking in Victorian Furniture

The steampunk matter onstage for the *Time Machine* tour was largely functional, if wholly fanciful, in a "Victorian Retro" sort of way. The three large wardrobe-looking things with knobs, dials, and a grill that make up Lifeson's backline actually housed Hughes and Kettner two- by twelve-inch cabinets, each tied to a powerful Hughes and Kettner amp in a rack offstage. Two of those amps are Lifeson's signature models; a third is a version called the Coreblade, which is kicked in almost as an effect on select portions of songs, like the end of the "Limelight" solo, during which the end note lingers and layers over Lifeson's return to the main riff.

Lifeson's rigs are some of the most complicated ones you will find in rock and roll. When I interviewed him about it for *Premier Guitar* magazine, he had to explain it twice before I could make sense of it.

On final legs of the *Time Machine* tour Lifeson had augmented his rig in a way that still causes controversy among his legion of guitar player fans—he stopped using speaker cabinets altogether. Instead, he opted for a Palmer Speaker Simulation setup, similar to that found on Geddy Lee's rig. Lifeson mentions in a MusicRadar gear feature that forgoing the cabinets addressed stage mix issues, something no one but Rush and their crew would have known about. Given Lee's bass rig could only be heard onstage via in-ear monitors, while Lifeson was using standard amplification, the claim makes sense. Regardless, all instrument amplification being relegated to tiny earpiece monitors is controversial, to say the least. Guitarists all over the world consider speaker types and cabinet styles a good deal responsible for their sound. But if you were onstage during the last leg of the *Time Machine* tour, you would have had to rely on monitors to hear the full band.

Geddy Lee Goes Orange

After years of using simulators and no power amps or speaker cabinets, Geddy Lee reverted back to a traditional amp and cabinet rig for the *Time Machine* tour. Well, sort of. The glorious return of the bass amp and cabinet (both by the classic amp company Orange) actually make up only one-fifth of Lee's live sound. And while the addition of the amp and cabinet were met with praise from bass purists, the cabinet is actually offstage, its signal fed to the front-of-house mixing desk responsible for blending Lee's five sound sources into a single amazing one. Indeed, rock's most intense and original bass player has been employing one of the most intense and original live bass rigs ever since the *Vapor Trails* tour. For the *Time Machine* tour, it was even more complicated and, arguably, better sounding.

The sound heard on *Time Machine 2011: Live in Cleveland* is a composite from multiple sources (the same goes for the previous two tours). An Avalon preamp and a Palmer Speaker simulator still make up the lion's share of Lee's sound, as they have as far back as *Rush in Rio* and the *Vapor Trails* tour. The Avalon signal delivers Lee's warmer tones, and much of the midrange—some of Lee's favorite frequencies for bass. The Palmer delivers a very clean and pure tone, and is responsible for delivering the bass's bottom end, which the simulator is great at extending. The remaining three channels contain various degrees of bass distortion. One of these comes courtesy of emulation software called Eleven (named after Spinal Tap's Nigel Tufnel's desire to have all amps go to eleven instead of ten). Eleven offers very detailed simulations of any bass rig imaginable, and the one processing Lee's bass signal is dialed in to emulate a classic Fender Bassman amp (a much sought-after vintage rig from the late fifties). Lee's Sansamp signal, dating back to the *Rush in Rio* era, is also still in the mix. The Sansamp has higher amounts of distortion than the Bassman / Eleven signal, but it's also down in the mix. Finally, there is the Orange amp and cabinet, which is set to stun as far as the overdrive and distortion go. This signal is also processed through a Palmer speaker simulator before it makes it to the board, where it can be mixed with the other four signals. Once the five signals are mixed together, they are compressed and then run through a vintage EQ emulator, living as software inside that massive mixing desk. The end result, as heard live during the *Time Machine* tour and on the *Time Machine 2011: Live in Cleveland* media, is Lee's best bass sound yet. Tonally, it is a work of art. "Vital Signs," "YYZ," and "Leave That Thing Alone" are just a few examples of the stunning sound realized with the stunningly complicated setup.

Lee's Jazz

For *Time Machine*, Lee stayed with a bass he proudly admits that he covets—Fender Jazz Basses. He uses three different Fender Jazz Basses, including a model from the seventies, his own signature model, and a red de-tuned one for *2112* material (it brings those high notes within range). Absent was his Rickenbacker 4001, the bass Lee is most known for despite now having his own line of Fender Jazz Basses (and having played Fender almost exclusively during the past couple decades).

The Fenders seen on *Time Machine 2011: Live in Cleveland* have a few cosmetic differences: a fancier pick guard finished in white pearloid, an alchemical symbol, and block inlays on the neck. The Jazz is a classic bass popular across many genres of rock music. Lee uses the traditional tonewood alder, a popular choice for bass. Alder is somewhat on the lighter side as far as tonewoods go (basses are big instruments, after all). It also produces an excellent bottom end and very warm mids. Its highs are present, but far from harsh. The maple neck on Lee's Jazz Basses offers excellent definition, ample brightness, and a very snappy response that is felt when playing and heard via articulation.

Victorian Vending Machines

The time machine / steampunk themes served Lee and the band well. Their backline for the *Time Machine* had the best symmetry and uniformity since Lee started using anything but bass amps onstage. They replaced the chicken roasters, automats, and dryers with something out of an H. G. Wells or Jules Verne classic, which just plain fits. But now, of course, with Rush's sense of humor fully unleashed, Lee added sausage-making to his side of the backline. In goes the meat on Peart's side, and out comes the sausage on the other side. (It wasn't real sausage, of course, just sort of a cheesy prop like what you'd find in a theme park diorama for spiced meats.) The sausage theme ties in to the intro and intermission videos, not that they needed tying in.

Time Machine Production

The production of the *Time Machine* tour continues the ever-rising trajectory of the high-end Rush show fans have come to expect, at least since their triumphant return (the *Vapor Trails* tour, 2002). Each show since then has leveraged what was learned from the tour before, along with emerging stage-production technologies. Bigger touring budgets have also helped Rush continue to deliver bigger and better shows over the past decade. And, yes, higher ticket prices play a role in that as well, but at least it's money well spent.

On the rear screen, the band employed about the same number of separate videos for certain songs (about fifteen total), plus video graphics used as frames whenever Lee, Lifeson, and Peart were featured live on the rear screen. While these treatments took up valuable rear-screen real estate, they served the highly thematic style of the *Time Machine* tour, and were a net positive for the night. These treatments also translated very well to the *Time Machine 2011: Live in Cleveland* media.

When the rear screen was not showing members of Rush as they tore through their three-hour set, they featured those videos especially designed for select songs. Many were highly thematic, and the brilliant stage lighting complemented these visuals to make the two elements—lights and video—appear seamless.

The rear-screen video used for many of the *Moving Pictures* songs seemed to tie together, even though they were produced by different artists, including the one used for "The Camera Eye," which had been directed and photographed by Rush's late photographer and friend, Andrew MacNaughtan. It seems that from their earliest days to the present, the band has made—and continues to make—smart choices when it comes to working with third parties to help realize the great Rush experience. For the *Time Machine* tour, the band used over a dozen different video artists to deliver what fans saw as they listened to the music being made. That it all worked so well, and was all of such wonderful quality, speaks to the talents of Geddy's brother Allan Weinrib, executive producer for the rear-screen video. Weinrib was also one of the producer's for the *Time Machine 2011: Live in Cleveland* DVD and Blu-ray, and has executive producer credits for *Snakes and Arrows Live* and *R30* as well.

The *Time Machine* Glow—It Moves

Snakes and Arrows Live had such a clean look, with the production building over time. It was highly effective, as noted earlier. It really allowed Lee, Lifeson, and Peart to be the focus—what their hands and feet were doing, how they moved, the faces they made, the moments they smiled or grimaced (mostly the former), and those rare glimpses when, by witnessing their interaction outside of their mutual virtuosity, fans witnessed a bond as deep as any three people could possibly have. *Time Machine* is a different story altogether. There is a lot to take in: the myriad steampunk props, the dazzling and highly stylized rear-screen art, all those videos before, during, and after the show, and all those beautiful lights, timed perfectly to deliver the right moods and energy for any given moment. And while the production had momentum to match that music, it peaked at a greater height than anything any Rush fan had witnessed before. And, once again, credit is due to Howard Ungerleider, Rush's longtime lighting director.

Ungerleider has become a master of the craft, and an important cog in the Rush touring machine. The *Time Machine* lighting is the best Rush has ever had to date, and they've all been pretty damn great. In fact, the *Time Machine* tour is a big step forward from *Snakes and Arrows*' stellar lighting production. Like that tour, it wasn't just the use of color, or just the timing or placement of the lights, although all these things mattered enormously. It was the movement. During the *Snakes and Arrows* tour, the lights themselves seemed to come alive, like a grouping of dumbstruck aliens coming out of a hyper-sleep. For the *Time Machine* tour, the lighting rig directly over the heads of Lee and Lifeson behaved like a giant spider awakened and crawling on invisible gossamer. Ungerleider had this animated lighting rig remain stationary through a good part of the show—just a rig with brilliant lights. And then, when it started moving, it caused the crowd to actually cheer—for the *lights*. It is a peak moment in the show, and it comes after the crowd is fully captivated by the music and the production. It really is an additional element that no one in the audience saw coming. The rig's arms swoop down slowly, bending in the middle like the jointed legs of an arachnid. The lights on them add a sentient quality to the animated rigging, and its focus is clearly on what is happening beneath it, as if awakened by some life-form caught in its web. Ungerleider does a great job of not overdoing the effect—and he applies that same restraint to the rest of the night. He has the patience and confidence to let things unfold at a natural pace, a pace he helps dictate with his lighting techniques.

Given all the steampunk doodads, video-based visuals, and of course, amazing music, Ungerleider was wise to up the ante considerably for the *Time Machine* tour. And, as big a step as the *Time Machine* tour was from the *Snakes and Arrows* tour, the *Clockwork Angels* tour was even bigger.

Sound Over Picture

The sound of *Time Machine 2011: Live in Cleveland* is top notch, and since the 2004 *R30* tour, Rush has been living in the sweet spot when it comes to capturing a live concert. That sweet spot has a few degrees of wiggle room, of course. The *Time Machine 2011: Live in Cleveland* sound has a bit more audience and, therefore live-ness to the audio tracks compared to *Snakes and Arrows Live*, which likewise sounds great. The instruments sound as great as ever; Peart's new kit and custom Paragon cymbals are perfectly placed, and their rings, smacks, and crashes all resonate smoothly and with discernible pitches. Lifeson has been riding a wave of great tone that cuts and balances clarity with heavy rock fatness. And five channels of Geddy Lee bass deliver perhaps the best tone he has ever had live. The whole thing works. We have known that since *R30* (would have been *Rush in Rio* if it weren't for weather and unexpected glitches), Rush no longer needs to twiddle the knob back and forth between too much of this or not enough of that. They are a mature band who sound great in their live recordings, and at this stage of their career, it would be a real shame if they did not.

16

The Gospel According to Rush

The Words of Neil Peart

When Neil Peart (aka, the new guy) joined the band in 1974, he brought more than his drumming chops. He also brought a strong, literary style of lyric writing that was a perfect fit for the band's music. Those lyrics hooked Rush fans every bit as much as their music. Even though critics have mercilessly lambasted his fantasy-laden, often grandiose lyrics, what other words would have served Rush's muse? Imagine, for a second, the bombast of *2112* with words about broken hearts, sex, or drugs—three themes that dominate hard-rock lyrics. Yeah, Robert Plant was clearly channeling a somewhat randy version of *The Lord of the Rings* and Norse mythology through much of Zeppelin's music, and critics didn't care for that too much, either. But they forgave Plant for it, perhaps because of his brilliant singing. Or perhaps it was because he and his band were cool in ways Rush simply are not. There were a few other bands of Rush's ilk that were singing about things more meaningful than sex, drugs, and rock and roll: Yes, the Who, and King Crimson come to mind. And thanks to Neil Elwood Peart, Rush was able to join their legion, instrumentally as well as lyrically—fine company, indeed. And despite the expected negativity from critics who earned their biscuits being snarky, Rush fitting into that club (as much as Rush could ever fit into *any* club) helped them earn credibility among a certain segment of rock fans early in their long career.

Peart's first serious stab at fantasy prog-rock lyrics, at least in recording order, starts with those eight words immortalized by Rush's appearance on *The Colbert Report*: "The Tobes of Hades lit by flickering torchlight." Imagine being the vocalist in a band and the new guy hands you *that* to sing. The song, of course, is "By-Tor and the Snow Dog" from 1975's *Fly by Night*, and it's one of Rush's first multi-part epic numbers. The lyrics are relatively few for an eight-minute song. There are only eighteen lines over three stanzas, and none repeat. It consists of four main sections: "I, At the Tobes of Hades"; "II, The River Styx"; "III, The Battle" (originally titled "Of the Battle" on the vinyl record version from *Fly by Night*); and "IV, Epilogue." "The Battle" is the longish instrumental section consisting of the four subparts: "i, Challenge and Defiance"; "ii, 7/4 War Furor"; "iii, Aftermath"; and "iv, Hymn of Triumph." The "7/4" mention in the "War Furor" refers to the time signature—one of Rush's favorites early on. Typical rock time signatures are 4/4, which counts out as 1, 2, 3, 4–1, 2, 3, 4—a zillion rock ditties fit that, whereas 7/4 counts out as 1, 2, 3, 4, 5, 6, 7–1, 2, 3, 4, 5, 6, 7, and so on (try snapping your fingers to *that*). Quite a lot of Rush songs employ this time signature in pieces, rarely in whole.

"By-Tor and the Snow Dog" has some of Peart's best lines from a prog-fantasy standpoint. *Fly by Night*, Rush's second album, and the first with Peart, would be their last not to include printed lyrics. Nonetheless, it is the words from "By-Tor and the Snow Dog" and most of the remaining songs from the album, including the opener "Anthem" (Peart's first foray into Ayn Rand–inspired Individualism), "Beneath, Between, and Behind" (more medieval than fantasy), and the lilting ode to the world of J. R. R. Tolkien—"Rivendell," that helped young Rush fans find solace and refuge from the daggers of youth. It was 1975—the Internet wasn't even a word, let alone a thing. Air conditioning was a luxury item in both cars and houses. Phones hung from walls and most used a dial instead of buttons. Vietnam was finally ending its savage destruction of young men unlucky enough to get caught in the draft, and since time immemorial, parents and grownups failed to understand what it was like to come of age in your own goddam generation, even though they did it once themselves. A lot of youth chose drugs as their means of escape; others chose fast cars for which to chase attainable women. A few had sports. Some discovered *Lord of the Rings*, and some found its musical equivalent—Rush—and a handful of other prog- and heavy-rock bands. Because of all progressive music offered as an escape, it was a complete experience—wizard bong totally optional. It also complemented other means of escape by way of a soundtrack to the grind of teenage existence and its constant chiseling away of innocence.

And that's why, critics-be-damned, Peart's lyrics mean as much as Lifeson's solos, Lee's bass playing, and all those drums.

The Mis-Education of Neil Peart

Rush fans know that Neil Peart is a sponge when it comes to knowledge and experience. He's a seeker in the classic sense; the subject hardly matters—if it catches his fancy, he's going to learn gobs about it faster and deeper than most folks can absorb a potboiler detective yarn. And that brings us to Ayn Rand.

During Peart's young days struggling in England, he was stung by the cynicism of those around him and that of the music industry at large in the UK with its heartless, emotionless all-business-no-art method of trying to find hits to sell instead of artists to cultivate. Peart discovered Rand's writing, primarily her book *Anthem*. Rightly or wrongly, he interpreted her views on individualism as an antidote to that which was barring his goal of becoming a drummer in a successful rock band. To Peart, the philosophy meant it was noble to throw yourself into something. To believe in something you wanted to manifest completely and utterly, damn all the rest. It was also about believing in one's self, something Peart held steadfast to despite all those doors that had failed to open to him. It wasn't about stepping on others, or selfishness in deed. It was about being singular in focus—keeping one's eye on the prize and doing all one must—within moral reason, to accomplish that goal.

It's quite ironic that on *2112*, the album to which Rush had applied a do-or-die intensity during the writing and recording process—the highest level of focus they'd given any album up to that point in their brief history, an album that they made *their* way, serving their muse and their muse alone with the only tools they knew how to use while their record company exhibited a practiced cynicism in their art-be-damned demand for profits

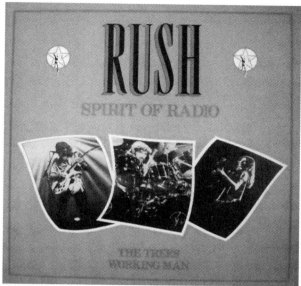

"The Spirit of Radio" was heavily promoted by Rush's label to radio stations. The track is both celebratory and cautionary (and ultimately prophetic) regarding the music-broadcast industry. *Courtesy of Joe Pesch*

(hey, it's a business . . .)—Rush delivered one of the most important albums of their career. And thus it is no coincidence that in the liner notes of *2112*, Peart acknowledges "the genius of Ayn Rand." Say what you will about Peart's interpretation of Rand's philosophies and writings, at a minimum, it inspired him to help create the Rush album that bought the band their freedom. It's even a reasonable assumption that, without *2112*, all those other Rush albums would never have been made.

Peart's interpretation of Rand's philosophies was not so far off the mark for its time, or at least his time. He was living the "portrait of the artist as a young man" life. A life where ideals reigned unchecked, like wild horses on the run. And where cynicism was a cruel poison to youth, to art, to identity, and to the freedom of making mistakes—such an important thing to self-discovery and finding one's muse. Given what Peart was trying to do, and the painful concoction of talent, innocence, and failure he was forced to consume like a puritan forcing down flagons of bitter ale, the young man was destined to uncover some new philosophy, some historic teaching that fortified his quest to remain true to his vision. And thank God for that. For without such fortification, Peart may have been known simply as "that guy at the farm equipment dealership who's a bitchin' drummer."

In Rand he found the courage of persistence, and a belief in self that is a trait among all the best personal success stories. That's a trait he shares with Geddy Lee and Alex Lifeson, and even Ray Danniels.

While we're on the subject of Rand and Peart, it's worth mentioning that her newest legion of followers—small in numbers but loud in voice in American politics, have taken her vision to a darker place than anything Peart had imagined. Peart is a self-described bleeding heart Libertarian who believes in a noble obligation to do well by your fellow man, and to serve your own interests with a passion, but without harm. In his words from a *Rolling Stone* interview in advance of the band's *Clockwork Angels* release, Peart succinctly describes Rand's influence as "an affirmation that it's alright to totally believe in something and live for it and not compromise. It was a simple as that." The current Randian Objectivism-inspired Libertarian movement that helped birth the USA's Tea Party movement is more in line with Rand's rejection of ethical altruism. This marks the major disconnect between Peart's ideals (at least as much as he has shared and can be interpreted from his writings) and the modern Libertarian movement. And yet, Libertarians make up a measurable portion of the Rush fan base, in part because in Rush, and especially in the songs "2112," "Anthem," and "Bastille Day," they found some very big music that, at some level, gave voice to their political leanings—a rare thing indeed, given rock's general proclivity for peace and love, sex and drugs, and when those things have failed, anarchy.

It's also worth remembering that Peart was only twenty-three when *2112* came out. And having twenty-something world views define someone for the rest of his or her life hardly seems fair.

"2112"'s World of Words

Peart's grand vision in the form of the song's story, both in lyrics and in the prose contained in each of the songs' seven suites, has as much to do with the power of "2112" as does the music. The song "2112" has one of rock's most fleshed-out storylines. Indeed, the only thing keeping it from being considered a rock opera is its lack of repeated musical themes and lyrical passages, like those found in the Who's *Tommy*, the benchmark for rock operas. And "2112" has enough ambiguity to remain subject to interpretation. For those unfamiliar with Rush's first "great work," the story takes place in a dystopian future, where all aspects of life in the Solar Federation (a group of planets under one rule) is controlled by the great priests and their massive computers in the Temples of Syrinx. Rush fans, especially those who joined up during or after *Moving Pictures*, should be very familiar with the line from *2112*'s Suite II, "The Temples of Syrinx." Less familiar is the prose prior to this suite describing regulated life against the gray walls of the Federation city.

Rush's *2112* came out in 1976, when vinyl records ruled, and a half-a-dozen albums fit under your arm and did not fit by the hundreds in your pocket. Thanks to this all-but-lost medium, as well as how music was consumed during vinyl's heyday, those who owned *2112* were all but guaranteed to sit down and read it from cover to cover, including the prose in between the lyrics that propel the *2112* story and help create its atmosphere. Music on vinyl albums was consumed the same way novels are read—from start to finish, in the expected order. What's more, fans of album rock generally read the lyrics and liner notes as the music was playing on the turntable. This made for a highly impactful artistic experience. A tradition lost to, or, perhaps, replaced by, modern technology. (Try doing this on a CD booklet without a magnifying glass, or on the lyrics tab of your smart phone's streaming app.)

As a whole piece, *2112* was, despite its fantasy sci-fi themes, totally and unequivocally "of its age." And its story of disillusionment amid one of humanity's (and rock and roll's) well-known themes of conformity and rebellion is timeless. Dig: The song's hero, a teenager teeming with optimism and wonder, and yet seemingly happy with the intensely controlled lifestyle of the Solar Federation, visits a waterfall, hidden in a cave. It is his secret place—a place of solace teenagers could no doubt both relate to and desire fervidly if they had yet to find their own version of such a place. Behind the waterfall, the hero discovers a secret room, and there discovers a thing of great mystery and beauty—a guitar.

Reading Peart's words here while listening to the sound of "Suite III—Discovery," where Lifeson musically dramatizes the discovery of the instrument and the hero's exploration into learning how to make beautiful music with it is genuinely chill-inducing for fans seeking a similar solace from the pressures of teenage life. This moment in the song also mirrors how many rock guitar players, Lifeson included, learned their instrument—through discovery, not education. Again, the combination of Peart's words, especially his prose, which was not sung by Geddy Lee, whose timbre on "2112" serves both the alien and alienated themes of the work as well as the urgency and oppression of its characters, makes "2112" more than a song,

The back cover of *2112* features the haunting story of Megadon and three weird-looking guys in kimonos.

Courtesy of Max Mobley

and for millions, makes Rush more than a band. This part of the story is told from Lifeson's tender approach of plucking strings and finding the instrument's voices, and from the text found in the album jacket. Those who owned the vinyl album version of *2112* know this story. Those only exposed to *2112* via CD or download, generally do not, or at least not in as much detail as Peart had intended. (Listen to the album in Spotify, the popular streaming music service, and you have to find an app to even display them.)

Getting back to our young hero, he soon learns how to play this strange device. And as many rock and roll guitar players know, the thing is actually easier to play than it looks. Guitarists also know that, with a little work, the sounds just plain take off. The eager young hero, probably dressed in his best white kimono, runs to tell the priests about his discovery. He humbly presents himself and his "ancient miracle" to the priests, led by Father Brown. The priests react by screaming angrily (Geddy Lee style) about being all too aware of this stupid, dangerous toy that does not fit their master plan of control. The hero has annoyed the priests and, being priests, they let him know about it. Father Brown crushes the guitar to bits, according to the story between the lyrics, and worse still, crushed the young hero's dreams. After experiencing music and art for the first time—a truly liberating experience that shatters the complete notion of life as it was known up until then—the anonymous hero now sees the Solar Federation and its priests for what they are—a body politic controlling every aspect of life at the expense of individuality and personal freedom. The similarity here to parents and grown-ups is obvious and perhaps even heavy handed, but to the psyche of a teenager discovering refuge in rock and roll, it's seriously heavy stuff.

This key point of the "2112" story is encapsulated by Peart on the back of the album cover, just beneath the infamous picture of Rush in their satin kimonos. The paragraph speaks of twin moons, a gray landscape, a place called Megadon, where life is spent watching Templevision and reading the Temple evening paper. The last line of this paragraph is a sort of Rush prophecy for the band, for their fans, and for the hero of the "2112" story. The line is about finding something (music) that changes everything.

Imagine a time long before the Internet, smart phones, and personal computers, with cable TV being the hottest new thing you hope comes to your town (the arrival of a McDonald's being a good sign . . .). Now imagine being a frustrated teenager in that time and in that cable-TV-less town. And as that teenager, imagine that you discover, lurking in a record bin teeming with Grand Funk Railroad, Peter Frampton, and the prior year's Led Zeppelin release (*Physical Graffiti*, which you probably already own), an album cover with a distant year printed on it floating above a dangerous-looking star in dangerous red. And on the back of that album cover you read that mystical, sci-fi paragraph that makes you realize that teenagers in the future may have it every bit as bad as you do. How do you, as that teenager, not buy that? How does a disaffected youth trying to come of age not become altered by listening to it and reading the "2112" story in time with the music—*that* music, and all those words that are as literary as anything you'll find on any rock and roll record? While Peter Frampton was asking via a talk box if you felt like he did, Neil Peart and Rush were allowing young teenagers to practice self-discovery through two of their favorite mediums—rock music and fantasy / sci-fi fiction. Rush did not tell teenagers how to feel with "2112," nor did they have to ask. They just let it be known, through art, that they understood. That they knew exactly how you feel.

And then . . .

The hero flees the temples, distraught and disillusioned. His dreams and his innocence are both shattered through the shocking destruction of a most precious sacred relic. He eventually makes it home, where he has a dream about a world where instruments like that guitar are made, and where people play them to help express their joy and their pain. This is "Part V, Oracle: The Dream," and in that dream the temples are destroyed, and the planet is saved by those who fled it decades ago. These are the same beings who believed in music and art as keys to a beautiful life—the ones who left that guitar-relic behind. The hero gets the lesson, but it is so painful he returns to his secret place, his cave, his waterfall, and the found room behind it. Too distraught to leave this, his only true place of solace, he does the unthinkable—he kills himself.

The prose and the lyrics end here, but the music carries on into "Part VII, The Grand Finale." The sound is that of a battle—Rush knows how to do this well as shown in "By-Tor and the Snow Dog," though this time it is without sound effects (cannon fire notwithstanding). Then a voice (created by Lee and Lifeson experimenting with recordings of their voice to tape) announces the end of the priests rule.

It is another metaphor for what "2112" meant to Rush, and what Rush meant to their new legion of male teenage fans.

The tone of the announcement leaves room for interpretation. Our hero is dead (and Rush dodged a bullet with the tales of suicide delivered to an impressionable audience. Thankfully, they did not glorify the act.). In his stead some powerful force has taken control of the dreaded Solar Federation—but was it the priests retaking control? No, there would have been no need for a final battle had that been the case. As Peart confirms in the making of *2112* documentary, it was an elder race that had overtaken the priests. The ancestors of the instrument that started the whole mess, and they were back—if only our hero would have waited it out . . .

As a work of fiction, "2112" has holes aplenty. But it was not created to solely be read, it was created to be heard. It is not a work of fiction, it is a song. In other words, more poetry than prose, though it contains ample amounts of both. And, therefore, any holes where listeners have to connect the dots should not be considered flaws, but rather an aspect of the medium.

2112, the Graphic Novel

Late in 2012, a graphic novel version of *2112* was released as part of a deluxe edition of a *2112* album re-release. This release includes a 5.1 surround-sound mix and a high-definition audio version on Blu-ray and DVD (since standard audio CDs are locked at a lower fidelity sample rate of 44.1 kHz). The graphic novel only uses Peart's words for "2112," both his lyrics and the prose in between. It also uses that teaser paragraph found on the album jacket. It was illustrated by Tom Hodges, who has also worked on several *Star Wars* comic books. Intermingled with Peart's homilies, Hodges does a great job of telling the story visually in contrast to the story being told by Rush musically.

Hodges version does not stop at the "2112" saga. He continues on, creating graphic interpretations of all the songs from *2112*—the stoner anthem "A Passage to Bangkok," "The Twilight Zone," the poetic and less-popular "Lessons" and "Tears," and another song seemingly inspired by Rand, the very ballsy "Something for Nothing."

The Mis-Education of Peart Fans

More than a few present-day followers of Ayn Rand continue to include Peart in their camp, as if he was frozen in time and forever a young man lost in London (not that he ever subscribed to Rand's core ideology). This is to be expected, and Rush does not discriminate—all are welcome. And in the current American political climate where members of the two main parties just can't seem to get along, it's comforting to know that there is one place where all sides can rock out together—a Rush concert.

And like all rock and roll lyricists, from John Lennon to Sting, Neil Peart has had his lyrics misinterpreted. Perhaps the most significant example lies in the lines of one of Rush's biggest FM classics: "The Spirit of Radio," from 1980's *Permanent Waves*.

Many Rush fans and classic rock fans who like Rush, but don't really gobble up the band's albums and media or attend their concerts, still mess up the song's title. It is not "The Spirit of *the* Radio," but rather and simply—"The Spirit of Radio." It's a song about the medium, and not about some ghost trapped in the dashboard of your dad's car.

The misunderstanding is partly due to grammar—putting "the" before the noun "radio" feels right—but it ain't. This error is also due to a misinterpretation of the lyrics. "The Spirit of Radio" is really a song that looks at both sides of FM rock-and-roll radio. There is the bright side—the spirit of the medium if you will, such as those magical moments when your favorite song come on when you need it most, or the DJ weaving a story through his playlist that fits your mood, or, more likely, shapes it. And there is the negative side, the business side—making playlists for profits, DJs celebrating songs they hate in order to sell air time. Interestingly, this is a theme that runs through much of Rush's work. Similar bouts of artistic integrity fueled the making of *2112*, and every Rush album thereafter.

Most of "The Spirit of Radio" is a tribute to the magic of a medium that today finds itself clinging to relevance. But its last two stanzas speak to radio's corporate side: putting the lowest common denominator on the airwaves in order to sell to the largest demographic—art be damned. In the line that mentions profits, the word is often misconstrued as *prophets*, which dramatically changes the meaning. Peart touches on the subject in an interview with *Billboard* magazine where he acknowledges the confusion, right down to radio salesman misunderstanding the lines as an endorsement of their drive for profits over everything else.

Peart's "The Spirit of Radio" lyrics, while profitable for the band—the Rock and Roll Hall of Fame named it one of 500 songs that shaped the genre; and it hit #13 on the UK singles chart—was also prophecy. In 1980, when *Permanent Waves* was released, most deejays still worked out of individual radio stations, and with the occasional exception, their shows were live and local. In the digital age, many shows are pre-recorded onto a hard drive, and there is little that is live about it. This makes sense from an ease-of-use and cost-saving point of view (aka, glittering compromises), but it comes at the expense of the magic Peart was writing about. Those forty and over should remember a time when an FM rock radio show was exactly that—a show. It was live, and the deejay literally spun out his stories via rock and roll. He was a friend on the airwaves, sitting in a small building somewhere, lining up your entertainment for the night. For those who remember, there truly is something magical about this dying art form. Today, once you get past the obligatory "morning zoo," it's a collection of songs (heavy on the Aerosmith, Bad Company, and Nirvana) that have been analyzed to help sell ads. And on their way to your car, where most radio is consumed (at least in the US), it is compressed to sound louder than it was recorded, and EQ'd to help make your car radio speakers resonate atonally at low frequencies. So not only are the deejays digitized, the music is not even broadcast as the artist meant it to be heard. It's a business, and that has its place, though amuck it may have run. Thankfully, despite its controversial evolution, the magic can still be found—like when one of the many Rush FM staples comes on, like "Freewill," "Closer to the Heart," "Working Man," "Subdivisions," "Limelight," "Tom Sawyer," and, of course, "The Spirit of Radio."

Some of Peart's Best Words

Neil Peart is best known for the lyrics of Rush's "bigger" more epic tunes, like "2112," "By-Tor and the Snow Dog," "Xanadu," and "Cygnus X-1 Books I and II (Tale of the Hemispheres)." These works tend to be adored by fans and maligned by critics. The more literary the work (as in these examples), the more Peart is reviled by the press. And for his tighter works, he still can't buy a break, and is often accused of a malignant form of pedagogy. The thing is, that is what Rush fans love about the band's (and Peart's) words—the lessons.

Peart tends to comment on observations in many of his lyrics—from the fruitless heartbreak of trying to fit in to the use of religion as either armor or sword. But the societal commentary found in many Rush lyrics is really not that different from the messages in the lyrics of critical darlings such as Joe Strummer or Eddie Vedder. The difference is really a stylistic one. Strummer and Vedder have (*had* in the case of the late Joe Strummer) the hearts of poets. That's a heart once broken and beaten down. Peart, despite his ability to create masterful timbres and rhythms in his lyrics, is extremely analytical. His words cut, and they color, but due to that analytical pragmatism, they can be extremely direct, though still poetic. He does not always wield his metaphors with the grace of rock's most popular lyricists, yet, in the best cases on both sides, his message is the same.

"The Pass"

From 1989's *Presto*, "The Pass" is exemplary of Peart's best lyric-writing. The song is about the penchant for teens suffering from the ills of their generation to romanticize suicide. Peart's tender words, backed by some of Lee's and Lifeson's most restrained riffs, make it clear that those who commit such a selfish act are not heroes (the overuse of the word "hero" is a bit of a running theme for Peart). As is the case with many of Peart's best lyrics, his phrases were inspired by literature. In the case of "The Pass," it was Oscar Wilde's play, *Lady Windermere's Fan*. Wilde's line from the play, "We are all in the gutter, but some of us are looking at the stars," was riffed on by Peart, who modernized it and made it his own as part of "The Pass." The same passage from Wilde was also lifted, practically wholesale, by Chrissie Hynde for the Pretenders' "Message of Love," released nine years earlier. Oscar Wilde also inspired Peart in the song "Resist," from 1996's *Test for Echo*.

"The Pass" is Peart at his lyrical best. The song is also a fan favorite.   *Courtesy of Max Mobley*

"Bravado"

As mentioned earlier, this song is arguably one of Rush's most poetic. From a pop- and simplified-songwriting structure, "Bravado" is one of their best. Of course, calling a Rush song *pop* may be considered sacrilege in some circles, though with one of Rush's most repetitive structures—one that is quite beautiful and works incredibly well—the pop categorization fits, albeit with some prog undertones, like the polyrhythmic underpinnings of Peart's drumming. The hooky lyrics were inspired by post-modernist novelist John Barth. Barth's work is highly regarded among literary circles, and is not for the casual reader (and thus a natural fit for the Professor).

"Marathon"

"Marathon," from 1985's *Power Windows* is a classic example of Peart's use of metaphor. In this instance, the metaphor can be found in the song's theme as Peart uses a marathon as a metaphor for life itself. "Marathon" reveals Peart's exercising his poetic, not his analytical, side. Peart has remarked that the song was really an introspective one—a reminder that life is too short to do all the things that have captured his attention. And yet, life is long enough, so don't burn yourself out. During a press junket for *Power Windows*, Peart mentions the song was inspired by the old Chinese proverb: "A journey of a thousand miles begins with a single step."

"Mission"

In some ways, "Mission," from 1987's *Hold Your Fire*, could be considered "Limelight," part two. This time no great author or pithy proverb was responsible for the lyrical inspiration. This time it was simply a conversation Geddy Lee and Neil Peart shared with an anonymous person or persons lamenting how bad their life was by comparison to that of "rock stars." "Mission" is an eloquent statement about the relativity of human existence. The lyrics sheds light on the reality that pain and

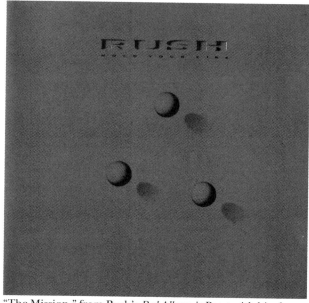

"The Mission," from Rush's *Red Album*, is Peart with his always-hopeful eye on humanity.   *Courtesy of Max Mobley*

joy are not exclusive to any particular economic class. Lee, Lifeson, and Peart sacrificed greatly for their music and their muse (like many artists, not just the well-known ones). They've worked their asses off to make it happen. They've spent months at a time away from their families, risked financial disaster, suffered the frustrating tedium of life in a suitcase—life on the road, mostly in a hotel room except for those few hours on the glorious stage. "Mission" offers the cold reality that realizing one's dreams doesn't change the fact that you're human, and life sometimes just plain sucks. The song's golden message is that since the pain of life is inescapable, and joy is not privy to just the wealthy—reach for your dreams with everything you've got, since you've really got nothing to lose.

"Entre Nous"

Though Peart has been accused of being a machine, in large part because of his astounding drumming ability, songs like "Entre Nous," from 1980's *Permanent Waves*, proves he's a machine with a big heart. "Entre Nous" (French for "between ourselves") is Peart's first truly personal Rush lyric, but not the first (nor the last) example of one of his favorite themes: the frailty of the human condition and our inherent need to explore life, which satisfies our equally important need for growth. If "Entre Nous" is one of Rush's love songs (it's hard to tell), then it's a cautionary one. It speaks to the secrets only closest confidants know about each other, and the need to preserve individualism (another favorite Peart theme) in order to grow strong together. It's hard to think of any other love song that looks at love in such a way, and yet it's hard to find a lasting relationship that does not honor that concept. For the never-ending supply of teenagers seeking solace and understanding of the human (teenager) condition in music, "Entre Nous" could easily be a song about a teenager's need for establishing his or her own identity while still managing the love of family—especially parents reluctant to let the flowers they've grown fully bloom.

"Afterimage"

Grace Under Pressure, from 1984, was a dark album despite being Rush's most reggae / ska-influenced venture. It was synth heavy, but unlike *Power Windows* and *Hold Your Fire* which followed, the synth sounds on *Grace Under Pressure* are dark and thick. That may have as much to do with Geddy Lee's choice in chord voicings. "Afterimage" is one of the darker songs on *Grace Under Pressure*, second only to the Holocaust-survival song (inspired by Geddy Lee's parents' actual experiences), "Red Sector A." "Afterimage" was written after the band lost one of its own, their friend Robbie Whelan, who was also the assistant engineer on *Moving Pictures* and *Signals* (and was also mentioned in the *Permanent Waves* liner notes).

"Afterimage" is a survivor's song in a different way than "Red Sector A," which speaks to personal survival against all odds. Instead, "Afterimage" speaks to those left behind when a loss occurs. Peart does a remarkable job of calling out the sudden shift in perspective of having someone close in one's life, and then suddenly gone. For those who have experienced that odd and tragic reality-challenging sensation, and the flood of simple memories (footsteps and echoes) it evokes, the lyrics to "Afterimage" resonate.

Different Stages, the 1998 live album that was released while Peart was dealing with personal, life-changing tragedy, borrows the opening lines of "Afterimage" as a sort of tribute: "Suddenly you were gone, from all the lives you left your mark upon (In loving memory of Jackie and Selena [Peart].)"

"Open Secrets"

Also from *Hold Your Fire*, "Open Secrets" was another of Peart's songs inspired by a conversation with some anonymous person. The lyrics touch on the importance of communicating the hard stuff, not just the easy stuff. In other words, *opening* secrets instead of sheltering them as a requirement for (once again) growth and the strengthening of bonds. Peart, being thorough, also touches on being receptive to such deep truths—the hard ones not easily said, and perhaps not easily heard. During interviews for *Hold Your Fire*, Peart mentioned that many of his lyrics come from personal conversations that inspire contemplation, and, in some instances, introspection, to see if the concepts or ideals ring true on a personal level. At the same time, Peart is quick to point out that any lyrics borne from conservations and the thoughts they inspired are by no means personal. It's social commentary at best, or just the man's take on a different point of view. Taking that into consideration and measuring it against many of Peart's lyrics, including the incredibly beautiful and poignant "Open Secrets," it seems that it is his poetic side that causes many fans to assume the point of view is Peart's. Fans can be forgiven for such indiscretions, and sometimes they are right.

"Roll the Bones"

Yes, "Roll the Bones," the single from the 1991 album of the same name. Some fans will no doubt consider this sacrilege due to its controversial bridge. Though at times it may be pedagogic, "Roll the Bones" also crystallizes one of Peart's key philosophies that has guided him, his writings, and Rush—life is random and that is scary as hell, but because of that fact, one may as well go for it (i.e., roll the bones).

"Roll the Bones" also deserves mention because it has strong ties to Peart's more recent work on *Snakes and Arrows*. "Roll the Bones" is one of Peart's first overt attempts at calling out the futility of religion in a world in which children

As rap is considered the polar opposite of rock, some fans did not care for Rush's prog-rock rapping on the title track to 1991's *Roll the Bones*. The music video, featuring a rapping skeleton, helped some.   *Courtesy of Joe Pesch*

are born into suffering. Such sentiments would be right at home on *Snakes and Arrows.*

Of course, none of these reasons are why fans would be surprised or even in violent disagreement over the fact that "Roll the Bones" is included in a chapter about Peart's best lyric writing. The trouble with "Roll the Bones" is that it contains a rap section. Yep, Canadian prog-rock rap was a thing for about one minute in a Rush song. And some fans could not stand it. Once again, it was a bold move for Rush, given that in 1991 rock and rap were the musical equivalent of oil and water. Rockers hated rap for a perceived (and certainly at times justified) lack of musicality. So, inserting a rap into a Rush song was a controversial move, and one can only assume that the band knew this but, in hail to the muse, did not give a damn.

As it should be.

Peart was inspired by rap's elevating forms via artists like Public Enemy, so he took a stab at it, and the rap lyrics are actually quite decent. They contain very interesting imagery, and rap's obligatory sense of machismo (something quite unusual considering Rush's *oeuvre*) while staying on target with regard to the song's themes and overarching metaphors. In other words, whether you like rap or hate it, in "Roll the Bones," the prog rap works.

Geddy Lee admitted that the rap was a stretch as far as song construction goes. The band considered keeping it satirical, and using someone like John Cleese to perform it. They also considered keeping it legit by having a serious rap artist perform it (the words are good enough, and to this day it would be something very much worth hearing). In the end, they punted. The rap was performed by Lee. His vocal was detuned and processed to sound like it does on the record.

"Armor and Sword"

The huge impact of 2007's *Snakes and Arrows* is still resonating somewhere in the universe, like a meteor crashing into a liquid planet. Yeah, the heavy riffs and excellent production play a significant role in that. As does the songwriting and the lyrics. This chapter is meant to call out some unique and significant lyrical highlights, and every song from *Snakes and Arrows* could have been included. And, even then, it would be impossible to put them in any sort of impactful order. "Armor and Sword," from *Snakes and Arrows*, is covered here first because it connects so strongly with the previous song, "Roll the Bones." Yes, "Armor and Sword" is about religion as is much of *Snakes and Arrows*. This is due to the fact that Peart had spent much time riding back roads through many American small towns where religion looms large, for better (armor) or worse (sword). Peart also happened to be riding during one of America's most difficult eras. The country was in the midst of two painful and contentious wars waged in the aftermath of 9/11. A controversial and largely unpopular president was nearing the end of his term, and the country's first serious-contender African American presidential candidate was on the campaign trail, bringing out in some places the country's latent, and even inherent, racism while key factions of the party in power tried to break down the walls separating church from state. These dramas were being played out on church billboards and marquees that Peart rode by daily. The result made it into much of *Snakes and Arrows*' lyrical content, including "Armor and Sword."

"Armor and Sword" contains some of Peart's most polemical lyrics. And yet in it, one can read between the lines that Peart really is rooting for us despite our flaws, our fears, and our failures. The song does not question the comfort of religion, but rather calls out how easily it can turn into something dangerous on both personal and cultural levels. In many ways, "Armor and Sword" sums up what Peart has been writing about since "2112"—the need for personal responsibility, the dangers of cult-thinking, be it sanctioned and global or secreted, the heartbreak of the day-to-day struggles we face, and our obligation to keep our chin up and do our best.

"Far Cry"

Like many rock-and-roll bands, Rush "saves" their best for first. First cuts, that is. If these were consolidated into a mix tape, it would be one helluva a compilation. Think about it: "Anthem," "Bastille Day," "2112," "The Spirit of Radio," "Tom Sawyer," "The Big Money," "Dreamline," "Animate," and, of course, "Far Cry" from *Snakes and Arrows*.

"Far Cry" is about as big and heavy as a Rush song can get (and that's saying something). Like "Armor and Sword" and the other ten tracks on *Snakes and Arrows* containing vocals, it features Peart at his lyrical best. The verses of "Far

Cry" shout out the madness and mess we find ourselves in, while its choruses are where Peart once again roots for that ultimate underdog, the human race. Because of this, "Far Cry" contains a remarkably deft look at the duality of humanity—our inability to collectively stop train-wrecking our species, followed by a "we won't give up, we won't stop trying" mentality. Like "Armor and Sword," it's another timely track inspired by Peart's American road trips. But it could have just as easily been written after watching too much cable news.

In some ways, the lyrics to "Far Cry" question our ability to evolve, while reminding us that we have little choice but to keep trying if we are to succeed, no matter how battered we may feel. Even in lyrics filled with such dark (and darkly real) imagery, Peart can't seem to help but keep hope alive. Perhaps that's why his lyrics resonate for so many fans who discovered Rush during the challenging teen years. Peart has no problem coloring the darkness in ways that are utterly relatable, both personally and in regards to the outside world. And, yet, not once has he given up on us. There is always at least one powerful line of hope. No matter what critiques one has for Peart's ability to craft lyrics, no one can ever accuse him of not rooting for the home team, even when that team has let itself down.

17

Peart's Prose

And He's a Darn Good Travel Writer, Too

or anyone who has spent time reading Rush lyrics, the fact that Neil Peart would jump into writing books comes as no surprise. As of this writing, Peart has published five books, all memoirs of sorts. In order of publication, the titles are: *The Masked Rider: Cycling in West Africa*; *Ghost Rider: Travels on the Healing Road*; *Traveling Music: The Soundtrack to My Life and Times*; *Roadshow: Landscape with Drums: A Concert Tour by Motorcycle*; *Far and Away: A Prize Every Time*.

Previous to these mainstream publications, Peart had written five books between 1985 and 1988 that were published privately for friends and family: *Riding the Golden Lion*, *The Orient Express*, *Pedals Over the Pyrenees: Spain and Spokes and Trains*, *Raindance over the Rockies: Across the Mountains by Bicycle*, and *The African Drum*. These books all involved Peart's bicycle travels in foreign lands and the not-so-foreign Colorado Rockies. In each instance, the publishing was homespun, the page count low, and the photos all black and white. They are undoubtedly precious gifts, given their homemade and from-the-heart nature.

The Masked Rider

The Masked Rider: A Cycling Tour of Africa was originally published on a very small scale, in 1996, with just enough copies published to place the book on store shelves in Canada, and in the merchandise booth at Rush concerts. In 2004, the book was reissued by Peart's primary publisher, ECW books. ECW's first run was riddled with mistakes—missing pictures, grammatical errors, and at least one incorrect map. Peart discovered the errors at a tour stop in Milwaukee, at which point he demanded (and received) a reprinting. Via Rush's website, Peart offered to exchange

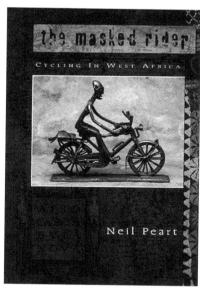

Peart's first published book, *Masked Rider*, covered his bicycle tour in Africa. Initially it did not take off, but there was newfound interest after the success of his next book, *Ghost Rider: Travels on the Healing Road.*　　*Courtesy of ECW Press*

reprinted, personally autographed books to the unlucky (or lucky) few buyers who bought the problematic editions. At least two fans took him up on the offer.

The Masked Rider's re-release comes after *Ghost Rider*, which garnered enough sales for Peart to make *The Masked Rider* available globally. This travel memoir is considered by many to be one of Peart's best books. While describing the beauty of cycling through Africa with a mixed bag of a fellow cyclists (from the capable to the whiny), Peart is very honest about his experiences—including his bout with dysentery, and the armed guards who had no qualms about handling trouble, real or perceived, with a heavy hand. The title comes from the arduous journey shared between strangers that provided insight into the various masks those strangers wear in civilization, and more importantly, what lies underneath them. Peart, the ultimate "constant reader," took two heavy books with him on this trek, Aristotle's *Nicomachean Ethics*, and Vincent van Gogh's autobiography, *Dear Theo*. As such, both authors and their books make appearances in *The Masked Rider*.

In *Ghost Rider: Travels on the Healing Road*, Peart took on the difficult task of writing about recovering from personal tragedy. There was talk about turning it into a movie, but, in the end, it was simply too painful a subject to revisit.   *Courtesy of ECW Press*

The Ghost Rider

Ghost Rider: Travels on the Healing Road—the sad tale, the brave tale. Just looking at this book and understanding why it was written and why the journey it tells was taken reminds one of Peart's bravery. His lyrics reveal a man with a big brain and a heart to match. *Ghost Rider* reveals a man tough enough to survive profound tragedy, revisit it by writing about it, and then defy his intensely private persona by publishing it.

Peart doesn't dwell on the tragic events in this book. But he seems to get that, being a key part of the story, he must include it. And then he quickly gets back to the long roads covered here. Riding from Alaska to Belize on a BMW motorcycle is a story in itself, and Peart makes great use of that. He also is also very frank about his struggles to find any joy in anything once the bike stops. Brutus, his trusty traveling companion (and occasional bodyguard), factors heavily into the story. Warm and vibrant Mexico seems to be the land where the spark finds its way into Peart's heart again, and the story ends more or less happily, at least as happy as this true story could—with a renewed sense of life, purpose, and love (albeit a fragile one) for Peart, thanks in large part to meeting his new wife (Carrie Nuttall Peart), introduced to him by the late Andrew MacNaughtan. Another key to Peart's recovery involves his reuniting with Lee and Lifeson to continue their musical exploration, which Peart reopens with a phone call to Lifeson claiming a need to "find honest work."

Traveling Music: The Soundtrack to My Life and Times

Go figure that the man constantly banging all those bang-able things center stage at a Rush concert is not one to hold still when off the road. Peart seems happiest when he's on the move, as illustrated by his 2004 tome *Traveling Music.* This time, instead of a BMW motorcycle, he's driving a slick BMW Z-8 roadster. And instead of fleeing horrors like a character from a Stephen King novel, or exploring exotic lands like a latter-day Marco Polo, Peart just wants to listen to music and be "in the drive" behind the wheel of a highly engineered driving machine. Peart's musical tastes are quite diverse—he listens to everyone, from critical darlings like Linkin Park and Radiohead to the classic American music greats Frank Sinatra and Patsy Cline. The road trip (from LA to Texas, which is a pretty dry route), seems little more than a means to listen to hours of music on end without sitting still, and that music, which plays a

In Peart's third book, *Traveling Music: the Soundtrack to my Life and Times*, fans learn of his eclectic musical tastes based on songs chosen for a road trip across the American Southwest, this time on four wheels instead of two.

Courtesy of ECW Press

bigger role in the book than the road itself, is a catalyst for memories and musings from one of rock's greatest minds.

Roadshow: Landscape with Drums: A Concert Tour by Motorcycle

Finally, what fans have been waiting for, or so it seems: Peart writing about Rush, and about concert touring. The only problem here is, 2006's *Roadshow* doesn't quite deliver on that expectation, or if it does, it's not in the way fans had anticipated. And, really, where did that expectation come from anyway? Peart? The fans? The title and cover of the book? Make no mistake, Peart does write about touring, as promised in the title, but it takes a back seat to Peart writing about his travels in between shows. *Roadshow* primarily takes place during the grueling *R30* tour, which had the band playing fifty-seven shows in nine different countries—no wonder one of the chief criticisms of the book is that Peart does not sounding gloriously excited while describing the tour. What fans should take away from this book, however (aside from Peart becoming quite an excellent travel writer), is that, except for the few hours spent onstage, touring is a tedious endeavor interrupted by drudgery such as laundry, paperwork, checkpoints, and little else. Had Peart not been able to ride in between shows, there would be remarkably little to write about. After all, it's not like Rush is known for their drug-fueled, sexed-up escapades and hotel room–trashing excess.

With *Roadshow*, one does get a certain sense that Peart wasn't ready to write about his job. That perhaps he was attempting to honor a "big ask" from his fans. It is a lot to ask of the guy—not only did he have to have his mind on the big game of being one of the best rock drummers of all time for fifty-seven nights,

Rush's drummer is known to spend more time on his BMW motorcycle than his tour bus. Both are featured here, taken backstage during the *Time Machine* tour.   *Courtesy of Tina Davey*

but he was somehow supposed to have a writer's eye throughout, and capture those mental videos of details and feelings and story elements so he could later write them down. All this while remembering fills and beats and dynamics while retaining enough presence of mind to handle the unexpected curve balls and change-ups that are part of a live show. This sounds all but impossible to do on the job. Perhaps writing about Rush would best be served if done during a time when the Rush concert tour machine had been stilled for some time. If given the choice, no doubt fans would prefer that the machine stay powered up, not rested long enough to distill and disseminate stories. Rock's best memoirs have this advantage—Keith Richard's autobiography is a shining example, though given the spirit of the Stones, there is so much more to write about than there ever will be about Rush, who really are just three decent fellows who happen to seriously worship one very progressive muse.

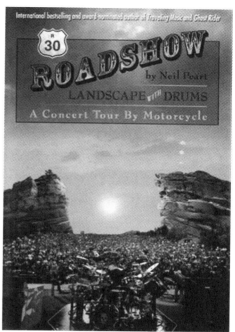

Roadshow: Landscape with Drums: A Concert Tour by Motorcycle reveals the highs and lows of a being at the center of a big concert tour. Fans were hoping for an insider's look about being in Rush, but, not being comfortable with fame and accolades, Peart wrote about his motorcycle rides between shows as much as (if not more than) the shows themselves.

Courtesy of ECW Press

Far and Away: A Prize Every Time

Far and Away: A Prize Every Time, released in 2011, contains twenty-two stories from different tours, places, and times in Peart's life, and features the Professor at his all-time writing best. This is the book that really proves Peart could have made a fine living as a travel writer. It contains the best elements of his other books, with a more resonant voice. *Far and Away* is tightly written but looser in attitude, making it a faster read than his previous efforts. The book is really a collection of Peart's best essays from his website. There is a chapter about life at home, told through his preoccupation with a hummingbird family—a metaphor for the start of his own family as his pregnant wife, Carrie, nears her delivery date. He even devotes chapters exclusively to drumming, including his

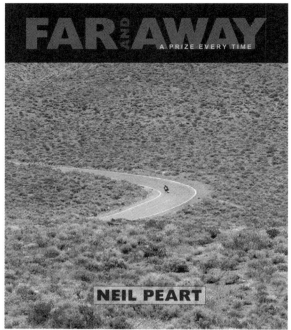

Peart's most recent book, *Far and Away: A Prize Every Time*, is a collection of essays and stories from his personal website. It contains some of his best prose writing.

Courtesy of ECW Press

work on the *Hockey Night in Canada* theme, where Peart beats heavy rhythms into the theme song for one of Canada's most sacrosanct traditions. The mere fact that Peart was allowed to participate in this event speaks volumes of how.

Clockwork Angels, the Novel

The novel *Clockwork Angels* is based on the 2012 studio album of the same name. That record, Rush's twentieth studio effort, happens to be Rush's first full-length concept album (hard to believe, isn't it?). As such, it includes Peart's prose inspiring the story in between the lyrics, just as Peart did with "2112," and "Cygnus X-1 Book II, Hemispheres." The record is reminiscent of both in terms of scope and format. However, *Clockwork Angels* has a bigger concept than anything Rush has attempted previously.

The book version was written by popular sci-fi author Kevin J. Anderson, whose work includes the *Dune* prequels, a series of *Star Wars* books, and his Nebula Award–nominated *Assemblers of Infinity*. Peart's contribution to the novel is predominately inspiration in the form of lyrics and story found in the

The steampunk concept from Rush's *Clockwork Angels* album is the foundation for *Clockwork Angels, the Novel*, helmed by author Kevin J. Anderson and co-written by Neil Peart.
Courtesy of ECW Press

Clockwork Angels album. The book also contains illustrations by the brilliant Hugh Syme.

Anderson is a natural fit for the book, having had success with new stories about well-loved tales, such as *Star Wars*. The book *Clockwork Angels* maintains the steampunk theme set forth by Peart and the band in their recent tours (The 2012–13 *Clockwork Angels* tour, and the 2010–11 *Time Machine* tour). The story is vivid and fits Rush's style quite well. Its themes of order-versus-chaos harken back to "2112," and Peart's lyrical work in general since that record. This is Peart's second work of fiction, the first being the short horror story *Drumbeats* about (coincidentally) a drummer traveling through Africa on a bicycle. That story was also co-written by Kevin J. Anderson. While Anderson calls it a truly collaborative effort, Peart is more humble about the project, citing that his contributions were limited to a bit of background on Africa, and some French dialog.

18

Rush Collaborations

Key Contributors to the Rush Experience

As of this writing, Rush has nearly 140 songs to their name. This includes a handful of songs that may not quite belong in the Rush canon, such as "You Can't Fight It" and "Garden Road" (technically, "You Can't Fight It" appears on their early Moon Records single from 1973). That number also includes Peart's standalone drum compositions like "Der Trommler" and "O Baterista." That's an astounding body of work by any measure. Nearly all of these were created and originally recorded by Lee, Lifeson, and Peart, and only a select few of those involved outside collaboration. Rush has prided itself on being a three-piece band, doing whatever it took to make all that music with the just the three of them and a whole lot of playing. And yet two of their most well-known tunes, "Tom Sawyer" and "Closer to the Heart," were written with the help of outside collaborators. More on that in a bit.

Hugh Syme on Keys and Paintbrushes

An integral piece of the Rush machine, Hugh Syme is mostly known by fans as the man behind Rush's album artwork as far back as 1975's *Caress of Steel* (and every album since). But he also deserves collaboration credit as a principal synthesizer programmer and keyboardist before Geddy Lee incorporated synths and keys into his rig, which began with 1977's *A Farewell to Kings*. Syme had a hand in creating the iconic opening soundscape that kicks off *2112* (both the song and the album). He also played Mellotron on "Tears" from the same record, the beautiful piano part on "Different Strings" from *Permanent Waves*, as well as the rock piano chops on "The Spirit of Radio." Syme is also credited with the keyboard "noises" heard on "Witch Hunt" from *Moving Pictures*.

Syme's work as Rush's artist-in-residence and the art director for their albums has become a key part of the band's experience. Their now-iconic starman logo was his design. The richly detailed street scene with the man juggling fire found in the jacket fold of *Hold Your Fire* exemplifies the high level of his work. That work was handcrafted by Syme, who created a miniature version of the dark, wet city street scene containing symbolic references to previous Rush albums. The scene is richly detailed, with the photo of the fire juggler layered in with care. For many entrenched in the digital age, it is hard to fathom the artistry involved in creating such a work without Photoshop or the digital safety

If Rush had a fourth member, it would be hard to find a better candidate than Hugh Syme, whose album artwork matches and complement's the tone of each album it graces (all but the first two). This poster, featuring the fire juggler from the inner fold of *Hold Your Fire*, is an excellent example.

Courtesy of Max Mobley

net of "undo" and copy and paste. That is the brilliance of Syme. Even the word *Rush* on the cover of *Hold Your Fire*, which looks liquid and lush in the same red as the rest of the cover (hence, *Hold Your Fire* being called "the Red album" by some fans), was handmade by Syme. He created a mold of the Rush name, and filled it with rich, red paint. Being an album-oriented band, Rush has been fortunate to count Syme as part of the family. He is also the designer of Peart's book covers. Syme has done work for other artists, though with one exception, he is best known for his rich body of work with Rush. That one exception is the album cover for Iron Maiden's *The X-Factor* album from 1995. It features Iron Maiden's well-known mascot, Eddie the Head, dissected and clamped onto some wicked-looking torture device. What's so unusual about the cover is that it is the first time an oil painting of Eddie had not been used. Syme went for a very graphic model or puppet of Eddie the Head. It looked grotesquely vivid. So much so that the album was released with an alternate, less-disturbing cover design. This kinder version was offered in regions where Syme's original version was considered just too much.

Andy Richards

Andy Richards was the man behind all those synth and sample parts on both *Power Windows* and *Hold Your Fire*. His impact on those albums was so big that band members had to face questions around adding a fourth member to Rush, and, if so, would that fourth member be Richards? Such questions have been a part of Rush interviews since their earliest days, but Richards is perhaps the first collaborator named as a potential new guy. When Peart was asked this question in a 1986 interview for the *Chicago Tribune*, he politely quelled such notions, accurately citing a need to preserve the band's chemistry.

After his stint in the eighties as the go-to guy for amazing synth and sampler parts (in addition to eighties Rush, he can be heard on records by Frankie Goes to Hollywood and Pet Shop Boys), Richards has made his living primarily making music for film. *Power Windows* and *Hold Your Fire* would not sound like they do without him. And those albums have as much to do with Rush's trajectory as anything that has come after, making his collaborations with the band quite significant. Arguably, he made Lee a better synthesist and programmer, largely because he helped Lee (and Rush fans) understand what keyboards can do for (and perhaps to) a band.

Jack Secret (and Other Keyboard Secrets)

The name Jack Secret is a bit of an enigma for many Rush fans. It's a name that has been peppered throughout many of the band's albums and tour books. As mentioned previously, Jack Secret is actually the nickname for Tony Geranios, one of the band's dearest and most trusted stage technicians. Geranios helped Lee quite a bit when he was discovering sounds lurking in the analog-synthesizer world. Not only did he maintain Lee's rigs on the road (and invent ways to get them to work together), he also helped Lee understand the world of analog-synth programming. Back when digital memory (i.e., RAM) was expensive and highly limited, Jack Secret was the guy loading sounds into samplers backstage in time for Lee or Lifeson to fire them off live. When mentioning Jack Secret, one has to also mention Jim Burgess, owner of the legendary music store Saved by Technology in Toronto, Canada. Though this book makes no bones about putting the members of Rush onto a fairly high pedestal, it is also important to note that they are musicians. And musicians need music stores. And every musician who spends considerable time honoring their G.A.S. (Gear Acquisition Syndrome) has that guy or gal in their favorite music store whom they can count on to talk shop, set them straight, and solve the revolving doors of music-tech dilemmas. For Lee, that guy is Jim Burgess. He has worked with Lee for decades on getting the right keyboard rigs set up the right way for Rush's music.

While on the subject of keyboards, it is important to note that Rush has never shied away from having a hired gun come in and play a few bars. As much as Lee wanted to be a keyboardist, he is a bass player—one of popular music's all-time best. While Rush would probably never invite another guitarist bassist or drummer to sit in on a recording session as there just is no need (if Rush can't play it on their native instruments, it doesn't belong in a Rush song) they have no qualms about using the right musician for keyboard duties in the studio (but never live). This was especially true after realizing what someone like Andy Richards can do for their sound.

After *Hold Your Fire*, Rupert Hine earned keyboard credits on the two Rush albums he produced (*Roll the Bones* and *Presto*). Rush "family member" Jason Sniderman also earned keyboard credits on *Presto*. Sniderman has been a friend of the band for years. His father was the owner of the famous Sam the Record Man shop in Toronto (formerly a chain, now reduced to a single link thanks to the MP3 age). Sniderman also fueled the discussion with members of Rush that resulted in the recording of *Feedback*, the 2004 EP of classic-rock covers that Rush recorded in celebration of their thirtieth anniversary. Perhaps most significantly, Sniderman played the poignant piano interludes on *Clockwork Angel*'s "The Garden."

Lastly, John Webster, of the Canadian-based act Red Rider, performed the barely heard keyboard segments on *Counterparts*, which are really little more than some minor moods and textures. As Peart points out in a 1994 interview with *Canadian Musician* magazine, Webster was very much the go-to guy during the *Counterparts* era (early-to-mid-nineties), having also performed keys on albums for Aerosmith and Metallica.

"Losing It" by Finding Mink

Among musos, Ben Mink is somewhat of a living legend. The multi-instrumentalist spent five years in the prog-fusion band FM (the Canadian one, not the British one), where Mink played electric violin and electric mandolin. FM had opened for Rush on 1979's *Permanent Waves* warm-up tour (Semi-Tour of Some of The Hemispheres), and 1981's *Moving Pictures* tour, giving the musicians ample opportunity to work together. Mink has also been nominated for his work with k.d. lang and Feist. Most recently, he worked with the band Heart, and can be both heard and seen on their live DVD, *Night at Sky Church*. He also produced their 2010 album, *Red Velvet Car*. That album includes a credit in the liner notes for none other than Geddy Lee. The credit is for a whistle on the track "Death Valley." Rush fans sussed out this credit, but hearing no actual whistle on the track, contacted those who worked on the album until they could get a satisfactory answer. According to Ben Mink, Lee's whistle credit is an inside joke. After hearing some high-pitched sound during the mix of "Death Valley," Mink quipped, "It's probably Geddy whistling."

Whistles and jokes aside, Mink's first involvement with Rush as a guest artist was on 1982's *Signals* album. Mink is the virtuoso responsible for the emotive electric violin part on the melancholy track, "Losing It." "Losing It" is a bit of a sleeper track on *Signals*, mostly due to the fact that there are so many popular songs on the record, and many share a certain ska / reggae-goes-prog vibe. "Losing It" has its own feel. It is super-keyboard heavy (the heaviest on what is quite a keyboard-rich album), and also quite forlorn both in musical feel and lyrical content. In some ways, "Losing It" feels like it belongs on a different album, such as the decidedly darker *Grace Under Pressure*, the studio album that follows *Signals*. Peart's words about artists losing their ability to follow their muse are sentimental and somewhat tragic, and Mink's ethereal electric violin sounds really complement the mood established by the lyrics and Lee's keyboard parts. The song's electric violin solo is nothing short of fantastic. Without losing the song's morose mood, it takes flight, like a trapped bird flying into the bars of its cage as it refuses to surrender its greatest gift. As the solo takes flight, it becomes the counterpoint for the tragedies of the song's two characters—the dancer whose body burns to dance but aches from the physical toll of a life spent dancing, so much so that it must remain still, and the writer too feeble to capture the torrent of words that once gave him his voice—a writer who can only stare dumbfounded at the empty page. Such genuine sadness (arguably Peart's most dramatic work, even more dramatic than "The Pass" or "2112") requires an intense sonic escape to punctuate the tale. That is what Mink's performance delivers, and thought Lifeson no doubt would have nailed the right part equally well, Mink's melancholy and otherworldly-yet-somehow-familiar sounds take the song where it needs to go.

Mink also makes an appearance on *Snakes and Arrows*, playing strings on "Faithless." Mink is an artist worthy of a Rush fan's attention. His guitar work can be heard on Lee's solo album, *My Favorite Headache*.

"Closer to the Heart"

"Closer to the Heart" is the first Rush song to feature a collaborator beyond performance and programming. Little is known about Peter Talbot, though he is credited with co-writing the lyrics to this classic Rush song. One of Peart's friends, he came up with the song's title and first verse. Talbot is also mentioned in the liner notes of *All the World's a Stage*.

Pye Dubois

Poet Pye Dubios was the chief lyricist for Canadian band Max Webster, and much of Webster front man Kim Mitchell's work. Veteran Rush fans will recognize Max Webster as the Canadian act that opened for Rush at countless shows during the band's early tours (up through *A Farewell to Kings*). For Rush fans whose door to discovery was the mighty *Moving Pictures*, Dubois is better known than Max Webster, for one very significant reason—he and Peart co-wrote the lyrics to "Tom Sawyer." Where Rush alumni like Hugh Syme and Andy Richards helped shape Rush's sound, Dubois helped shape Rush's message, or at least its delivery. Peart loves to be inspired and share his inspirations, and in working with Dubois, Peart's inspiration was that of one poet inspiring another. "Tom Sawyer" was not just a turning point for the band, it was also a turning point for Peart's lyric writing. Though Peart's early work had a literary feel to it, his work post-"Tom Sawyer" contained more allegory and metaphor, having found in his poet's voice that wonderful ability to say more with less.

As a collaborator, Dubois returned to the Rush family in 1987 for "Force Ten" on *Hold Your Fire*. Here, Dubois's contribution came at the last minute. The band was a day and half away from walking into the studio to capture the songs they believed they had lined up for *Hold Your Fire*. According to a 1987 interview with Lee for *Rockline*, Dubois had submitted some lyrics to the band, and in a push to have a tenth song on the album, Peart reworked and embellished Dubois's verses at the eleventh hour, the result being track one on *Hold Your Fire*.

Max Webster wasn't just a signature opening act during Rush's early days; their members also helped shape the band's trajectory.

Courtesy of Joe Pesch

Dubois's beautiful poem "A Lake Between Sun and Moon," inspired not only the Rush song "Between Sun and Moon" from 1993's *Counterparts*, but also inspired themes found on the album—the existence and need for counterparts, and the space between them (man and woman, actor and act, sun and moon). This extends to the mystery one perceives from the other—the mystery of woman from a man's point of view, and vice a verse. It also explores the existence of counterparts as a balancing point in nature, with the magical experience lying in that mysterious place between them.

Rush's Collaborative Present and Future

If 2012's *Clockwork Angels* and its subsequent tour are any indication, fans can expect collaborations on Rush's music to continue. This concept album features some nice string section arrangements courtesy of Canadian David Campbell. Campbell is no stranger to working on rock records; he's worked with artists such as Metallica, Muse, and Evanescence. His son is the one and only Beck, as in "I'm a Loser," and "Two Turntables and a Microphone." Campbell arranged and conducted the *Clockwork Angels* string sections, and helped create the Clockwork Angels String Ensemble that Rush took on the road for the tour in support of the album.

The Clockwork Angels String Ensemble, shown here at a Michigan stop of the *Clockwork Angels* tour, was an integral part of both the tour and the studio recording.

Courtesy of Joe Pesch

19

Clockwork Angels Live and in Studio

Rush's Biggest Live Production Heralds the Return to Bigger Stories

C lockwork Angels is, by any measure, a monster of a rock album. It signals the return of Rush to their high-concept roots despite the fact that the album contained some of their shortest songs and tightest arrangements (the longest is the seven-and-a-half-minute title track). In many ways, *Clockwork Angels* is the ideal effort to follow 2007's *Snakes and Arrows*, which many Rush fans treat as a triumphant return to what the band does best—throw it down hard and keep the surprises flowing in the form of riffs and arrangements. There is no doubt that *Snakes and Arrows* was an invigorating enterprise for Rush—the songwriting, the performances, taking residence in a studio like the "good old days."

Clockwork Angels was a team effort that included producer Nick Rasculinecz and engineer Rich Chycki. Like the best Rush albums, elements of the band's diverse *oeuvre* can be found on *Clockwork Angels*, from the raw bombast of Rush's oldest records to the refined bombast of *Snakes and Arrows*, and almost everything in between.

Clockwork Angels Tour

The *Clockwork Angels Tour* album (CD) and DVD and Blu-ray concert video was released in November 2013. A deluxe edition containing all three formats was released at the same time. It was the most anticipated live release by the band—perhaps ever.

Clockwork Angels, from 2012, was Rush's first full-length concept piece.
Courtesy of Max Mobley

This is, after all, the first Rush product post-Rock and Roll Hall of Fame Induction. It is also the documentation of Rush's most successful tour, a tour that featured a truly arresting stage production. The live video also premiered across the US in select theatres for a single night, even in IMAX at some locations. Capturing the concert was a bit of a last-minute decision for the band. They were thinking about doing something late in the second leg of the seventy-four-show tour. Rather than make a "production out of the production," they chose, instead, the next few stops amenable to filming. Those ended up being three consecutive shows in the American Southwest: Phoenix, Arizona, on November 25, 2012 (US Airways Center); Dallas, Texas, on November 28, 2012 (American Airlines Center); and San Antonio, Texas, on November 30, 2012 (AT&T Center). Most of what is seen on the *Clockwork Angels Tour* concert film was from the Dallas show, with a few songs rotated in and out of the setlist, taken from the Phoenix and San Antonio performances.

Like Nothing Seen or Heard Before

While the *Clockwork Angels* studio record features the best of Rush from both prog rock and performance perspectives, the *Clockwork Angels Tour* breaks new ground in the Rush concert experience, and it does so right out of the chute.

After the obligatory opening video—featuring Lee, Lifeson, Peart and their techs preparing for the show, told in what can only be described as steampunk slapstick—the band opens with a song which had never once been featured in the opening slot: "Subdivisions." That is a familiar live song for sure, having been played on sixteen different tours, including the *Exit . . . Stage Left* tour, when the band played an early pre-*Signals* version of the track. It's been number two on quite a few setlists, but the *Clockwork Angels* tour marks the first time it was used as an opener. It's a unique move for Rush to kick off a concert with keyboards instead of guitar, or the whole band. "Subdivisions," as an opener,

Songs like "The Anarchist" satisfy Rush fans' lust for both heavy-sounding and high-concept material.

Courtesy of Max Mobley

was symbolic of the show itself—expect the unexpected, and expect lots of keyboards. Though the *Clockwork Angels* album contains very few keyboards (mostly due to the choice of a live string ensemble instead of a digital one), the tour in support of the album featured several songs from Rush's keyboard-heavy era—"The Big Money," "Force Ten," "Grand Designs," "The Body Electric," and "Territories," among others. These are songs two through six in the twenty-nine-song *Clockwork Angels Tour* set. Lee mentioned in interviews around the release of the DVD that modern technology made playing keyboards live on Rush's most synth-heavy material much simpler. What he doesn't mention, but what is plainly heard on the live album and DVD (and in person for the thousands who saw the show) is that these versions of Rush's keyboard-dominant material were mixed with guitars on top. The results are dramatic. On some songs, the keys are relegated to the back seat. On others they seem to serve Lifeson's guitar parts as opposed to the reverse. And what guitar parts they are! The guitar-oriented mix gives these songs (and others, such as "Middletown Dreams" and "Manhattan Project," available as special features on disc two) a whole new energy. As such, this tour seems to be a form of redemption for Alex Lifeson, who took it on the chin when his guitar parts were struggling for oxygen among all the digital glass and color from Rush's synth period. To drive that theme of redemption further, the fan (and band) fave from *Clockwork Angels*—"The Garden," one of Rush's mellowest and prettiest numbers, featuring a beautiful piano interlude by Jason Sniderman, was played on the *Clockwork Angels* tour by Lifeson himself.

This substantial change in how these songs are heard also reveals what Lifeson fans knew all along—the material from Rush's synth era (*Signals* through *Hold Your Fire*) contain some of his most innovative and interesting parts. The man had worked so incredibly hard to make the guitar work on tracks laid heavy with synthesizers and orchestral parts, and in the *Clockwork Angels Tour*, those parts are finally given their rightful place up in the mix, and with chunkier, heavier rock guitar tones to boot. Placing those guitar parts on top changes the feel and dynamic of these songs to the point of making them entirely fresh takes on music well known to fans.

Blonde Fire

Each officially captured live show has something special. And capturing a live show adds stress to an event that needs no additional weight. All those additional cameras serve as a reminder that what happens that night will forever be captured for posterity. Wanting to deliver a product the band can be proud of and that their fans will enjoy for years can alter the mood and subsequent focus when walking onstage. And Lord knows that in our YouTube world, failures live on for millions to view and comment on over and over again. However, on the nights captured for the *Clockwork Angels Tour* media, Lifeson is on fire for most of the night. He's always been great live, especially on the official live recordings. But, for the *Clockwork Angels* tour, he appears to be a man possessed. This is especially noticeable in the solos of many of the tracks that happen to require much more Floyd Rose whammy than any previous setlist. On some numbers, such as "Where's My Thing?" and "Force Ten," Lifeson is given additional room for riffs and soloing, and he makes excellent use of that in what appears to be an improvisational way. The *Clockwork Angels Tour* DVD arguably shows Lifeson as the star of the trio (if any one member could ever stand above the others in such a band). That may be the result of the traditionally non-guitar heavy material being treated to a guitar-heavy mix.

Two More Fires

One of the things that make Rush's live performances work so well is how the three members feed off each other's energy. Lifeson being afire means Peart and Lee will also be raising their game, and vice versa. On that score, the *Clockwork Angels Tour* has some great Neil Peart moments. This is largely due to having a camera mounted right by Peart's hi-hat cymbals. It's probably unintentional, but many moments are captured when Peart is blazing on drums while staring, glaring, and often smiling at that camera. Like boosting guitar on synthy tracks, this perspective changes how the viewer takes in Peart's always-fascinating drumming. It gives viewers a better sense of what the man is really doing behind all those drums, the outward grace he possesses while doing it, and how incredibly hard he works throughout. Because of this camera placement (along with a few others), the *Clockwork Angels Tour* has, pound for pound, more smiles from the Professor on the drum kit than any other Rush product or moment ever. Seeing a man smile while smacking drums so hard the whole kit shakes is truly unforgettable. It catches a glimpse of that young man in St. Catharines for whom everything was a drum or cymbal to be hit in time.

While Peart is captured by the glam of the camera, and Lifeson is playing his best parts with the wisdom of a veteran and the intensity of someone under the influence of his muse, Geddy Lee is very busy. He is busy singing. He is busy playing keyboards and bass with his feet. He is busy playing bass guitar and keyboards with his hands. He is busy bopping about with his mates and with Rush fans. And he is busy filling extended intros, outros, and breaks with bass riffs no else can play. His infectious energy (again, Lifeson seems to have started this outbreak) is like that of some poor sot learning he has just won the lottery. In an interview with *Rolling Stone*, Lee admits that knowing a show is going to be filmed often results in the band playing harder and, therefore, better. On the *Clockwork Angels Tour*, he is having the time of his life, and you can see it and hear it in all the things he does.

Ensemble Fire

As mentioned earlier in this chapter, a running theme throughout the *Clockwork Angels Tour* video (and the tour itself) is to leave all expectations behind. This could not be truer than when the Clockwork Angels String Ensemble takes to the stage for set two.

Having additional musicians on stage is a huge first for Rush. Having eight virtuosos (not counting Rush) seemed a bit dangerous. As a trio, things had been working well for nearly forty years. So why muck with it now? Previously, when a string ensemble or an orchestra joins a rock band for a live event, it rarely works. Metallica did it and it seemed kind of lame at best, and pretentious at worst. Kiss, Aerosmith, and others did it, and it just plain did not work. Peter Gabriel did it, but forgot the rock band, and his music lost its rhythmic and progressive complexity (though it w as a great show if you like dark, orchestral music). Fans know Rush's experiments can sometimes backfire, and adding a string ensemble seemed dangerous indeed. And so it was such a pleasant surprise that it worked so amazingly well.

And fans walked out of the venue hoping Rush would do it again.

The eight musicians on cello, viola, and violin had all spent time in support of rock and roll. Some had even worked with *Clockwork Angels'* producer Nick Rasculinecz when he produced Evanescence and, of course, the *Clockwork Angels* studio album. Some of the performers were serious Rush fans, and all had a deep respect for their musicianship—a feeling that was mutual as far as Rush was concerned. The string parts arranged by David Campbell were tastefully done, and familiar to fans playing the hell out of the *Clockwork Angels* studio album. It was clear that Lee, Lifeson, and Peart were stoked to have them on their backline (well, behind the new round of steampunk props, anyway). And when they came to life on the set two opener, "Caravan," history was made—for the better. The eight musicians chosen by both Campbell and Rasculinecz had a great look, and they knew how to rock. They perfected the balance between rocking out and not stealing the show. They were incredibly into their music, which helped them add feeling instead of just playing the quavers on the charts. That may have been where other rock bands attempting this feat failed—by adding great musicians who were not fans of the band or the kind of music they were to augment. With the Clockwork Angels String Ensemble, it was clear that they loved what they were doing every bit as much as the members of Rush love playing live.

Ten of the twelve songs from the *Clockwork Angels* studio release kicked off set two of the *Clockwork Angels Tour*. Each was accompanied by the string section. After that, the string ensemble joined Rush on classics such as "YYZ" and "Dreamline." This worked every bit as well as the *Clockwork Angels* material, which was recorded with live strings. The impact on "YYZ" was especially profound, giving the song a bit of tasteful Beethoven bombast.

The members of the string section looked like they were rockers at heart, especially when the fifteen-foot-tall flames went off right behind them. The heat from those flames was felt in the first ten rows—easily. When they went off, fans looked at each other and reacted vocally as much to the heat as to the look. Fire has been a part of Rush's stage show since it was started by the dragon on the

Vapor Trails tour. One can only imagine what it felt like for the members of the string ensemble, who, after a couple nights, anticipated the event and edged as far as they could to the front of their riser.

The Look of the *Clockwork Angels Tour*

The intense and infectious moments described above are wonderfully captured on the *Clockwork Angels Tour* video. And that they are so prominent also has to do with the filming and editing of the video. This video does a great job showing Lee and Lifeson do more than play their guitars. It shows them playing their foot pedals, switching through effects, swapping out guitars, and generally performing all the wizardry lost (but heard) past the fifth row of a Rush concert. On that score, the *Clockwork Angels Tour* video has a distinct look compared to all previous live Rush videos.

The editing is somewhere between the manic cuts of *Rush in Rio*, and the long, highly composed feel of *Snakes and Arrows*; it alternates effectively between the two extremes. Unlike any previous Rush concert video, *Clockwork Angels Tour* brings the viewer into the Rush concert experience in two distinct ways. The beginning and ending of the film, along with a few segments scattered throughout, show the members of Rush behind the scenes—what it's like to wait and prepare, what it's like between sets, and how fast Neil Peart flees from kit to bus (he practically has to jump on the thing as it pulls out of the venue). It also shows what it's like to be in the crowd. More than a few shots are from handheld cameras in the middle of the audience, looking at the band from between air-drumming arms and bobbing heads.

The sound and video quality of the *Clockwork Angels Tour* DVD is actually spotty in places, as if the last-minute decision to make a film extended to the overall quality. In the end, this is more of a plus than a minus. There is a somewhat raucous and raw look to the video, which adds a certain feel befitting a rock-concert experience. In this age of fans recording camera phone video for entire shows, it actually seems a bit silly to complain about how high the definition of Rush's latest Hi-Def video.

The *Clockwork Angels* Visual Feast

In many ways, what *Moving Pictures* was to Rush's studio albums, the *Clockwork Angels Tour* video is to Rush's DVD releases. Not only does it have an immersive live feel to it, it also captures Rush's most imaginative stage production. Things tried over previous tours were improved upon and modernized for this tour. Lee and Lifeson had updated their steampunk backlines (now both members forgo traditional amps and speaker cabinets, causing some of the most expensive seats in the house—those nearest the stage—to have the worst sound experience in the building). The lighting was bigger, more intense, and more colorful than any prior Rush show. The rear-screen video elements had an updated, 3D CGI

The visual feat that accompanied much the *Clockwork Angels* tracks was a beautiful mar-
riage of sight and sound.   *Courtesy of William Clark*

vibe that extended to a series of light and video rigs floating and moving above
the stage. The production was the biggest thing Rush had ever done before by
a large margin. It was probably the most expensive as well, which may be why
the tour played more large arenas this time out as opposed to the traditional
amphitheaters they had been fond of in previous years. That may also be a
symptom of Rush's increasing popularity, and the venue requirements for
hosting such a spectacular stage show. The lighting production, helmed once
again by Howard Ungerleider, was truly a show surrounding the show. It tied in
so deeply with the material, and the visuals were so effective that, this time out,
the best seats in the house were twenty or so rows back, where one could take
in the production accompanying the performances.

   The *Clockwork Angels Tour* visual production was so big it was hard to capture
on video. However, producer Allan Weinrib, and director Dale Heslip captured
it the best they could, and they largely succeeded. In keeping with the live flavor
of the video, the film even cuts to lighting director Ungerleider in action—to
great effect.

Three Is Better Than One

Another dramatic change in the tried-and-true attractions of previous Rush concerts concerned Peart's solo drum work. Fans are accustomed to one fairly long,
highly composed drum-and-percussion opus, mixed with samples, improv, and
a big-band finish. This has been a hallmark of Rush concerts for decades, and

it's been good enough to be nominated for a Grammy in at least one instance. It's a moment fans eagerly anticipate, as it is also a part of the concert when audience participation in the form of air-drumming is *de rigueur.*

That was not to be the case on the *Clockwork Angels* tour. This time out, Peart played three solos, spread out across the entire night. The first, "Here It Is," comes as an interlude to the set-one, Grammy-nominated instrumental, "Where's My Thing?" from 1991's *Roll the Bones.* (This time they lost to guitar hero Eric Johnson and his "Cliffs of Dover.")

Once it becomes apparent that this first solo is not just an extended drum break, the crowd erupts, seeming to cheer on their favorite drummer while simultaneous reacting to another one of the *Clockwork Angels Tour*'s surprises. The solo is wholly fresh, stilling the arms of all but a few brave (and perhaps overeager) air-drummers in the audience. There is nothing to relate to here from previous drum solos, except perhaps its snare paradiddle intro and the heavy snare ending, which occurs while Peart is playing an entirely separate rhythm with his feet. Tempting as it is to describe the solo as one of Peart's most original and inventive, this seems premature based on what's in store later in the night for unsuspecting fans. "Here It Is," despite having some organic synth textures provided via triggers, has roots in traditional drum solos that favor technique over melody.

"Drumbastica" is the title given Peart's second solo, and it comes near the end of *Clockwork Angels*' "Headlong Flight." Other than the fact that it is played on the same drums by the same guy who played the previous drum solo, "Drumbastica" has little in common with the previous solo. It makes great use of Peart's ability to add melody to his solos via samples fired off by drum triggers place around his kit. Traditionally, this is how the big-band music that traditionally accompanied the end of his solos was played. But, in yet another surprise for fans, Peart fires off samples of Lifeson's and Lee's riffs from "Headlong Flight" itself. With these riffs played via drum triggers, Peart creates an entirely different musical structure from a song the band was in the middle of performing. Mind-bending in its way, it's also an excellent use of the technology and the moment. Though fans would probably have happily gone along with another decade of big-band excerpts to end a Peart solo, this wholly fresh take was fitting for a tour teeming with fresh ideas.

Peart's third and final solo of the evening is a standalone piece that sounds like anything but a drum solo. It is a two part number: "The Percussor (I), Binary Love Theme (II), Steambanger's Ball." The two sections lean heavily on samples intermingled with Peart's ability to create simultaneous multiple rhythms across his vast kit.

Combined, the three solos feature Peart at his most inventive and most melodic. They are not about how fast he can play, or how many drums he can hit. Drum fans looking for that would have to visit Peart's older solos. On the *Clockwork Angels Tour*, it's not about Peart's enviable technique, it's about what drums and a drummer can do, and where they can take music. The answer, at least as far as Neil Peart is concerned, is still being written.

There was plenty of gear on Rush's backline for the *Clockwork Angels* tour, but none of it made any sound. *Courtesy of William Clark*

Clockwork Angels Tour Gear

Another tour, another chance to take new gear out on the road, along with some old favorites.

Peart's is easy to cover—same kit as *Time Machine*, right down to the riser, though this time the kit rotates mid-song. This gives him a brief opportunity to say hello to the string section, sweating and rocking behind him, before switching thrones without losing a single beat.

Peart's *Time Machine* kit fit perfectly among the steampunk aesthetic of all things *Clockwork Angels*. It also had a huge sound. *Courtesy of William Clark*

Lerxst Sound

The biggest changes come in the guitar department, with Lifeson's redesigned amp-and-effects rig. This time out, Lifeson uses three different amp heads. The familiar Hughes and Kettner Coreblade, for his heaviest tones, is the sole remnant from previous tours. For clean tones, Lifeson has added the versatile Mesa Boogie Mark 5. Mesa Boogie is best known for some intense distortion sounds, but the Mark 5 is also designed to offer some very clean tones without breakup. The bulk of Lifeson's distortion tones come from his custom Lerxst Omega amps, made in North Carolina. These handmade amps were the result of Lifeson's desire to capture the same tones used on the *Clockwork Angels* record. For that record he used a 1987 Marshall Silver Jubilee, which was modeled after the revered Marshall JCM 800, though it really has its own mojo, and a greater range from crunch to full-on distortion. However, these amps are very hard to find, and being over twenty years old, not the most reliable tour-wise. The Lerxst Omega amps were designed and built by Steve Snyder of Mojotone, and modeled after the Silver Jubilee.

As the *Clockwork Angels Tour* backline denotes, Lifeson has joined Lee in forgoing typical speaker cabinet rigs, opting instead for a series of Palmer Speaker Simulators, which go direct to the in-ear monitors and the front-of-house mix. For effects and additional crunch and tone, Lifeson used two Fractal Designs Axe FX II signal processors, and, in what may be considered controversial for a live rig, a host of guitar software apps running on Apple laptops.

Guitar-wise, Lifeson relied heavily on his signature model Les Pauls. The versatility of these guitars is quite obvious thanks to the setlist. Check out the guitar parts on "Where's My Thing?" the instrumental from set one to hear the myriad tones Lifeson creates from a single guitar. Also worth noting on that track is the guitar switch at the drum solo (solo I: "Here It Is") to his faithful companion, his Gibson ES-355. The drum solo in the middle of this instrumental allows for the change, and allows fans to grok the tonal differences between Lifeson's signature Les Pauls and his most classic axe. It's actually quite odd to have a guitar change mid-song (barring a string break). The impetus here appears not to be tonally motivated, but to accommodate the back-to-back transition from "Where's My Thing?" / "Here It Is" to "Far Cry," the only song played from *Snakes and Arrows*.

Lee Sound

Geddy Lee's rig changed little from the *Time Machine* tour, at least as far as the multi-channel outputs to mixer and in-ear monitors. That part is virtually identical, including the Orange amps. What *is* quite different are the basses Lee has brought out for the *Clockwork Angels* tour. This time, Lee puts four different basses through their paces, with a spare in case something goes kerflooey. They are all Fender Jazz Basses, most from the early seventies. Previously, Lee changed bass guitars when the band tuned down or tuned differently for a certain song. While that still applies here, Lee also switches to his various Fender Jazz Basses for tonal purposes. Some of these basses are nearly entirely stock with original Fender electronics. In addition, some have had their Fender electronics beefed up, and some have had those electronics replaced with customized parts specified by Lee.

One beautiful addition to Lee's axes on this tour is a surf-green '72 reissue coming out of Fender's Custom Shop. Lee's main bass for this tour, a black '72 Fender, was used heavily on previous tours. That bass is on its third neck, one chunkier than previous necks.

Gnomes, Dwarves, and Other Special Features

Seeming to have learned from the overlong videos of the *Time Machine* tour, the interstitial videos for the *Clockwork Angels Tour* are more to the point, and avoid competing with music time. The humor is still there, of course, although not so much laugh-out loud funny as odd and quirky funny. It is, as mentioned earlier in this chapter, "steampunk slapstick," that more or less works because of the look and stylistic elements as opposed to the script (if there was one).

On the main concert disc of the *Clockwork Angels Tour* DVD, the video largely retains an audience POV. On disc two, the videos are available separately, as are outtakes from the filming.

What makes disc two a valuable addition is the inclusion of songs rotated in and out of the *Clockwork Angels* tour setlist: "Middletown Dreams," "The Pass," "Manhattan Project," and a sound-check version of "Limelight." Found as bonus additions on the DVD of the *Clockwork Angels* tour, they are also available in the live-album CD version.

Disc two also features "Can't Stop Thinking Big," a tour documentary produced by SRO-Anthem alum Meg Symsysk. There is some excellent insight here into the world's greatest Canadian prog-rock power trio working with rock's best string ensemble.

20

Vapor Trails' Trials and Tribulations

Making Right an Important Wrong

W hile it may never be considered one of Rush's greatest albums (though as of this writing, the remixed version of *Vapor Trails* has only been out a few weeks), it is, by all accounts—including Rush's, one of the most important albums Rush has ever made. While not the triumphant return that was 2007's *Snakes and Arrows*, it was certainly one of the bravest events in the band's history—climbing back onto a horse that had thrown Peart (and by extension, the whole Rush machine) into one of the darkest ravines known to man.

The *Vapor Trails* sessions were said to be marked by the pain of recovery, mixed with the joy of rediscovery. Where six or seven months was considered a long Rush recording process (*Grace Under Pressure* and *A Farewell to Kings* come to mind), *Vapor Trails* took an astounding sixteen months to record and mix. The band first got back together in 2002 for a meeting (held on egg shells) to discuss making a new album. Having so much of a history, yet hardly seeing much of each other over the five years after Peart's loss, it was a matter of just getting comfortable again, and letting those bonds of love reestablish themselves. It's easy enough to say "I love you, man," over the phone or in a letter, it's different saying it face to face, especially after such a long gap. In most instances, band-mates share a rare bond like no other—love, respect, a level of communication deeper than conversation, a sort of intercourse and intimacy. For the return of *Vapor Trails*, Rush wisely knew they had to get together to reinvigorate that connection. It wasn't that Lifeson, Lee, and Peart had stopped loving or caring about each other, it had just become both cautious and remote, given the circumstances. For it to work at all, Peart had to be able to love again and let himself be loved, without feeling like it was a setup for another tragedy, and without it feeling like he was cheating on the memory of the deepest loves he had known and tragically lost with the passing of his wife and daughter. And Lee and Lifeson had to learn how to be gentle while still being themselves with someone truly important and significant in their lives. In so many ways it was like starting over again. And on that score if for no other, *Vapor Trails* is praiseworthy just for being finished and released.

Too Tenebrous to Schedule

Normally, the Rush songwriting and recording process was tightly scheduled—so many weeks for writing, so many weeks (or months) for recording, so many weeks for mixing, and then the fast track to mastering and release. It was how the band had worked on pretty much every other Rush album. As Peart said in a *Circus* magazine interview from the seventies, the band thrives under pressure. Perhaps, understandably, the band decided not to put any time restrictions, and therefore any pressure, on the making of *Vapor Trails*. Given the delicacy of the situation, they decided the least they could do was let the album take as long as it needed to take—after all, much was at stake, and much had happened. While this may have been the only way they could have made this particular album, the lack of a codified schedule was, in hindsight, part of *Vapor Trails*' problem. The months of songwriting delivered a lot of subpar material that had to be tossed out or revised. ("Earthshine" was rewritten three times.) The band's muse, it seemed, had gone into hiding, and it took the band's groove with it.

Part of climbing back into the saddle involved Peart getting comfortable behind the kit again. The man had not picked up a stick (except perhaps to throw it) in years. The last time he played drums he was considered one of the best to ever do so. Being someone who tends to push to be the best he can be, it was probably difficult for the man to not feel the pressure of being, well, Neil Peart. The early days of the *Vapor Trails* project consisted of Lee and Lifeson writing music in one room, and Peart learning to be great on drums again in between writing lyrics sometimes too painful to read. By the time they were ready to record the album, their hearts were already committed, and so there would be no turning back.

As is often the case, a certain kinetic energy overtakes bandmates in the studio. They're in an environment designed to capture their craft. Since music is an art form, created and experienced over time, it makes sense that those making it love going back and hearing what they had made. They do not have the luxury a painter has of being able to study his work as the paint dries, and for as long as it takes to discover the flaws and accomplishments of his or her work. For musicians, the note or beat is played, and then it's gone. Because of this, studios are like churches dedicated to capturing and playing back art as it passes through time. Once in the studio for recording *Vapor Trails* (Reaction Studios in Toronto), the band started having fun again. Still, they needed to take it slow. They weren't out of the woods just yet, and, in some ways, the hardest times still lay ahead.

Again, with no schedules to be their carrot or their stick, the band's recording efforts kept taking longer and longer. No doubt the band also took some time off during the recording process in order to let their ears and instincts freshen. But after months attempting to gain the courage to soar again, and relearning how to do so, the band became so immersed in the project and committed to its outcome that, even during time spent away from the process,

The original *Vapor Trails* album cover. While most Rush fans owned it, few played it due to its technical flaws.

Courtesy of Max Mobley

their thoughts were still on the record.

Lifeson once described album making as birthing process. It's as good an analogy as any, surely. And if that is the case (and it is), then songwriting is the conception, the recording process the contractions, the mix the delivery, and the mastering is the smack on the newborn's ass to illicit the first of many breaths. In the case of *Vapor Trails*, the conception was arduous and tenuous; the recording was nearly a year of painful, incessant contractions. By the end of it, it was impossible not to see the thing through and deliver the son of a bitch. Lee himself admits that the band should have taken a break between recording and mixing in order to gain some much-needed perspective on the project. But they were too close to it at the time to be able to do that. Their hearts were in it, for better and worse. They needed to see the damned thing done—seemingly at any and all costs. By the end they were just sick of it—two different mix engineers, and over a year of work without a firm grasp of the quality of the final product. At this point they could barely stand to hear it—something that remains true for Peart, as he admits, to no one's surprise, that it dredges up painful memories. Once the mix was finished (or perhaps *surrendered* is a better word), the band was so ready to be done with the record that Lifeson took off on a golf trip, Peart just took off, and the all-important mastering was left to Lee, alone.

Lifeson stayed in close communications via telephone while Lee managed the daunting task of mastering a baby that was reluctant to be delivered, and yet so important to the Rush family. In the mastering process, Lee started hearing what would become the well know flaws of the record. Some of the issues were from heavy-handed mastering, and some resulted from the mix itself. In the middle of the mastering process, Lee made the tough decision (with Lifeson's unwavering support) that some songs had to be remixed. It was a rare and difficult choice, certainly.

In the thick of making the record, the band was at times unsure if it could even be made. And if not, what would that mean for Rush?

Indeed, during the final steps when the baby is supposed to live and breathe on its own, it looked like that fear was prophecy. But Lee soldiered on.

Weeks went by, and after what had to be one of the longest mastering processes of a first release, the album was ready to hit music store shelves, which in the intervening years between Rush's most recent record (1996's *Test for Echo*) and this one, were becoming fewer and farther between. Lee sent a disc of the final version of *Vapor Trails* to Lifeson, who was on vacation with his family in Hawaii. He held on to the disc for two weeks before he was ready to listen to the damn thing. Sitting on a beach, Lifeson listened to the disc via headphones, and, like any good parent, was proud of the baby that was so hard to bring into the world—flaws and all.

Vapor Trails Live

Yes, *Vapor Trails* sounded different than anything that had come before, but that's not unusual for a Rush record. And, yeah, it had some serious technical flaws. But of all the criticisms of the record, few, if any, were levied against the songs themselves. The key ingredients of a great Rush record were there. They had just been sabotaged by the horrible sound of digital clipping and over-compression.

Quick sidebar here—analog distortion is often pleasing sounding; it has an organic quality to it (John Lennon's "Instant Kharma" is an excellent example of this, as are many of Lifeson's guitar sounds). Analog clipping contains a bit of magic because it's a physical phenomenon—there is a place for that clip to go, albeit at the expense of fidelity and certain frequencies. Digital clipping is another matter. When a digital clip happens, there is neither a place nor any mechanism for that overage to be absorbed or accommodated. Full scale is full scale, just like no matter how hard you try, a twelve-ounce glass will never ever be able to hold thirteen ounces of liquid. 0db (ironically, the loudest signal in the digital domain, the rest are minus dBs), is full saturation of the binary words (zeroes and ones) carrying the audio. So when digital clipping occurs, a really horrible noise is made. It has been described as an alligator farting in a swamp, or someone dropping an anvil onto a steel plate. It's one of the few sounds in existence that has no musical quality whatsoever. So why wasn't the problem obvious? Among audio engineers and many musicians familiar with the woes (and joys) of working in digital, it more or less was. But, key to this phenomenon is how music is played in a digital environment. In analog—tape or vinyl records—the music exists in a linear fashion, the magnetic imprint or the long circular groove filling an LP. Digital audio has no true linearity. A track on a CD, for example, contains 44,100 individual snapshots of audio playing one after the other every second. At that speed (called sample rate) it sounds linear. It sounds like music since humans cannot possibly hear .00044100 of a second. Many of us can't even hear one-tenth of a second (ten milliseconds). And those god-awful clips on *Vapor Trails* were happening at that sample rate speed in groups of ten, or a hundred, or even a thousand. So, instead of hearing alligators farting, we just get tired of listening, a phenomenon known as *ear fatigue*. When these clips happen often enough in a track (as they do on *Vapor Trails*), some listeners refer to that as razor blades to the ears. There is an overall distaste for the sound that is felt as much as it as it heard. And that was the monstrous side of the *Vapor Trails* studio album. But live, well, it was hard not to love those song's live.

For many Rush fans, *Rush in Rio* or the *Vapor Trails* tour was the first time they really heard and, therefore, appreciated *Vapor Trails'* music. Specifically, "One Little Victory," with its big dragon-and-drum opener, played as the kickoff to set two, and a brilliant version of "Earthshine," on *Rush in Rio*, that remains a fan favorite. "Secret Touch" and "Ghost Rider" (alternated with "Ceiling Unlimited" during early parts of the tour) were also heard live, and it allowed fans to get a perspective on the power lurking beneath *Vapor Trail's* layer of glitches. "Earthshine" made it onto the setlist for *R30*, as did "Secret Touch," which also made an appearance on the *Snakes and Arrows* tour.

The Vapor Trails of *Vapor Trails*

Whether or not *Vapor Trails* fell short of being the cathartic enterprise the band needed can be debated. But through the prism of hindsight, it was clearly a part of the catharsis that allowed forces to realign, and the muse and the magic to re-emerge. The making of the *Vapor Trails* album was the opportunity for Lee, Lifeson, and Peart to get to know one another again—to learn how to react to and adapt to the different people they had become after that horrible tragedy. It was a requirement, in other words, for everything that followed. This is why *Vapor Trails* is such an important album, one deserving of a remix.

It just so happens that the glorious part of this multi-year cathartic experience did not happen in the studio; it happened on the *Vapor Trails* tour, especially during its huge finish in front of those amazing Brazilian fans. Upon conclusion of the tour, a grueling one with some sizable glitches during the South American leg, Rush dubbed it one of their best times on the road, ever. They were back, they were made whole again, and they were healed. And if that is not triumphant, then what the hell is?

Vapor Trails, the Remix

The album cover of the remixed version of *Vapor Trails* features a white background instead of the black one found on the original, flawed version. That's quite fitting given the remarkably different sound of the record. It really is the difference between lightness and darkness.

The remixing job was given to producer David Botrill, who is best known for his work with the band Tool. Botrill was a strong contender for the original *Vapor Trails* sessions, but, wanting to help Peart feel as secure as possible when they ventured back into the studio, the band opted for their friend Paul Northfield, who had worked on seven previous records as far back as *Permanent Waves*. That is not to say the problems with the original mix and mastering were Northfield's fault. Such things are a team failure, not attributed to any one person.

Fortunately for all involved, especially the fans, the songs that make up *Vapor Trails* really lend themselves

The *Vapor Trails* remix revealed a new sound the band had created, but one that initially got lost in the mix.
Courtesy of Max Mobley

to Botrill's touch. For those familiar with the original version of *Vapor Trails*, when listening to the remix, a definite space and openness can be heard, resulting in better definition for each song's separate parts. These improvements do not need to be sought out, they are obvious. For those unfamiliar with the original version, *Vapor Trails*, the remix, just sounds like a new, well-mixed, well-produced Rush album. It could be a new album on that score—it sounds current in every way, though it is not as heavy as *Snakes and Arrows* or *Clockwork Angels*.

There are a lot of parts and layers to the *Vapor Trails* cuts, and Botrill is able to find a place in the stereo field for all the ones that matter. There are guitar solos that were never heard before, and vocal harmonies that were previously lost in the sludge of over-compression. All in all, *Vapor Trails Remixed* is one of Rush's best-sounding records, and one of their most unique. Rush (and specifically Lee, who drove the project to fruition—once again) did right by the material it contains. There are some great Rush tracks here, and few of the band's albums are as important. Fans should not be surprised to see Botrill's name associated with future Rush projects.

21

Le Studio—Rush's Abbey Road

Ruins of a Prog-Rock Holy Site

L e Studio, just outside the quaint village of Morin Heights in Quebec, an hour from Montreal, was the birthplace for seven Rush albums: *Permanent Waves*, *Moving Pictures*, *Signals*, *Grace Under Pressure*, *Presto*, *Roll the Bones*, and *Counterparts*. Le Studio was where the rise of synthesizers in Rush's music gained momentum (*Moving Pictures*, *Grace Under Pressure*), with the band relocating to the UK for their synth peak found on the albums *Power Windows* and *Hold Your Fire*. Le Studio was also where the synth period dimmed back to its rightful place under Lifeson's vaunted riffs (*Presto* through *Counterparts*).

If there is a mecca for Rush fans, it would be Le Studio. Some sixty-one Rush songs were recorded in its live rooms, where, through its many windows, the Laurentian Mountains stand like sentinels in the distance. Some of Rush's most famous and most cherished songs (not always one and the same; just ask a Rush fan) came to life here: "Tom Sawyer," "The Spirit of Radio," "YYZ," "Subdivisions," "The Pass," "Red Sector A," "Bravado," "Between Sun and Moon." So did three of the songs from the Fear Series: "Witch Hunt," "The Weapon," and "The Enemy Within."

Le Studio saw both the peak and the end of the Terry Brown era. It also saw the beginning of the ever-changing producer era. It saw the end of the sidelong (or many minutes long) concept pieces, and the beginning of the one-instrumental-per-album era. Le Studio was where some of Peart's most beloved and oft-quoted lyrics were put

Alex Lifeson soloing on his black Hentor at Le Studio during the *Moving Pictures* sessions. Notice a smiling Terry Brown in the control room. *Courtesy of Yaël Brandeis*

down on tape, where the elastic, moving solo of "Limelight" was recorded, along with the *Superman* street sounds that open "The Camera Eye."

It was where Kevin "Caveman" Shirley and Alex Lifeson almost came to blows over Lifeson's reverb-and-guitar effect demands during the *Counterparts* sessions (to this day, *Counterparts* remains one of Rush's best-sounding records). It was where Rush boasted about chef André's amazing culinary skills, and where the music video for "Tom Sawyer" was filmed. It is also where Geddy Lee's highly controversial foray into rap transpired during the making of "Roll the Bones." That much-maligned break was boldly satiric, highly musical (for rap), contained some of Peart's best plays on words, and also has some excellent guitar textures—so what's the problem? For original Rush fans and those who joined up after *Permanent Waves* and *Moving Pictures*, the Rush albums recorded at Le Studio are usually personal favorites.

Rolling Stones in Glass Houses

Le Studio was a highly regarded recording spot to those outside the world of Rush as well. It was designed by André Perry in 1974 and built under the stewardship of Perry and his business partner and wife, Yaël Brandeis. Le Studio's design broke many conventions when it came to acoustic engineering for recording studio space. It was one of the first "environmental recording studios," meaning that the state-of-the-art facility was designed to also be a temporary residence for artists using the space. The goal was to give artists and the

Le Studio was not just a place for creativity the building itself was a sprawling, creative marvel, as shown here during a Canadian winter.   *Courtesy of Robert Digioia*

Andre Perry's Le Studio was one of the most beautiful recording environments on the planet, as shown in this image.   *Courtesy of the André Perry collection*

technologists responsible for production and recording a comfortable place to live, and a welcoming environment where the artist's muse was free to roam and loom large. It was designed to be a sanctuary where ideas could be hashed out and captured whenever they appeared. An environment dedicated to the art of making and recording music. Perry succeeded brilliantly in his goal, and in its heyday, Le Studio was as respected and cherished as any recording studio in the world. While Rush may have been Le Studio's home team, David Bowie, the Police, and Keith Richards, among others, have called Le Studio their temporary home.

Tearing Down the Temples

As digital-audio technology became more refined and affordable, lush recording cathedrals such as Le Studio found it harder and harder to stay in business. A facility like Le Studio typically contains half a million dollars' worth of recording gear or more, plus the staff to run it, and the scientifically designed building to house it properly. By comparison, a fast personal computer with a couple of thousand dollars' worth of software and hardware can record rock and roll with good fidelity and precision. While the home digital studio does not offer the comfort of a collaborative artist's space like Le Studio, or the brilliant engineers with their solid-gold ears to do the recording, producing and mixing, it does offer unprecedented access and ease of use. And so, as the music world embraced recording and mixing "in the box" (i.e., inside a computer), places around the world like Le Studio were abandoned.

Perry and Brandeis sold Le Studio in 1988. The studio shut down for good around 2008. Today, it remains as an abandoned relic, a veritable rock-and-roll Parthenon in the Laurentian Mountains. It is a place for nostalgic Rush fans on a road trip to find and mourn and snap a few pics. A place that once was as alive as any on the planet, but is now dead, its remote location being the only thing saving it, thus far, from a bulldozer.

Geddy Lee and Le Studio founder and owner, Andre Perry, behind Le Studio's massive SSL console during its glory days.
Courtesy of Yaël Brandeis

Rush, Andre Perry, and friends enjoy Le Studio's Laurentian Mountains location for an outdoor meal.   *Courtesy of Yaël Brandeis*

22

Rush's Mainstream Acceptance Via the Rock and Roll Hall of Fame

Blah, blah. Blah blah blah, blah blah, BLAH!

O n April 19, 2013, the temperature in hell rivaled Green Bay, Wisconsin, on any given January night, and flying pigs had mucked up air traffic all across North America. These events clearly meant one and one thing only: Rush was being inducted into the Rock and Roll Hall of Fame (RRHOF). Finally. It was true. (Well, except for the flying pigs part. And the true temperature of hell on any given day is a highly guarded secret—thank God.) After years of angry letters and hate mail from legions of Rush fans to the RRHOF board members, four generations of prog-rock outsiders were finally welcomed inside the great temple (the Nokia Theatre in Los Angeles), at $100 a pop (for the cheap seats), to witness something many feared (and a few hoped) would never happen—Rush, the true kings of progressive rock and roll, were officially cool enough and important enough to earn a goddam trophy signaling mainstream acceptance. To fans, it was a mystery that Rush had seemingly been refused entry. To non-Rush fans, it was a mystery as to why anyone would even want the band within five hundred yards of the Rock and Roll Hall of Fame, let alone invite them inside and, God forbid, let them make their own music (even though it's located in the town where Rush first broke out—Cleveland, Ohio). To both Rush fans and non-Rush fans, the biggest mystery of all was expressed perfectly by former Nirvana drummer and current Foo Fighter leader Dave Grohl, who (along with Foo Fighter drummer Taylor Hawkins) inducted Rush into the height of mainstream popular music acceptance: *When did Rush become cool?*

To Be Cool or Not to Be Cool

Rush's induction into the RRHOF wasn't just another trophy night for the group, either. Despite being downplayed by the band, the award is genuinely prestigious—only 701 individual artists and music industry members have ever received one in the institution's twenty-seven year existence. By comparison, nearly three hundred Grammy awards are given out each and every year. It's also important to note that the only quantifiable requirement to be eligible for RRHOF induction is that twenty-five years must have passed since the inductee's debut album. For Rush, that span was nearly forty years, meaning they had been eligible since 1999.

Grohl's induction speech aptly summed up what the night was about. Rush never gave a damn about being cool, fitting in, or being accepted by the rock glitterati feted and seated at such events. Rush's only fault as far as mainstream-muso hipsters are concerned, is also the band's best trait as far as Rush fans and true rock and rollers are concerned. That is, the only thing Rush ever really cared about was the music, and they insisted on making music their way. Because that was honest, because that had integrity, and because that was what they knew rock and roll to be about—formula and suits be damned. And their millions of fans feel the same way. Rush fans don't care about being cool, they just care about the songs—especially when they're played LIVE. If they did care

As shown in this T-shirt artwork, many Rush fans did not take lightly the Rock and Roll Hall of Fame's perennial snub of their favorite band.

Courtesy of Joe Pesch

about being cool, they'd hide their Rush T-shirts instead of wearing them with pride. And they would have ditched 1991's *Roll the Bones* for 1991's *Nevermind* by Nirvana—two great albums that couldn't sound more different, even though on April 19, 2013, those two albums became intrinsically and permanently linked. That's why Rush's induction into the Rock and Roll Hall of Fame was such a huge night for Rush fans—it's the music, silly.

The members of Rush have already earned every award imaginable for their revered musicianship—in this there is no controversy. But as a single entity—as songs and albums and a voluminous body of work, Rush's music was due the appropriate acknowledgment given to them that night. So was their work ethic, with over forty years of heavy touring—sometimes as many as 250 shows in a single year—bringing it hard and strong every night regardless of sickness, fatigue, or gear behaving badly—because the fans paid their money and held high expectations. Rush's forty albums and countless solos, time signature changes, riffs, words, drum fills, screams, feedback, power chords, and emotional highs and lows, all of which measurably influenced modern music as much as any act before them, have, through the sum of those parts, clearly earned rock music's greatest honor. So it is no wonder that Rush fans had taken the RRHOF snub personally—it was always the music, never the kimono. And that's probably why Rush graciously accepted the award on their fans' behalf.

The 2013 Rock and Roll Hall of Fame list of inductees was incredibly diverse, as shown in this T-Shirt graphic created to celebrate the event.   *Courtesy of Joe Pesch*

So maybe record low temps in hell and skies filled with flying swine aren't such a bad thing.

And as is often the case—the rarer the event, the more precious and memorable it is.

From Loathed to Loved

April of 2013 found Rush getting ready for the spring leg of their 2013 *Clockwork Angels* tour, and subsequently kicking the tour off in the days following the RRHOF induction ceremony. During this time, Geddy Lee, a huge Major League Baseball fan, made time to attend the April 2nd home opener for his team, the Toronto Blue Jays, where he threw out the first pitch. Later in the month, with his buddy Lerxst, the two made time for the usual pre-tour press. Only those interviewers never really discussed the tour. Instead they focused on the upcoming RRHOF ceremony. It seems that Rush's snub, and their fans' insistence that it be rectified, was big news. As a result, Lee and Lifeson spent quite a lot of time talking with the press about the event instead of the excellent sales figures and overall success associated with all things *Clockwork Angels*. In these interviews, the band downplayed the snub and subsequent award, and put the focus on—what else?—the fans. Of the many print and

Rush and their fans are key to the economic success of the music industry, as shown in this promo pass for Record Store Day in the US. Perhaps that played a role in the band finally making it as Hall of Famers. *Courtesy of Joe Pesch*

radio interviews given, the following quote from Alex Lifeson from the *Hamilton Spectator* newspaper (Hamilton, Ontario) sums up nicely the band's take on the event:

> We kind of wore it as a badge of honor that there was a core inside the committee that did not want us in there. . . . But our fans were very insulted by it. . . . Now they feel vindicated by it. Certainly not all of them do. There's certainly a lot of Rush fans who think we should ignore it. But the proper, courteous thing to do is to go and accept it graciously, try to make everybody happy, move on and never have to deal with it again.

Having been overtly snubbed for a decade and a half, Lifeson's feelings are understandable. When you factor in how cruelly the band (and prog rock in general) had been treated by the mainstream rock press, it is understandable that Rush could be perceived as graciously bitter (that also happens to be the name of the *Hamilton Spectator* piece from which the Lifeson quote was lifted). The following snarky quote from RRHOF board member and *Rolling Stone* senior editor, David Wild, reveals how Rush had taken it on the chin: "It ain't ever gonna happen. Regardless of their success, Rush have never achieved critical acclaim and no one will ever vote for them . . . most of it gives me a headache."

Ouch.

That quote from a senior editor of rock and roll's signature rag—despite Rush being one of the most musically honest bands in rock and roll history, despite a work ethic unrivaled by any performer in the history of the genre, despite only the Beatles and the Rolling Stones having earned more gold and platinum records, and despite their now-legendary influence on rock bands over the past four decades—reveals that maybe the RRHOF isn't all it's supposed to be. Perhaps *The Rolling Stone Magazine Hall of Fame* would be a more fitting name. (Speaking of *Rolling Stone*, since Rush's induction, the band has appeared regularly in the magazine's online edition.)

The day before the ceremony, Wild, having eaten his words graciously (and perhaps bitterly, too), tweeted: "#GodBlessRush. Many people never thought their day would come. I know because I was one of them. I was wrong. . . #RockHall"

Rock fans (and prog-rock haters—you know who you are . . .) who still believe Rush are not Hall-of-Famers, have claimed that the votes were tabulated differently for 2013, resulting in Rush's inclusion—as if it were an accident, or perhaps as if the hacker group Anonymous was behind it. They are referring to the 2013 induction process including votes from fans. However, it is important to note that it was still up to the Hall of Fame board. Those fan votes only counted as a single vote on the voting committee—that does seem appropriate since, as previously mentioned, other than a career spanning twenty-five years, all other artist milestones and contributions to that hoary beast of rock are subjective and based solely on the voting committee's opinion. And Lord knows that much of the serious music press feel the Clash was the only band that mattered.

The Inspiration of Critical Darlings

Foo Fighter's Dave Grohl and Taylor Hawkins were fitting choices for inducting Rush into the Rock and Roll Hall of Fame. Their introductions were perfect. In them they cited each member's musicianship, and what it was like to be a devout Rush fan even though it was considered seriously uncool (as a legion of Rush fans can attest; Grohl spoke about how the album *2112* changed him and filled him with the urge to rock out. He also mentioned how the back photo of Lee, Lifeson, and Peart in kimonos and white silk pants—including Alex Lifeson's infamous camel toe—prevented him from sharing the album with friends. He and Hawkins reminded those who needed it that, in following their muse, Rush broke all the rules, which is what rock and roll is all about. Grohl closed his speech by asking when it became cool to like Rush. The answer is, of course, *always.*

When it came time for Rush's RRHOF performance, Grohl (on guitar) and Hawkins (on drums) were joined by Rush producer Nick Rasculinecz (*Snakes and Arrows*, *Clockwork Angels*) on a Rickenbacker bass for a rousing version of the "2112 Overture" while Rush looked on from the side of the stage. Not only did Grohl, Hawkins, and "Boojze" do a fine job riffing out the epic piece, they were wearing kimonos, silk pants, and wigs to match the *2112* band photo. The three super-fans nailed the look and the bombast of the era, while doing the song justice (even though Rasculinecz used a pick with the Ricky—something very unGeddy-like). Needless to say, fans loved the tribute to the point of nearly drowning out the music. (The Beatles on *The Ed Sullivan Show*, anyone?) Lee, Lifeson, and Peart—no strangers to self-deprecating comedy, were equally tickled. They joined the

Although Rush may not look like they did in this pic from the *2112* tour, thankfully they still sound amazing, and still work their damndest to give fans a great show filled with great music. *Courtesy of Donald Gadziola*

mock-Rush tribute shtick by the end of the tune which ended with Lee singing the infamous, "And the meek shall inherit the Earth." Rush (the *real* band this time, wearing "regular" clothes) went on to play heavy versions of "Tom Sawyer" and "The Spirit of Radio." They had also planned on playing "YYZ," but when they were approached by Grohl about playing "2112" as Rush, circa 1976, well, they couldn't say no to what they knew would be comedic gold mixed with rock and roll bombast—one of Rush's favorite combinations.

Lee, Lifeson, and Peart graciously accepted the accolades to the smiles and cheers of fans and their family—including their SRO-Anthem family. Lifeson, however, summed it up best in his speech, which was nothing more than a few minutes of him telling the saga and idiocy behind being snubbed then accepted into the controversial hall by repeating a single word—*blah.*

And to his point—and the feelings of Rush fans who preferred that their favorite band *not* accept the award—it does seem weird that Rush and the Eagles belong to the same club, and it's not just AARP.

Selected Bibliography

Magazines and Periodicals

"A Canadian Rush: The Metal Marvels That Took the Rock World by Surprise." *Circus*, February 14, 1977.

"Alex Lifeson—Different Strings." *Guitar Player*, September 1, 2007.

"Alex Lifeson Gear Interview: Rush Time Machine Tour 2011."

Barnes, Chris. "Close Look at the Rush Man's Steampunk Inspired DW/Sabian Set-Up." MusicRadar, January 19, 2011.

Barton, Geoff. "Rush: Progressive to the Core." Classic Rock Radio FM 97, September 2006.

Barton, Geoff. "Lifeson: Vapor Trails Is an Important Record—Our Return After a Horrible Nightmare." *Classic Rock*, October 2013.

Benarde, Scott R. "How the Holocaust Rocked Rush Front Man Geddy Lee." *JWeekly*, June 25, 2004.

Borden, Jamie. "Neil Peart Time Machine DW Drum Kit." *iDrum Magazine*, September 13, 2011 (video).

Bosso, Joe. "Alex Lifeson talks about Rush's first single." MusicRadar, October 24, 2011.

———. "In conversation: Chad Smith with Alex Lifeson." MusicRadar, May 13, 2013.

Buttner, Christopher. "Geddy Lee: The Reluctant Rockstar." *Bass Frontiers Magazine Archives*.

Chamberlain, Rich. "Neil Peart Gets Improvisational on new Rush Record; Drummer Discusses *Clockwork Angels*." MusicRadar, January 12, 2012.

Cohen, Elliot Stephen. "Alex Lifeson: Rush Keeps Rollin'." *Vintage Guitar Magazine*, February 2004.

Coryat, Karl. "Geddy Lee: Still Going." *Bass Player*, December 1993.

"Dear Superstar: Geddy Lee." *Maxim*, April 2013.

Greene, Andy "Q&A: Neil Peart on Rush's New LP and Being a 'Bleeding Heart Libertarian.'" *Rolling Stone*, June 12, 2012.

Guitar World Staff. "Alex Lifeson and Geddy Lee of Rush Choose 22 Songs That Inspired Them Most." *Guitar World*, July, 9, 2013.

Hammond, Shawn. "Interview: Rush's Alex Lifeson and Geddy Lee." *Premier Guitar*, October 8, 2012.

Hughes, Andy. "Geddy Lee Bass Guitar Magazine Interview: Like Clockwork." *Bass Guitar Magazine*, July 2012.

"Interview with Brad Madix." *Canadian Music Scene Magazine.*

Jennings, Steve. "All Access: Rush." *Mix*, January 1, 2013.

Jisi, Chris. "Geddy Lee: Full Steam Ahead." *Bass Player Magazine*, August 13, 2012.

Laing, Rob. "Alex Lifeson's Live Rig." MusicRadar, September 23, 2011.

Lloyd, Jack. "Sometimes Rush Is in a Hurry." *Philadelphia Inquirer*, May 1981.

Mobley, Max. "Interview with Rush's Alex Lifeson." *Crawdaddy!*, October 22, 2008.

———. "Interview: Alex Lifeson." *Premier Guitar*, March 17, 2009.

"The Moustache That Conquered the World." *Sounds*, April 1980.

"Neil Peart Time Machine Kit Tour." *Rhythm*, June 2, 2011.

Peart, Neil . "Rush—Presto." *Rush Backstage Club Newsletter*, March 1990.

———. "The Drummer Sounds Off." *Rush Backstage Club Newsletter*, September 1988.

———. "For Whom the Bus Rolls." *Rush Backstage Club Newsletter*, October 1981.

———. "Rush—Hold Your Fire." *Rush Backstage Club Newsletter*, January 1988.

———. "Rush Backstage Club Newsletter," January 1994.

———. "The News." *Rush Backstage Club Newsletter*, July 1985.

———. "Thrice Told Tales by Neil Peart." *Backstage Club Newsletter*, December 1983.

————. "Twenty-Five Questions." *Rush Backstage Club Newsletter*, December 1985.

Porter, Tom. "Neil Peart's DW Drum Kit Gets Steampunk Makeover." MusicRadar.

Reed, Ryan. "Rush's New Producer Talks About Having to Critique His Heroes in the Studio." *Ultimate Classic Rock*, May 10, 2012.

"Rock and Roll Hall of Fame 2013 Inductees: Rush, Public Enemy, Heart and Randy Newman." *Rolling Stone*, December 11, 2012.

"Rush Popular with the Fans, If Not the Critics." *Chicago Tribune*, April 4, 1980.

"Rush Remix Their Polarizing Album 'Vapor Trails'—Premiere." *Rolling Stone*, September 27, 2013.

"Rush Rock & Roll in the Classroom." *Circus*, August 4, 1977.

"Rush 'Rolls the Bones' as They Enter the 1990's." *Tunes Magazine*, February 1992.

"Rush: Still on a Journey of Discovery, 20 Albums On." *Total Guitar*, January 2012.

Musician's Friend, April 19, 2011 (video).

"The Rush Dilemma!" *Rockline!*, July / August 1984.

"Steampunk Cymbals." *Sabian Cymbals Newsletter*, January 2011.

Sterdan, Darryl. "Rush Drummer Uncomfortable with Fame." *Toronto Sun*, February 7, 2010.

Vaziri, Aidin. "Rush Front Man Wants to Put Time on Hold." *San Francisco Chronicle*, September 15, 2002.

Wilonsky, Robert. "Rush Guitarist Alex Lifeson Discusses the Band's Road Less Traveled." *Dallas News*, November 22, 2013.

Books

Banasiewicz, Bill. *Rush Visions: The Official Biography*. London: Omnibus Press, 1988.

Bergamini, Joe. *Neil Peart: Taking Center Stage—A Lifetime of Live Performance*. Emeryville, CA: Hudson Music, 2012.

Clockwork Angels (tour book). Toronto, Canada: Anthem Entertainment Group.

Collins, Jon. *Rush: Chemistry: The Definitive Biography*. Helter Skelter Publishing, 2006.

Gett, Steve. *Rush: Success Under Pressure*. Cherry Lane Music, 1985.

Menon, Vinay. *Rush, An Oral History*. Toronto: Toronto Star Newspapers Limited, 2013.

Peart, Neil. *Ghost Rider: Travels on the Healing Road*. Toronto: ECW Press, 2002.

———. *Roadshow: Landscape with Drums: A Concert Tour by Motorcycle*. Toronto: ECW Press, 2011.

———. *Traveling Music: The Soundtrack to My Life and Times*. Toronto: ECW Press, 2004.

Popoff, Martin. *Contents Under Pressure*. Toronto: ECW Press, 2004.

———. *Rush: The Illustrated History*. McGregor, MN: Voyageur Press, 2013.

Rush Time Machine (tour book). Anthem Entertainment Group.

Rush tour books, 1977–2004. Anthem Entertainment Group.

Video

Can't Stop Thinking Big. Producer: Meg Symsysk. Zoe Records / Pgd.

Rush: Beyond the Lighted Stage. Directors Sam Dunn, Scot McFadyen. Zoe Records.

Rush: Classic Albums: 2112 & Moving Pictures. Director: Smith, Martin R. Eagle Rock Entertainment.

The Boys in Brazil. Director Andrew MacNaughtan. Anthem Entertainment Group / Atlantic Records.

The Game of Snakes and Arrows. Director: Andrew MacNaughtan. Anthem Entertainment Group / Atlantic Records.

Internet

andrewolsen.com

blabbermouth.net

Blender.com

cygnus-x1.net

dailyswarm.com

Drummagazine.com

fender.com

Fender.com

freddysfrets.com

Gibson.com

Grammy.com

hughes-and-kettner.com

Idolator.com

IMDb.com

metalstorm.net

musicradar.com

NeilPeart.net

neilpeartnews.com

news.2112.net

orangeamps.com

Rush.com

rushisaband.com

Rushvault.com

Ultimate-Guitar.Com

vintagesynth.com

Index

THE FAQ SERIES

HAL•LEONARD®
PERFORMING ARTS
PUBLISHING GROUP

FAQ.halleonardbooks.com

1213